A Concise Companion to
Middle English Literature

Blackwell Concise Companions to Literature and Culture
General Editor: David Bradshaw, University of Oxford

This series offers accessible, innovative approaches to major areas of literary study. Each volume provides an indispensable companion for anyone wishing to gain an authoritative understanding of a given period or movement's intellectual character and contexts.

Published

Modernism	Edited by David Bradshaw
Feminist Theory	Edited by Mary Eagleton
The Restoration and Eighteenth Century	Edited by Cynthia Wall
Postwar American Literature and Culture	Edited by Josephine G. Hendin
The Victorian Novel	Edited by Francis O'Gorman
Twentieth-Century American Poetry	Edited by Stephen Fredman
Chaucer	Edited by Corinne Saunders
Shakespeare on Screen	Edited by Diana E. Henderson
Contemporary British Fiction	Edited by James F. English
English Renaissance Literature	Edited by Donna B. Hamilton
Milton	Edited by Angelica Duran
Shakespeare and the Text	Edited by Andrew Murphy
Contemporary British and Irish Drama	Edited by Nadine Holdsworth and Mary Luckhurst
American Fiction 1900–1950	Edited by Peter Stoneley and Cindy Weinstein
The Romantic Age	Edited by Jon Klancher
Postwar British and Irish Poetry	Edited by Nigel Alderman and C. D. Blanton
Middle English Literature	Edited by Marilyn Corrie

A Concise Companion to
Middle English Literature

Edited by Marilyn Corrie

WILEY-BLACKWELL

A John Wiley & Sons, Ltd., Publication

This edition first published 2009
© 2009 Blackwell Publishing Ltd

Blackwell Publishing was acquired by John Wiley & Sons in February 2007.
Blackwell's publishing program has been merged with Wiley's global Scientific,
Technical, and Medical business to form Wiley-Blackwell.

Registered Office
John Wiley & Sons Ltd, The Atrium, Southern Gate, Chichester, West Sussex,
PO19 8SQ, United Kingdom

Editorial Offices
350 Main Street, Malden, MA 02148-5020, USA
9600 Garsington Road, Oxford, OX4 2DQ, UK
The Atrium, Southern Gate, Chichester, West Sussex, PO19 8SQ, UK

For details of our global editorial offices, for customer services, and for
information about how to apply for permission to reuse the copyright
material in this book please see our website at www.wiley.com/wiley-blackwell.

The right of Marilyn Corrie to be identified as the author of the editorial
material in this work has been asserted in accordance with the Copyright,
Designs and Patents Act 1988.

Library of Congress Cataloging-in-Publication Data

A concise companion to Middle English literature / edited by Marilyn Corrie.
     p. cm. — (Blackwell concise companions to literature and culture)
  Includes bibliographical references and index.
  ISBN 978–1–4051–2004–3 (alk. paper)
  1. English literature—Middle English, 1100–1500—History and criticism.
2. Great Britain—Civilization—1066–1485. I. Corrie, Marilyn.
  PR260.C665 2009
  820.9'001—dc22
                                                    2008044519

A catalogue record for this book is available from the British Library.

Set in 10/12.5pt Meridien by Graphicraft Limited, Hong Kong
Printed in the United Kingdom

1   2009

Contents

List of Illustrations   vii
List of Contributors   viii
Acknowledgements   xi

Introduction   1
Marilyn Corrie

Part I   Key Contexts   7
  1   Signs and Symbols   9
      Barry Windeatt

  2   Religious Belief   32
      Marilyn Corrie

  3   Women and Literature   54
      Catherine Sanok

  4   The Past   77
      Andrew Galloway

Part II   The Production of Middle English Literature   97
  5   Production and Dissemination   99
      Alexandra Gillespie

Contents

6   The Author   120
    Jane Griffiths

Part III   Writing in Middle English; Writing in England   143
7   Language   145
    Jeremy J. Smith

8   Translation and Adaptation   166
    Helen Cooper

9   Contemporary Events   188
    Helen Barr

Part IV   Middle English Literature in the Post-
            Medieval World   209
10 Manuscripts and Modern Editions   211
    Daniel Wakelin

11 The Afterlife of Middle English Literature   232
    David Matthews

Index   253

List of Illustrations

Figure 1.1   Woodcut from *The Art of Good Lywyng and Deyng*,
              printed in Paris, 1503.   14
Figure 6.1   Title page of the 1527 edition of John Lydgate's
              Fall of Princes, printed by Richard Pynson.   121
Figure 9.1   The Westminster Abbey portrait of Richard II
              (1390s).   198

List of Contributors

Helen Barr is Fellow and Tutor in English at Lady Margaret Hall, University of Oxford, where she teaches Old and Middle English literature, the history of the English language, and Shakespeare. Her books include *Signes and Sothe: Language in the Piers Plowman Tradition* (D.S. Brewer, 1994) and *Socioliterary Practice in Late-Medieval England* (Oxford University Press, 2002). Her primary research interest is in relationships between textualities and cultural practices.

Helen Cooper is Professor of Medieval and Renaissance English at the University of Cambridge. Her books include *The Canterbury Tales* in the Oxford Guides to Chaucer series and *The English Romance in Time: Transforming Motifs from Geoffrey of Monmouth to the Death of Shakespeare* (Oxford University Press, 2004).

Marilyn Corrie is a lecturer in English at University College London. She has published essays on early Middle English literature and manuscripts, Sir Thomas Malory's *Morte Darthur*, and the history of the English language in the medieval period. She is currently writing a book about Malory's *Morte Darthur* and religion in the late Middle Ages.

Andrew Galloway has taught in Cornell University's English Department since receiving his PhD (UC Berkeley) in 1991. He has written numerous essays on Middle English poetry, especially that of

Chaucer, Gower and Langland, and on medieval chronicles. Recently he completed *The Penn Commentary on Piers Plowman: Volume One* (University of Pennsylvania Press, 2006) and *Medieval Literature and Culture* (Continuum Press, 2007).

Alexandra Gillespie is an Assistant Professor of English at the University of Toronto. She specializes in medieval and early Tudor literature and book history, and is the author of *Print Culture and the Medieval Author: Chaucer, Lydgate, and Their Books, 1473–1557* (Oxford University Press, 2006), and the editor of *John Stow (1525–1605) and the Making of the English Past* (British Library, 2004) and a special issue of *Huntington Library Quarterly, Manuscript, Print, and Early Tudor Literature* (2004).

Jane Griffiths is a lecturer in English at the University of Bristol. Her book *John Skelton and Poetic Authority: Defining the Liberty to Speak* was published by Oxford University Press in 2006, and she has also published essays on fifteenth- and sixteenth-century English poetry and poetics in *Huntington Library Quarterly, Mediaevalia & Humanistica, Renaissance Studies* and *The Yearbook of English Studies*.

David Matthews is a lecturer in Middle English at the University of Manchester. He is the author of *The Making of Middle English 1765–1910* (University of Minnesota Press, 1999). Recently, he has co-edited *Medieval Cultural Studies* (with Ruth Evans and Helen Fulton) (2006) and *Reading the Medieval in Early Modern England* (with Gordon McMullan) (Cambridge University Press, 2007). He is currently working on political verse of the thirteenth and fourteenth centuries.

Catherine Sanok teaches in the English Department at the University of Michigan. She is the author of *Her Life Historical: Exemplarity and Female Saints' Lives in Late Medieval England* (University of Pennsylvania Press, 2007). Her essays on Middle English literature have appeared in *Exemplaria, Journal of Medieval and Early Modern Studies, New Medieval Literatures* and *Studies in the Age of Chaucer*.

Jeremy J. Smith is Professor of English Philology at the University of Glasgow. His publications include *An Historical Study of English* (Routledge, 1996), *Essentials of Early English* (Routledge, 2005, 2nd edn) and *Sound Change and the History of English* (Oxford University Press, 2007).

Daniel Wakelin is a lecturer in English at the University of Cambridge and a Fellow of Christ's College. He has published a book on *Humanism, Reading and English Literature 1430–1530* (Oxford University Press, 2007) and articles on Middle English manuscripts, the history of reading, carols and early Tudor writing. His current research concerns corrections and correctness in Middle English books and literature.

Barry Windeatt is Professor of English at the University of Cambridge and a Fellow of Emmanuel College. His books include a parallel-text edition of *Troilus and Criseyde* (Longman, 1984) and a Penguin Classics edition of Chaucer's poem (2003); the Oxford Guides to Chaucer critical introduction to *Troilus and Criseyde* (1992); an annotated edition of *The Book of Margery Kempe* (Longman, 2000) together with a Penguin Classics translation (1985); and also an edition of *English Mystics of the Middle Ages* (Cambridge University Press, 1994). He has created the 'Medieval Imaginations' website of images of medieval English visual culture (http://www.english.cam.ac.uk/medieval/) and is writing a study of text and image in later medieval England.

Acknowledgements

I would like, first and foremost, to thank all of the contributors for their tolerance of my often considerable demands, and for their patience in waiting for the book to appear in print. I would especially like to thank Andrew Galloway for his help and encouragement from the inception of the project to its very last stages.

A number of my colleagues in the English Department at University College London have helped me in a variety of ways. I am very grateful for advice provided by Rosemary Ashton, John Mullan and Henry Woudhuysen, and for the continuous help and encouragement of Susan Irvine. I could not have completed the project without the kindness and support of Neil Rennie. Anita Garfoot sorted out many issues that I was unable to sort out myself. I would also like to thank Nicola McDonald at York, Francis O'Gorman at Leeds, Corinne Saunders at Durham and Marion Turner at Oxford for invaluable assistance with different aspects of the book. Thorlac Turville-Petre gave generous and useful feedback at an early stage; Elisabeth Dutton and Christina von Nolcken provided crucial and greatly appreciated help much later in the day. Emma Bennett at Wiley-Blackwell has been a kind and astute editor, and I have benefited too from the expertise and patience of Annette Abel and Sue Leigh. Lastly, I would like to thank my friends for both practical help and moral support. I am especially grateful to Emma Barker, Georgia Brown, Gordon McMullan and Melanie Mauthner, and to Clarence Liu and the Barbican, London for providing ideal working conditions.

Much of the research for Daniel Wakelin's chapter was conducted with the aid of a Francis Bacon Foundation Scholarship at the Huntington Library, San Marino in 2006.

Introduction

It has become fashionable for literary studies to blur the boundaries that have traditionally been used to distinguish one period of literature from another. Scholars of medieval literature have explored both the transmission of Old English literature in the period of Middle English and its study in the Middle English period by people who could no longer read it with ease (see, for example, Franzen 1991). More recently scholars have blurred the boundaries between the Middle English and the 'early modern' periods, examining the transmission and presentation of the writings of late fourteenth- and fifteenth-century English authors – especially Chaucer and Lydgate – in the sixteenth century, after printing had become firmly established (Gillespie 2006), or the continuing interest in medieval romances as late as the early seventeenth century (Cooper 2004). Interests and ideas that have been thought to be new in the early modern period have also been discerned in writing and in manuscripts that were produced in the fifteenth century (Strohm 2005; Wakelin 2007). As David Matthews discusses in this volume, recent literary histories that treat the medieval period have chosen as their starting point the mid-fourteenth century, and have continued their surveys well into the sixteenth century – or have begun their surveys in the Old English period and continued them up to the mid-fourteenth century. There are reasons for splitting the period of Middle English in two, as such surveys do: in particular – as has long been recognized – it is in the second half of the fourteenth century that the English language becomes widely used for great literary writing, including the works of Chaucer (and William Langland's great dream vision poem *Piers Plowman*, John Gower's *Confessio Amantis* and the anonymous *Sir Gawain and the Green Knight* and the other works in the manuscript in which that poem has been preserved). But there are reasons too for preserving the traditional 'fence' placed around the Middle English period, usually loosely defined as the centuries between 1100 and 1500. Those reasons are the subject of this book.

The subjects covered in the various chapters of the volume, which are by different authors, have been chosen with a view to elucidating issues that are likely to be unfamiliar to people approaching Middle English literature for the first time, or who have only limited experience of that literature. Those issues need to be appreciated if Middle English texts are to be understood on their own terms. At the same time, each of the chapters offers new insights on its subject, and the contributors consider material that will be unfamiliar even to experts in Middle English literature, or look at more familiar material from new perspectives. This is a book, therefore, for more advanced readers of Middle English texts as well as new ones.

Chaucer, the best-known Middle English author, figures prominently in the volume as a whole, and is discussed in detail in many of its essays. But Chaucer's writings are considered in the context, and the light, of other writing of the period: an approach that enables readers to appreciate both how Chaucer is typical of the age in which he was writing and, in a number of important respects, how he departs from, and sometimes implicitly queries, many of the conventions of writing in the Middle English period (see in particular the essays by Catherine Sanok, Andrew Galloway, Alexandra Gillespie, Jane Griffiths, Helen Cooper and Helen Barr; compare also Daniel Wakelin's and David Matthews' chapters).

The book is, first and foremost, about Middle English literature – but several of the subjects with which it deals also inform medieval literature in languages other than English. I have grouped those subjects of which this is especially true at the start of the volume, under the title 'Key Contexts'. The chapters here consider such issues as the compulsion to read symbolic significance into the phenomena of this world in the Middle Ages, evidenced, as Barry Windeatt discusses, in Middle English writers ranging from the female visionaries Margery Kempe and Julian of Norwich to Sir Thomas Malory, the author of *Le Morte Darthur*, as well as in the Middle Scots writer Robert Henryson; the responses of medieval people to the religious beliefs that they were taught to hold, scriptural, doctrinal and otherwise, exemplified strikingly, but far from exclusively, in writing by the *Gawain*-poet and Langland; ideas about women in the Middle Ages, which infuse writing both by men and by women themselves, and which are one of the most conspicuous ways in which Chaucer engages with debates that were, by his day, traditional (although they remained current); and thinking about the past in the period, which was regularly seen, especially, not as something separate from the present, but as something that was, in fact, inseparable from it, as was apparent to the anonymous playwrights of the mystery cycles that were performed in prosperous English towns in the late Middle Ages, amongst other people. There is an important exception to the applicability of the points made in this part of the book not just to Middle English literature but to medieval literature more generally, and that concerns the response to religious teaching that prevails in Middle English literature in the fifteenth century. This is the product of circumstances that were particular to England, the result of the backlash of the Church in England and the English state towards teaching that had already been branded heretical. Discussion of this issue is included in the second chapter of the book, on 'Religious Belief'.

The second group of chapters discusses issues that distinguish the production of Middle English literature from the production of writing in other periods. The first of the chapters in this part considers the contexts in which Middle English literature was both produced and disseminated – orally and in writing, in (and from) religious milieux, especially monasteries, and secular milieux too, including the royal court, aristocratic households and, late in the period, the environment of the administrative centre of England at Westminster and the adjacent city of London. The second of the chapters discusses the engagement of Middle English literature – including, again, Chaucer's writings – with the distinctive medieval ideas surrounding the role of an author in the production of a text. By the end of the medieval period something resembling many of the ideas about authorship that prevail today had emerged; and yet even then traditional medieval thinking about authorship can be seen to linger in the ways that the authors of texts represent themselves.

The third part of the book covers subjects that are of particular relevance to writing in England in the medieval period. The first chapter here discusses the features of the Middle English phase of the English language. As Jeremy Smith points out in the chapter, it is to nineteenth-century historians of the English language that we owe the term 'Middle English'; they perceived that between the Norman Conquest of 1066 and the introduction of printing technology to England in 1476, English showed certain characteristics that set it apart from Old English on the one hand and early modern English on the other. The chapter explores what the characteristics of Middle English are, and how they are related to the functions that English performed in the years between the Conquest and its début in print. The second chapter in the section discusses the fact that a great deal of the Middle English literature that survives to us, from religious treatises to romances, is translated or adapted from writing in other languages, particularly French and Latin. Chaucer's works show a conspicuous and recurring interest in the issue of translation, and a more sophisticated attitude towards its practice than his famous branding as a 'grant translateur' by one of his French contemporaries may suggest. In the final chapter of the section, the historical 'background' to Middle English writing is discussed, and particularly the specific events in England and concerning England with which that writing engages. Middle English texts are vehicles – sometimes the only vehicles we have – for telling us about those events, and yet, as Helen Barr explains in the chapter, their presentation of them is far from objective: if Middle English literature is informed by certain events, it also 'produces' those events in various ways when it gives them textual shape.

The final part of the book addresses issues relating to the ways in which Middle English literature is perceived in the present day. The chapter 'Manuscripts and Modern Editions' discusses how the media in which Middle English literature is usually read now change the experience of reading it in important ways from the experience that people in the Middle Ages would have had when they read it. Modern printed editions of Middle English texts both add things to the manuscript forms in which Middle English texts circulated in the Middle Ages and take things away, and it is essential to be aware of the changes that they impose on the texts if we are to have a sense of the distinctive ways in which they were read, and the ways in which they circulated, in the Middle Ages. The book concludes by discussing how present-day perceptions of Middle English literature have been shaped by the changing ways in which it has been thought about and commented on since the Middle Ages. The chapter also ponders the future of Middle English literature, suggesting the appeal of its 'difference' from the literature of other periods and regretting some aspects of the current trends in academic scholarship that obscure that difference.

If the book deals with issues that define the distinctiveness of Middle English literature, it does not obscure heterogeneity in approaches to those issues amongst writers of the period, nor changes and developments across the four hundred years in which the literature was produced. The essays draw attention, for example, to the rise of the concept of 'poesye' in the late fourteenth century (see Andrew Galloway's chapter); the changes in the dissemination of Middle English texts that took place at around the same time (see Alexandra Gillespie's chapter); the appearance in Middle English writing of the late fourteenth century of new ideas relating to the role played by an author in the production of a text (see Jane Griffiths' essay); and new attitudes towards the copying and the presentation of Middle English texts in the late fourteenth and early fifteenth centuries (see Daniel Wakelin's chapter). Within the world of writing and the copying of that writing in England, various changes were taking place more or less simultaneously around the end of the fourteenth century, a parallel to the many changes that were taking place in the wider world at the same time (compare, for example, Staley 1996; see also my own chapter and Helen Barr's below).

It will have been evident from the above summary of the subjects covered by the book that, within the concise format necessitated by the demands of the *Concise Companion* series, the volume aims to provide a comprehensive (if not, of course, exhaustive) guide to the study of Middle English literature; it can also, however, be dipped into for consultation on specific topics. Each of the chapters aims to offer comprehensive coverage of its particular subject, again within a concise format. In all of the essays, contextual information about the subject that is being addressed is combined with the critical (or linguistic) analysis of a range of texts. The aim of the volume as a whole, then, is to offer a guide to its subject that is both useful and illuminating. If it is a concise companion to Middle English literature, it hopes, nonetheless, to be an authoritative and a stimulating one.

References

Cooper, Helen (2004). *The English Romance in Time: Transforming Motifs from Geoffrey of Monmouth to the Death of Shakespeare*. Oxford: Oxford University Press.

Franzen, Christine (1991). *The Tremulous Hand of Worcester: A Study of Old English in the Thirteenth Century*. Oxford: Clarendon Press.

Gillespie, Alexandra (2006). *Print Culture and the Medieval Author: Chaucer, Lydgate, and Their Books, 1473–1557*. Oxford: Oxford University Press.

Staley, Lynn (1996). 'Julian of Norwich and the Late Fourteenth-Century Crisis of Authority'. In David Aers and Lynn Staley, *The Powers of the Holy: Religion, Politics, and Gender in Late Medieval English Culture* (pp. 107–78). University Park: Pennsylvania State University Press.

Strohm, Paul (2005). *Politique: Languages of Statecraft between Chaucer and Shakespeare*. Notre Dame: University of Notre Dame Press.

Wakelin, Daniel (2007). *Humanism, Reading, and English Literature 1430–1530*. Oxford: Oxford University Press.

Notes on the contents of bibliographies; references; and abbreviations

The bibliography at the end of each chapter is divided into two sections: 'Primary texts' and 'Secondary sources and suggestions for further reading'. Primary texts are generally listed under the names of the editors whose versions of the texts the contributors have used; references within the text of each essay specify whose edition has been consulted. The possibility of including extensive bibliographies for each subject has been precluded by the demands of the *Concise Companion* series; where they have thought it appropriate, the contributors have, however, added some titles to the list of works that they reference within their chapters in order to indicate reading that they consider essential to their topic.

Quotations from Chaucer's works have been taken from *The Riverside Chaucer*, gen. ed. Larry D. Benson (Boston: Houghton Mifflin, 1987) unless stated otherwise; the line numbering of *The Riverside Chaucer* has also been used in the essays. References to quotations from *The Canterbury Tales* (or *CT*) are to the number of the fragment from which the quotation is taken, followed by the line numbering within the fragment, again as identified in *The Riverside Chaucer*. References to editions of texts and quotations from editions are given in the form (for example) '(ed. Vinaver 1990)' and '(ed. Vinaver 1990: 850)' respectively; references in the form (for example) '(Vinaver, ed., 1990: 10)' are to a statement made, or material contained in, an edition that is not part of the edited text itself. Unless otherwise indicated, references are to page numbers in the specified works. Italics in quotations identify material expanded from abbreviations in manuscripts, or material underlined in manuscripts; square brackets identify material supplied by editors or contributors themselves.

'EETS' stands for the Early English Text Society; 'OS' stands for the Ordinary Series of volumes within the publications of the Society, 'ES' for the Extra Series, and 'SS' for the Supplementary Series.

Part I
Key Contexts

Chapter 1

Signs and Symbols

Barry Windeatt

> Omnis mundi creatura
> quasi liber et pictura
> nobis est in speculum;
> nostrae vitae, nostrae mortis,
> nostri status, nostrae sortis
> fidele signaculum.
> (Alan of Lille, ed. Raby 1959: 369)

[All creation, like a book or a picture, is a mirror to us – a true figure of our life, our death, our condition, our lot.]

To the medieval mind symbolic significance might be read into almost anything, when all creation was a mirror, figure and script that pointed beyond itself, reminding of an otherworldly dimension that offered the only true and abiding perspective. In the variety of his works the fifteenth-century Scottish poet Robert Henryson can represent – by way of introduction to this chapter – the sheer range of uses of signs and symbols in medieval writings. His *Garmont of Gud Ladeis* reads moral conduct in terms of the symbolism of female attire, and in his *Testament of Cresseid* the disfiguring leprosy that punishes Cresseid for defiance of the gods draws on traditions that see sickness as an outward sign of inner moral condition. In his *Orpheus and Eurydice* Henryson plays his own variations on medieval traditions of moralizing classical mythology to expound a Christian moral. Here the hero and heroine symbolize intellect and desire respectively: when Eurydice flees through a May meadow from a would-be rapist shepherd, is stung by a venomous serpent and is summoned to hell, she flees from 'good vertew' (perhaps surprisingly to the modern reader) through the world's vain delights, and so descends into hell through excess of care for worldly things. Henryson's *Fables* include the grimly schematic symbolism of 'The Paddock and the Mouse', where a mouse (man's soul), in seeking to cross a river (the world) to reach better things, has no option but to be tied to a frog (man's body) that tries to drag her under and drown her, before both are seized by a kite (sudden death). Yet Henryson's interpretations may also signify challengingly, as in 'The Cock and the Jasp', where a cock finds a jewel (which betokens perfect wisdom and knowledge) but hankers instead for something edible (sensibly enough, for a chicken?) – only to be roundly condemned as an ignoramus on the basis of the otherworldly perspective that unifies the medieval reading of signs.

Sign Systems

> You can make a cross on the meal-table out of five bread-crumbs; but do not let anyone see this, except your wife. . . .
>
> *(Instructions for a Devout and Literate Layman,*
> trans. Pantin 1976: 398–422)

As St Augustine had remarked in *De doctrina Christiana* ('On Christian Teaching'), 'A sign is a thing which of itself makes some other thing come to mind, besides the impression it presents to the senses' (trans. Green 1997: 31). In the Middle Ages, the natural world, the human body, or society and its constructions all had their symbolism and were full of signs to be interpreted. Most human experience could be read as symbolic: the successive ages of man; the powers or defects of the senses (vision or blindness, deafness, sweetness); the sleep of sin; illness, medicine and healing, which were seen as signs of moral failing and regeneration. Conduct was often evaluated symbolically in terms of conflicts between vices and virtues (personified in morality plays and innumerable allegories). As for the natural world, there was a long tradition of 'bestiaries', illustrated texts that expounded the moral symbolism discerned in the behaviour of animals and birds, as one preacher explains:

> The Lord created different creatures with different natures not only for the sustenance of men, but also for their instruction, so that through

the same creature we may contemplate not only what may be useful for the body, but also what may be useful in the soul . . . For there is no creature . . . in which we may not contemplate some property belonging to it which may lead us to imitate God or . . . to flee from the Devil. For the whole world is full of different creatures, like a manuscript full of different letters and sentences, in which we can read whatever we ought to imitate or flee from . . .

(Thomas of Chobham (d. 1236?), *Summa de arte praedicandi* ('Manual of the Art of Preaching') (ed. Morenzoni 1988: 275))

The symbolism in plants, flowers, herbs and trees (and by extension in gardens and springs, and the character of the seasons) was also the focus of moralizing interpretations, while a science of astrological signs decoded the stars, and, as in Henryson's *Orpheus and Eurydice*, the ingenuity of medieval mythography read Christian symbolism into classical mythology. Analysed in texts called 'lapidaries', precious stones were credited with powers of healing and safeguarding, and gained symbolic meanings, as did both colours and also numbers, the subject of elaborate numerological symbolism (on all of which traditions the *Gawain*-poet draws). With their colours and gems, medieval clothes and jewellery, and above all ecclesiastical vestments, made symbolic statements, as did such accoutrements as armour and weapons. Heraldry developed a sophisticated lexicon of signs and signatures of kinship and descent. The regalia of kingship – crown, orb and sceptre – were replete with a symbolism of authority invested by coronation ritual, the most solemn amongst a system of symbolically charged ceremonies that included swearing of homage, and the dubbing and arming of knights, as also the observances and insignia of chivalric orders and the conduct of tournaments. In grander households some principal pastimes – hunting, jousting, feasting, dancing – were invested with symbolism, as were games and gift-giving, and all inform romance literature with its symbolic testings and questings. The quest draws meaning from a larger symbolism of movement and space: symbolic readings of journeys, and of the way taken, are especially resonant in the concept of the pilgrimage, as in romance, while architecture interprets built space in symbolic terms, in secular as well as ecclesiastical contexts.

Symbolism remained readable at different levels of understanding, education and literacy. Written explanations were provided even for medieval viewers of the 'typological' schemes of stained glass at Canterbury Cathedral, in which certain Old Testament episodes ('types') are read as prefigurations of New Testament episodes ('anti-types'),

11

and hence as signs that each episode in Christ's life fulfils a divinely ordained pattern (Michael 2004: 13, 25; see also Henry, ed., 1987). Since Jonah's three days in a whale's belly were understood to prefigure Christ's three days in the tomb (Matthew 12:40), Jonah's being spewed up by the whale offered a memorable symbol of Christ's resurrection, as did Samson's carrying off the gates of Gaza where he was captured and imprisoned (while visiting a prostitute, but typology often seized on parallels regardless of context). In *The Tale of Beryn* – a fifteenth-century sequel to *The Canterbury Tales* in which the pilgrims reach Canterbury – lower-class pilgrims 'counterfeting gentilmen' try interpreting images in the cathedral windows and squabble ignorantly over their significance (ed. Bowers 1992: 64). However baffled they appear, these humble pilgrims' conviction of symbolic meanings to be discovered reflects the wider typological awareness mirrored in the structure of mystery play cycles and throughout medieval visual culture.

Signs are for remembering: symbolism might prompt devout memorization by organizing knowledge, through pattern and tabulation, of core tenets of faith and cues for devotional observance, with no sign more central than Christ's body. Analysis of sins and virtues might be set out in the form of diagrammatic trees or wheels or other visual mnemonics. Always there is the structure lent by numerical pattern: the seven sacraments, seven works of mercy, seven deadly sins; Mary's joys and sorrows (variously, five, seven or fifteen); and Christ's five wounds, object of a fragmenting devotional attention that disassembled Christ's body into fetishized parts for veneration, focusing on separate images of wounded hands, feet and gaping side. Henry VI's confessor records how the king

> made a rule that a certain dish which represented the five wounds of Christ, as it were red with blood, should be set on his table by his almoner before any other course when he was to take refreshment; and contemplating these images with great fervour he thanked God marvellously devoutly.
>
> (trans. James 1919: 35)

The wounds become the 'Arma Christi', or 'Arms of Christ', quasi-heraldic badges of pain and shame ironically signifying glory, sacred insignia often conjoined with the 'Instruments of the Passion' – the emblematic objects and implements of torture that, by a kind of visual shorthand, prompt devout memories to recall man's ingratitude to Christ. Blazoned on bench-ends, screens, roof-bosses, in wall-paintings and external decoration, images of the Wounds and Instruments might be displayed dispersedly throughout churches. 'His body hanging on the cross is a book open for your perusal', declares a fourteenth-century contemplative, the Monk of Farne, likening Christ's body to a text, and for a contemporary mystic, Richard Rolle, Christ's bloodied body is 'lyke a boke written al with rede ynke' (ed. Farmer 1961: 76; Ogilvie-Thomson 1988: 75).

Since their influence was so potent, the role of devotional images could not go unexamined, although the traditional orthodoxy – that images 'been ordeyned to been a tokene and a book to þe lewyd peple, þat þey moun [can] redyn in ymagerye and peynture þat clerkys redyn in boke' – continued to be a mainstream view, and images were defended because: 'ther ben mony thousand of pepull that couth [could] not ymagen in her hert how Crist was don on the rood, but as thei lerne hit by sight of images and payntours' (ed. Barnum 1976–2004: Vol. I, Pt. 1, 82; Erbe 1905: 171). Written for advanced contemplatives, the anonymous *Cloud of Unknowing* deplores how some will form distracting mental images of a God richly attired and enthroned 'fer more curiously þan euer was he depeynted in þis erþe' (ed. Hodgson 1944: 105), but the *Cloud*'s contemplative contemporary Walter Hilton justifies images in a pastoral context because they prompt desirable devotional sentiments –

> Amongst which signs the Church sets up images of Christ crucified . . .
> in order that the Passion and also the martyrdoms of other saints may
> be recalled to memory by looking at these images; and thus slow and
> carnal minds may be stirred to compunction and devotion.
> (ed. Clark and Taylor 1987: Vol. I, 188; compare Figure 1.1)

Churches, therefore, in design, contents and adornment, came to present highly developed sign systems available to be read at different levels by different observers.

Signs of Devotion

> And þen anon is taken to hir a tabil [painted panel], ful wel depeynte
> with an ymage of oure Lorde crucifyed: and holdyng that open and
> vncouerd wiþ booþ handys, ful deuoutly she lokiþ . . . in þe same
> ymage with alle þe intente of hir mynde. And . . . sche is rauesched and
> waxes [grows] alle starke, holdynge þe tabil . . . And oþere-while þe same
> tabil is lenyd vpon hir breste, and some-tyme abouen her face, after
> dyuerse holdynges of þe tabil in þe bikumynge [attainment] of euery

Figure 1.1 From *The Art of Good Lywyng and Deyng* (printed Paris, 1503): an angel bids the dying man turn his soul away from impatience. Reproduced by courtesy of The Master and Fellows of Emmanuel College, Cambridge.

The image shows (left to right): Christ with the instruments of his scourging; God the Father with scourge and arrow; and four saints bearing the emblems of their sufferings – St Barbara with the tower in which she was imprisoned, St Lawrence with the gridiron on which he was roasted to death, St Catherine with the wheel on which she was tortured and the sword that beheaded her, and St Stephen with the stones with which he was pelted to death.

rauishynge. . . . And soo she durith a good space, wiþ incres of swetnesse, as semes to hem þat se right as she didde, in biholdynge of þe ymage, wiþ oþere hy3 tokens of deuocyone . . . but her countenance is stedfastly sette in consideracyone of þe ymage; so þat she byholdith no body nor noon oþere thinge but the tabil allonly. . . Whan alle this is doon, mykel moor solempnely and moor merueylously þan I can or maye write, sche keueriþ [covers] and closeþ þe same tabil and takith it to som body bisyde hir.

(*The Life of St Elizabeth of Spalbeck*,
ed. Horstmann 1885: 110)

In her rapt engagement with this painting the holy woman Elizabeth of Spalbeck exemplifies just how intense was the stimulus to devotion – and potentially to visionary experience – provided by images. In England *The Book of Margery Kempe* – the self-account of a Norfolk housewife and visionary – presents itself as recording the vivid experience of a comparably suggestible respondent to contemporary signs and symbols of devotion. (Indeed, Kempe's extravagant weeping is compared with the conduct of another Low Countries holy woman, Mary of Oignies, whose paramystical life appears in English translation alongside that of Elizabeth of Spalbeck). Kempe came to have God so constantly in her thoughts that she 'behelde hym in alle creaturys' (ed. Windeatt 2000: 320), and saw everything as a sign: nursing mothers and young children put her in mind of his Nativity, while witnessing animals or children being beaten reminds her of his Passion (164). Kempe's *Book* ignores or merges traditional dualisms – body and spirit, literal and symbolic – less because she is naïve or literal-minded than because inclusion matches better with experience. Moreover, Kempe acts out a medieval devotional tendency to see any one aspect of Christ's life as present in all others: she might have seen Annunciation images showing a beam of light descending to Mary – representing her sinless conception – while a small crucifix or a baby clutching a cross slides down the sunbeam towards her, encapsulating Christ's redeeming future death even at the instant of his conception (compare King 2006: plate I 2a). Or again, Kempe probably encountered the iconography of the 'Lily Crucifixion', an image which, in depicting Christ crucified on a lily flower, superimposes his anguishing death on to the lily identified with both the Annunciation and his mother (see Woodforde 1950: plate XXII). Everywhere repeated would be an Annunciation image where the dove of the Holy Spirit flies down towards Mary's ear when the Word is made flesh. One lyric confidently identifies which ear ('Blessed be, Lady, thy richt ere: / The Holy Gost, he liht [alighted] in there, / Flesch and blod to take'; ed. Horstmann 1892: 126); Kempe hints at identification with Mary when recalling how she heard the Holy Ghost like a robin redbreast 'that song ful merily oftyntymes in hir ryght ere' (197). Imagery of Christ's conception as a beam of light was represented – according to stage directions – very literally and concretely in one mystery play cycle, probably East Anglian and now entitled *The N-Town Play*:

> Here þe Holy Gost discendit with iij bemys to our Lady, the Sone of þe Godhed next with iij bemys to þe Holy Gost, the Fadyr godly with iij bemys to þe Sone. And so entre all thre to here bosom . . .
>
> (ed. Spector 1991: 122)

Incarnation of the triune God in Mary's womb was represented highly concretely in such 'vierge ouvrante' images as 'The Lady of Boulton', once in Durham Cathedral, where the belly of an image of Mary, like a cupboard, 'was maide to open . . . from her breaste downward', to reveal the Trinity enclosed inside, with an image of God the father

> holding betwixt his handes a fair & large crucifix of Christ all of gold . . . and every principall [major feast] daie the said immage was opened that every man might se pictured within her the father, the sonne, and the holy ghost, moste curiouselye and fynely gilted.
>
> (*Rites of Durham*, ed. Fowler 1903: 30)

Just as a lyric hails 'Marye, mayde mylde and fre, / Chambre of þe Trynyte' (ed. Brown 1924: no. 32), so Kempe records herself being thanked by Christ for receiving and seating the Trinity in her soul (373). Above all, Kempe exemplifies how meditative devotion encouraged the contemplative to 'Make the in thy soule present' at the Gospel scenes (as one of the most popular vernacular texts of the fifteenth century, Nicholas Love's *Mirror of the Blessed Life of Jesus Christ*, advises). In her mind's eye, Kempe steps through the frame and inside the devotional image. In her meditations she assists at the births not only of Christ but also of the Virgin and John the Baptist, relating as mother of fourteen children to these three differently miraculous births, and inserting herself into such devotional scenes as the Visitation and the early life of Mary. When in contemplation she wraps Jesus in his swaddling clothes (77), addressing the Christ Child while tearfully 'havyng mend [mind] of the scharp deth that he schuld suffyr', Kempe acts out her own performance of those English lyrics that take the form of lullaby exchanges between Mary's fears and her child's prophecies to her of his eventual death, so that Nativity and Passion images are superimposed into a kind of double exposure.

When Kempe records seeing in a Leicester church a crucifix 'petowsly poyntyd [piteously depicted] and lamentabyl to beheldyn' (228) and is prompted to 'pity and compassion' at the thought of Christ's Passion, her response exemplifies the effect of images that Hilton had endorsed. Similarly, in his *Testament* the monk John Lydgate recalls how as a boy of under fifteen 'holdyng my passage, / Myd of a cloyster, depicte vpon a wall', he saw a crucifix 'with this word "*Vide*" [Behold!] wrete there besyde', which moved him to write a poem in which Christ guides observers in contemplating his Passion (ed. MacCracken 1911: 356). Moreover, Kempe's other recorded reactions to artefacts, as well as her visions, reflect developments in devotional focus and the images that led and served this. In a Norwich church Kempe recalls seeing a 'pete' – a *pietà*, or image of Mary with the dead Christ across her lap – 'and thorw the beholdyng of that pete her mende was al holy ocupyed in the Passyon' (286); equally, one poem by Lydgate was evidently planned to accompany an image of a 'pyte' ('looke on this fygure . . . My bloody woundis, set here in picture . . .') and guide meditation upon it ('Whan ye beholde this dolerous pyte . . .': 250–1). In another poem Lydgate tells how, during a sleepless night, he 'Vnclosyd a book that was contemplatiff' and found a 'meditacioun' preceded by 'an ymage ful notable / Lyke a pyte depeynt' (268), which moved him to pen the ensuing work. Some lyrics narrate how what appears at first sight the painted and carved artefact of a *pietà* turns into the lamenting Mary herself ('In a chirche as I gan knele . . . / I saw a pite in a place . . . / Ofte she wepte and sayde "Alas" . . .', cited in Woolf 1968: 257). In *De arte lacrimandi* ('On the Art of Weeping'), while kneeling before a *pietà*, the poet's spirit is ravished from his body to see a vision of Mary, whose autobiographical account is punctuated by the refrain 'Who can not wepe, come lerne att me' (ed. Garrett 1909: 269–94). In one lyric the speaker, confronted with Mary cradling the dead Christ, confesses 'I said I cowd not wepe, I was so harde hartid', and is sharply reproved by Mary 'with wordys shortly that smarted . . . "Thyne owne fadder þis nyght is deed!"' (ed. Brown 1939: no. 9). To the priest who dryly reproaches her for weeping ('"Damsel, Jhesu is ded long sithyn"'), Kempe's riposte may represent her performance of the situation dramatized in such poems, where the *pietà* is a challenge to tears and compassion: '"Sir, hys deth is as fresch to me as he had deyd this same day – and so me thynkyth it awt to be to yow and to alle Cristen pepil!"' (286). The thrust of Kempe's retort is that Christ's life and death should be concurrent with our experience. As potent a focus for devotion as the *pietà* was that of the 'Imago Pietatis' or Man of Sorrows. In this image, the wounded post-Crucifixion body of Christ usually stands visible from the waist up in a tomb chest, surrounded by the instruments of the Passion. It is a version of this image that Kempe apparently describes in her vision of Christ appearing 'with hys wowndys bledyng as fresch as thow he had ben scorgyd beforn hir', as in succeeding visions of his body looming over her (368–70). Kempe's vision reflects trends to objectification of Christ's body in devotion. The 'Imago Pietatis' is a kind of freeze-frame picture abstracted from the Passion narrative without corresponding to any particular moment in it: a posed and arranged composition, selecting from both Crucifixion and entombment, which becomes the cue for innumerable poems and images (and may colour representations of the resurrected Christ as Man of Sorrows, as in the Wakefield *Play of the Resurrection*).

Kempe records being constantly at church when she had such visions reminiscent of the 'Imago Pietatis' (368–71), and the church fabric presented a system of such signs, serving the building's central focus on the Mass. The moment when the miracle of Eucharistic transubstantiation was displayed to the laity at the elevation of the Host is the focus of many lyrics and carols (declaring 'Thowgh yt seme whit, yt ys rede; / Yt ys flesshe, yt semeyth bred', or, more daringly, 'In Virgyne Mary this brede was bake, / Whenne Criste of her manhoode did take'; ed. Greene 1977: nos 319, 318). Like many visionaries, Kempe has her mysterious insight during Mass when she sees the Host fluttering at elevation, evidently suggesting the dove of the Holy Spirit, as the priest staggers under the miraculous manifestation of God with us (129). It was to celebrate how life thereby defeats and succeeds death that on Good Friday the Host was 'buried' symbolically in an 'Easter Sepulchre' (sometimes an elaborate tomb-chest), to be taken out again on Easter Sunday morning as a sign of the Resurrection, a ritual Kempe records witnessing with devout emotion (275–6). Near to an Easter Sepulchre was a favoured place for burial of the dead, mentioned in many medieval wills that plan for interment inside a church. The two-decker or 'cadaver' tomb – displaying above the deceased's effigy in stately dignity of royal, noble or ecclesiastical robes while below is carved a naked skeleton or partly decomposed corpse prey to worms and toads – gave plastic form to the message of a widespread medieval cautionary exemplum of a son converted by gazing into his father's grave. Another 'memento mori' was the theme of the 'danse macabre' (or Dance of Death), in which figures representative of various ranks and professions dance with their own skeletons (a motif overlapping with the 'carole' or dance-song symbolizing a courtly life of love and diversion, as in *The Romance of the Rose*). The Dance of Death famously depicted round the church-yard walls of the Innocents in Paris was imitated in St Paul's church-yard and accompanied by Lydgate's verses translated from the French poem inscribed at the Innocents. In Henryson's *The Thre Deid Pollis* ('The Three Skulls') the death's heads speak – with their fleshless skulls and hollowed-out eyes – reminding 'wantone yowth', fashionable ladies and 'febill aige' that all-devouring death makes a mockery of worldly distinctions (ed. Fox 1981: lines 43–4). In *The Three Dead Kings* – the one English poem treating the encounter of 'The Three Living and the Three Dead' – three kings out hunting together come face to face with the animated but decomposing corpses of their dead fathers, who warn their sons to live so that they do not fear Judgement Day ('Makis ȝour merour be me!') (ed. Turville-Petre 1989: 148–57). The repentant kings build a minster on whose walls their encounter is recorded; such scenes – in which the three figures may represent different ages of man and estates of society – were a frequent subject of church wall-paintings. Indeed, it is into scenes of hunting – emblematic of courtly society at play – that signs and tokens of mortality impinge (as in Chaucer's *Book of the Duchess*). In the lyric beginning 'In noontyde of a somers day' the narrator 'toke my hawke, me for to play' and sets off delightedly to hunt, 'My spanyellis renyng by my syde' (ed. Gray 1975: no. 80). Yet, in the midst of pursuing a pheasant, the jaunty huntsman stumbles, his leg torn by a briar, and, looking down, notices how the briar 'bare wrytyng in every leff – / This Latyn word, *revertere* [turn back]'. Forgetting pheasant and dogs, the hunter's 'hart fell down unto my to' and he sighingly reflects how, since 'This hawke of yowth' leads astray, 'than ys best *revertere*'. Also an admonishment, in the poem *Somer Soneday* (ed. Turville-Petre 1989: 140–7) the narrator, having become detached from the hunt in which he has been riding, encounters Dame Fortune rotating on her wheel the rising, falling and fallen figures of four kings – which might be captioned 'I shall reign', 'I reign', 'I have reigned' and (at the bottom) 'I am without a king-dom' – an image that also relates to wheel-like symbolizations of the ages of man's life. Drawing together such tokens of mortality, the alliterative romance *The Awntyrs off Arthure* opens by refashioning a well-known tale of how St Gregory encounters his mother's ghost who urges him to have Masses said for her soul. Isolated from their hunting party by a sudden storm, Gawain and Guinevere are confronted by a gruesome apparition of Guinevere's mother as a corpse prey to toads and serpents and risen from the grave and purgatory to warn the Queen to amend her life, to have Masses said for her mother's soul, and to warn Gawain of the coming downfall of the Round Table and its values ('Your king is too covetous'; ed. Hanna 1974: 264).

Following the Signs

In the mysterious *Corpus Christi Carol* the speaker laments that a falcon 'hath born my mak [mate] away' and carried him 'into an orchard brown':

> In that orchard ther was an hall,
> That was hangid with purpill and pall.
>
> And in that hall ther was a bed:
> Hit was hangid with gold so red.
>
> And yn that bed ther lythe a knyght,
> His wowndes bledyng day and nyght.
>
> By that bedes side ther kneleth a may,   maiden
> And she wepeth both nyght and day.
>
> And by that beddes side ther stondith a ston,
> '*Corpus Christi*' wretyn theron.
>   (ed. Greene 1977: no. 322A)

Inexhaustibly enigmatic, this image of a knight in a rich bed with his wounds constantly bleeding, and a kneeling maiden constantly weeping, summons up both a world of chivalrous endeavour and a suffering love and devotion, associating them with the Eucharistic sacrifice of blood and its mystery. For from ideas of Christ's Passion as a combat – as in William Dunbar's poem 'Done is a battell on the dragon blak' – waged out of God's love for mankind, a pervasive imagery developed of Christ as lover-knight jousting at a tournament of the Passion for his beloved, man's soul (see also Catherine Sanok's essay below). Christ's arms stretched wide on the cross could be viewed as a lover's arms outstretched to embrace, as in this advice to a female recluse on devotional images:

And as touchynge holy ymages, haue in þyn awter þe ymage of þe crucifix
. . . he is ysprad abrood to bykleppe [embrace] þe in his armes, in which
þu schalt haue gret delectacioun . . .

(ed. Ayto and Barratt 1984: 35)

Even Christ's assumption of human flesh in Mary's womb at the
Incarnation could be likened to a knight's donning armour with the
aid of a maiden, and his Deposition from the Cross to a disarming. St
Paul's allegory of putting on the armour of God generated narratives
of knightly arming for a spiritual quest. It is within such traditions that
Piers Plowman describes Christ coming to his Crucifixion to joust 'in
Piers armes, / In his helm and in his habergeon [coat of mail] – *humana
natura*' (ed. Schmidt 1987: XVIII.22–3)). In one poignant lyric Christ
calls the Cross his horse ('Mi palefrey is of tre / With nayles naylede
þurh me'; ed. Brown 1924: no. 51), and torturers in the Wakefield
Crucifixion play call on Christ to mount 'apon youre palfray sone',
jesting about his being so tightly tied to his horse when 'Ye must just
in tornamente' (ed. Stevens and Cawley 1994: 290). In some variations on this theme Christ speaks like a knightly lover, as in the lyric
beginning 'Mi love is falle upon a may, / For love of hire I defende
this day', where the narrator's passionate love is not to be denied ('Loue
aunterus [daring love] no man forsaket; / It woundet sore whan it
him taket . . .'; ed. Brown 1924: no. 73). In different tellings the lady's
response to the Christ-knight's loving sacrifice may range from indif-
ference to grateful treasuring of the knight's blood-stained armour, shield
or shirt – allegorically, the memory of the Passion – as in Henryson's
The Bludy Serk. Here a knight rescues a lady – abducted from her father
and held captive in a dungeon by a giant – but is fatally wounded and
begs his grieving lady 'Tak ye my sark [shirt] that is bludy, / And hing
it forrow [in front of] ye' (lines 75–6). A concluding moralization likens
'The manis saule to the lady, / The gyane to Lucefeir, / The knycht
to Chryst that deit on tre' (lines 99–101) and concludes 'Think on the
bludy serk' (line 120).

To think on Christ's bloodied body as our lover and knight might
make any other knightly endeavour seem vain, and many Grail
romances – like Malory's 'Tale of the Sankgreal' – exploit the outward
forms and conventions of a knightly narrative made up of adventures
and quests, except that everything has been transposed and reordered
to prompt discovery of otherworldly perspectives. Although Malory
has radically pruned much commentary from his French source, *La
Queste del Saint Graal*, retrospective explications by hermits and

21

recluses still promote the reading of all events as signs within a symbolic narrative, with adventures for the successful Grail knights – Bors, Galahad and Perceval – determined by marvellous signs and tokens that transcend and critique conventional knightly adventures. When Perceval's sister dies willingly, giving 'a dysshfulle of bloode' in order that another lady might be healed, this signals that the conventional way of abolishing such an oppressive 'custom of the castle' by male knightly challenge has been superseded by a Christ-like self-sacrifice of blood and life by a maiden ('And therefore there shall no more batayle be'; ed. Vinaver 1990: 1002–3).

Leaving behind their horses (essential to conventional knighthood but also sometimes symbolic of male sexuality), Grail knights move about now on mysterious ships – without sail or oar, and seemingly uncrewed and unvictualled – one of which names itself by an inscription, 'for I am Faythe' (984), and contains a sword destined for Galahad, among other marvellous artefacts (including spindles carved from the Tree of Life brought by Eve from Eden). Most of the ships are white, in a narrative where symbolism of whiteness and blackness – as of youth and age, or lions and serpents – is a key to spiritual significance. Nearly carried off to perdition by the fiend in the form of a supernaturally swift black horse, Perceval, alone with wild beasts on a sea-girt mountain, sees a lion battling a serpent, slays the serpent and dreams a 'mervaylous dreme' of a young lady riding a lion (she foretells that tomorrow Perceval must fight the world's greatest champion) and an old lady riding a serpent (she threatens '"I shall take you as he that somtyme was my man"': 914). A priest-like old man on a ship covered in white samite interprets the young lady as the New Law of Holy Church and the old lady and serpent as the Old Law and the devil. After the white ship has gone away 'he wyste nat whydir', it is succeeded by a ship 'coverde with sylk more blacker than ony beré'. Inside is a gentlewoman of great beauty – a shapeshifted Lucifer – who asks for Perceval's assistance ('"for ye be a felowe of the Rounde Table"') because, she claims, the greatest man of the world has disinherited her perpetually as '"I had a litill pryde, more than I oughte to have had"' (917). In sultry weather choice meats and potent wine are served 'and therewith he was chaffett [heated] a lityll more than he oughte to be . . . and prayde hir that she wolde be hys'. But, as the naked Perceval is about to lie down beside the naked lady in a pavilion, 'by adventure and grace he saw hys swerde ly on the erthe naked, where in the pomell was a rede crosse and the sygne of the crucifixe therin'. Making the sign of the cross on his forehead, he promptly sees the pavilion 'chonged unto a smooke and a blak clowde' as the lady and her ship go 'with the wynde, rorynge and yellynge, that hit semed all the water brente after her' (919). Declaring that since '"my fleyssh woll be my mayster, I shall punyssh hit"', Perceval drives his sword into his thigh in a token self-castration, before the old man in the white ship returns to identify the gentlewoman with the old lady riding on a serpent and with Lucifer ('"And that was the champion that thou fought withal . . ."': 920).

Such a spiritualizing narrative – featuring struggles between good and evil played out through knightly quests – unfolds through the symbolism of a black-and-white moral landscape, but within this evil may assume deceptive appearances. That Bors' visions are first interpreted falsifyingly – by a man seemingly in religious apparel but riding a horse 'blacker than a byry' (962) – highlights the significance in these adventures of the process of interpreting signs and tokens, as does the tragicomic shallowness of Gawain, who cannot be bothered to stay for a hermit's interpretation of his spiritual state (949). Early in his quest Sir Bors

> loked up into a tre, and there he saw a passynge [very] grete birde uppon that olde tre. And hit was passyng drye, withoute leyffe; so she sate above, and had birdis whiche were dede for hungir. So at the laste he [*sic*] smote hymselffe with hys beke, which was grete and sherpe, and so the grete birde bledde so faste that he dyed amonge hys birdys. And the yonge birdys toke lyff by the bloode of the grete birde. Whan Sir Bors saw thys he wyste well hit was a grete tokenynge . . .
>
> (956)

His further vision of a worm-eaten tree, which would have impaired the whiteness of two lily-like flowers (958), betokens the spiritual dilemma that Bors confronts when he must choose whether to save his brother Sir Lionel from being killed by his captors or save a lady from imminent ravishment by a knight. Prizing chastity above all, Bors prevents the rape and seemingly fails to prevent his brother's death. As an abbot interprets the signs, '"the sere [withered] tree betokenyth thy brothir . . . whych ys dry withoute vertu"', rotten because he '"doth contrary to the Order off Knyghthode"', while the two white flowers signify the knight and gentlewoman who escaped damnation (968). Most significantly, when Christ who bled his heart's blood for mankind on the Cross revealed himself to Bors '"in the lyknesse of a fowle . . . there was the tokyn and the lyknesse of the Sankgreall that appered afore you, for the blood that the grete fowle bledde reysyd the chykyns frome dethe to lyff"'. Here, the familiar Eucharistic symbolism of the 'pelican in its piety' (reviving its chicks with its blood) comes to represent the Grail. As for the bare old tree in which the bird is sitting, this '"betokenyth the worlde, whych ys naked and nedy, withoute fruyte, but if hit com of oure Lorde"' (967), and the barren tree as a sign of spiritual emptiness is applied not only to Lionel but to Gawain ('"in the ys neythir leeff nor grasse nor fruyte"': 949), and to Lancelot, who is '"lykened to an olde rottyn tre"' (898), in a parallel with the fruitless fig tree accursed by Christ (Mark 11:13–14). The only way forward is by penitence (Lancelot dons a hair shirt) and by confession; otherwise, a hermit warns Lancelot, he will never see the Grail ('"thoughe hit were here ye shall have no power to se hit, no more than a blynde man that sholde se a bryght swerde"': 927).

When Lancelot is, for the first time in his life, unsuccessful in a tournament – where he helps a company of knights in black whom he sees being worsted by knights in white – a recluse later explains that the tournament '"was but a tokenynge of oure Lorde"' in which Lancelot failed to distinguish good from this world's vainglory ('"hit ys nat worth a peare"': 934). For Galahad, chivalric narrative and Christian symbolism can be fused: at the Castle of Maidens – through his knighthood in overcoming seven knights – he abolishes the wicked custom of the castle and frees the captive maidens. As a hermit explains:

> 'the Castell of Maydyns betokenyth the good soulys that were in preson before the Incarnacion of oure Lorde Jesu Cryste. And the seven knyghtes betokenyth the seven dedly synnes that regned that tyme in the worlde. And I may lyckyn the good knyght Galahad unto the Sonne of the Hyghe Fadir, that lyght [alighted] within a maydyn, and bought all the soules oute of thralle . . .'
>
> (892)

By contrast, even when Lancelot reaches the site where he will see something of the Grail, at a castle unguarded 'save two lyons kept the entré and the moone shone ryght clere', he still trusts in his sword and draws it against the lions: 'so there cam a dwerf sodenly and smote hym the arme so sore that the suerd felle oute of his hand'; and Lancelot hears himself reproached for lack of faith ('"For He myght more avayle the than thyne armour, in what servyse that thou arte sette in"': 1014). At this castle, glimpses of the Grail are translated into the traditional iconography of visions during Mass, when it appears as if the Man of Sorrows steps forth from the Grail or Mass chalice 'bledynge all opynly' (1030). With blood from the spear – earlier identified as that which wounded Christ's crucified side – Galahad can heal at last the wounds of the Maimed King. Yet just as the focus of Malory's 'Sankgreal' implies honour for Lancelot despite his unfulfilled Grail quest – and a hermit interprets Ector's dream of Lancelot riding an ass as a parallel with Christ's entry into Jerusalem – so too in Malory's concluding part of *Le Morte Darthur* one of his few invented scenes allows, in the healing of Sir Urry, for Lancelot, a sinful, fallen man, to perform his own act of miraculous healing of a maimed knight, confirming the earlier remark of a recluse during the Grail Quest: '"of all erthly knyghtes I have moste pité of the, for I know well thou haste nat thy pere of ony erthly synfull man"' (934).

'The token of synne is turnyd to worshippe . . .'

> A God, and yet a man?
> A mayde, and yet a mother?
> Witt wonders what witt can
> Conceave this or the other.
>
> A God, and can he die?
> A dead man, can he live?
> What witt can well replie?
> What reason reason give?
>
> God, truth it selfe doth teache it;
> Mans witt sinkes too farr under
> By reasons power to reach it –
> Beleeve, and leave to wonder!
> (ed. Brown 1939: no. 120)

The Incarnation – in which God became flesh and suffered in a human body – could be not only a sign of mankind's fallen condition in need of redemption but also a token of how human bodily nature has the potential to rise above itself. A flamboyant Nativity carol – with its clarion opening (from Romans 13) 'Owt of your slepe aryse and wake / For God mankynd nowe hath ytake' (ed. Greene 1977: no. 30) – hails the consequences of God's taking on of human flesh as an empowering revaluation of humankind:

> And thorwe a maide faire and wys
> Now man is made of ful grete pris;

> Now angelys knelen to mannys servys,
> And at this tyme al this byfel.
> Nowel!
>
> Now man is brighter than the sonne;
> Now man in heven an hye shal wone;   dwell
> Blessyd be God this game is begonne . . .!

In her sixteen revelations of May 1373, recorded and subsequently meditated upon, Julian of Norwich presents extraordinary re-visionings and deconstructions: her 'shewings' not only transfigure signs and tokens that, seen through most other eyes, are commonplaces of devotional culture, but also thereby explore the empowering implications of the interrelationship between humankind and an incarnate God. Julian's shewings begin when a crucifix is held before her dying gaze, but her revelations develop when this painted artefact morphs into the cinema of moving image: as Julian watches, painted blood moves and trickles. Although Julian's shewings imply the devotional images of her day, both her descriptions and the contemplative inferences she draws always represent some intensifying transposition of contemporary images. In their photographic focus, close-ups and angled shots, her first and second revelations may reflect – yet develop far beyond – devotion to the crown of thorns and the cult of the Vernicle (an image of Christ's face, miraculously imprinted on St Veronica's veil, with which he wiped his face on his way to Calvary). The fourth revelation of streaming blood pans out boldly on all levels from devotions to the Flagellation and Christ's multiple wounds, just as the eighth revelation re-reads in clinical close-up what is implicitly the agonized and slumping crucified body of late-medieval visual culture. The tenth revelation that moves cinematically into Christ's side is a contemplative development from devotion to the Five Wounds, just as here and more generally Julian's alertness to a mutual enclosing – of us in God, and of God in us – imaginatively and spiritually transcends devotion to images representing the Trinity in the Virgin's womb. Julian's contemplation of God as our mother far transcends, yet still reflects, such advice to a recluse as that in *De institutione inclusarum* ('On the Instruction of the Enclosed') on how to read the image of the crucifix on her altar ('hys tetys beþ al naked ischewd to þe to ȝyue þe melk of spiritual delectacioun and confortacioun'; ed. Ayto and Barratt 1984: 35). Yet, despite the intense visuality of her revelations, Julian guards against misleadingly literal understandings of symbolism spatial and material

('But it is not ment that the son syttith on the ryte hond . . . for there is no such syttyng, as to my syte, in the Trinite'; ed. Glasscoe 1993: 81).

As in the symbolism of pilgrimage towards enlightenment in *Piers Plowman* or Hilton's *Scale of Perfection*, Christ shows himself to Julian 'as it were in pilegrimage, that is to sey, he is here with us, ledand us, and shal ben till whan he hath browte us all to his bliss in hevyn' (130). In interpreting what she has seen, Julian's own longest contemplative pilgrimage arises because: 'I saw our Lord God shewand to us no more blame than if we were as clene as holy as angelys be in hevyn' (71). To Julian's concerns comes a response 'shewing full mystily a wondirful example of a lord that hath a servant' (72), a symbolic sequence that only twenty years later does Julian see how to interpret. Julian had been shown a lord sitting at rest in a desert place and gazing lovingly at a servant standing by. The lord sends off the servant, who runs to do his will but falls into a valley and lies wounded, unable to look back at his lord. To the spiritual symbolism of each detail of colour, clothing, movement and position in this narrative image Julian's contemplative imagination returns to discover accumulating layers of implication. As she comes to see, 'in the servant is comprehended' both Christ and Adam, 'that is to say al man', although 'in the servant that was shewid for Adam . . . I saw many dyvers properties that myten be no manner ben aret [attributed] to single Adam' (74). The symbolism of the lord is duly interpreted ('the blewhede of the clothing betokinith his stedfastnes'), but it is the dynamically doubled entity of the servant – at once Adam, Christ and all mankind – that challenges Julian's contemplative commentary. In her vision the Fall of man and Christ's incarnation are daringly fused, conveying how the loving divine descent into human flesh and suffering identifies with our fallen humanity in order to redeem it. Yet Julian's vision also ennobles the servant Adam, now seen toiling outside Eden in a gardener's ragged, sweat-stained clothing, and – remarkably – passes over silently the whole tradition of human self-blame and guilt for the Fall (not to mention misogynistic condemnations of Eve). The lord's sitting on the earth is to signify that God 'made mans soule to ben his owen cyte and his dwellyng place', while the servant's thin garment of a single layer signifies 'that there was ryte [noght] atwix the Godhod and manhede' (79). From Adam we have our weakness and blindness, and from Christ our virtue and goodness, but because Christ has taken all our blameworthiness upon himself 'therfore our Fadir may, ne will, no more blame assigne to us than to his owen son'. Through Christ's triumphant return to heaven our human flesh that he assumed – 'which was Adams old kirtle, streyte, bare and short' – has been rendered by Christ 'fair, now white and bryte, and of endles cleness'. Astonishingly, as Julian sees it, 'our foule dedly flesh' is transfigured into something 'fairer and richer than was than the clothyng which I saw on the Fadir' (80).

Pondering her vision's symbolism, Julian comes to see that the beloved servant's fortunate fall is not only rewarded 'aboven that he shuld a ben if he had not fallen', but proves a source of honour (it is 'turnyd into hey and overpassing worship and endles bliss'). At once spiritual yet boldly humane, Julian's mystical intuition that 'the token of synne is turnyd to worshippe' (52) opens a theological perspective that can make a positive of the mingling of Lancelot's success with failure in Malory's 'Tale of the Sankgreal', or of the moment in *Sir Gawain and the Green Knight* when Gawain returns home determined to see the green girdle as a '"syngne of my surfet"' (ed. Andrew and Waldron 2002: line 2433) and '"þe token of vntrawþe þat I am tan inne"' (line 2509), whereas Camelot fashions the selfsame token into an elegant courtly blazon celebrating what his fallen humanity has accomplished. If Julian can proclaim that 'by the assay [experience] of this failyng we shall have an hey, mervelous knoweing of love in God without end' (99–100), then the girdle Gawain sees as '"þe bende of þis blame"' can be flourished simultaneously as an insignia of honour. Julian's visionary reinterpretation of the sinner – 'Thow he be helyd, his wounds arn seen aforn God, not as wounds, but as worships' (54) – suggests how contemporaries' appraisal of the transgression signalled by Gawain's neck scar might interrelate this-worldly and otherworldly, bodily and spiritual, literal and symbolic, in ways that champion both humanity and the divine without exclusion. Not unlike Julian, the Nativity carol quoted above simply occludes possible damnation at Judgement Day ('Now shal God deme both the and me / Unto hys blysse yf we do wel . . .'), whilst exulting 'That ever was thralle, now ys he fre; / That ever was smalle, now grete is she'. St Augustine's 'other thing' – which so many signs recall to the medieval mind – is indeed an otherworldly perspective that reminds of this world's vanity. Yet, as this exuberant carol-writer may exemplify, signs and symbols remind not only of humankind's sinfulness but of coming exaltation, when the signs are fulfilled. Here God can be buttonholed like a brother, and all heaven and earth shall bow as mankind passes on his way to the court of heaven to gaze not at symbols but upon the face of God:

Now man may to heven wende;
Now heven and erthe to hym they bende;
He that was foo now is oure frende;
This is no nay that I yowe telle.
Nowel!

Now, blessyd brother, graunte us grace
At domesday to se thy face,
And in thy courte to have a place,
That we mow there synge nowel.　　may
Nowel!

References

Primary texts

Andrew, Malcolm and Waldron, Ronald, eds. (2002). *The Poems of the Pearl Manuscript: Pearl, Cleanness, Patience, Sir Gawain and the Green Knight*. 4th edn. Exeter: University of Exeter Press.

Ayto, John and Barratt, Alexandra, eds. (1984). *Ælred of Rievaulx's De institutione inclusarum*. EETS OS 287. Oxford: Oxford University Press.

Barnum, Priscilla Heath, ed. (1976–2004). *Dives and Pauper*. Vol. I, Pt. 1: EETS OS 275; Vol. I, Pt. 2: EETS OS 280; Vol. II: EETS OS 323. London and Oxford: Oxford University Press.

Bowers, John M., ed. (1992). *The Canterbury Tales: Fifteenth-Century Continuations and Additions*. Kalamazoo: Medieval Institute Publications.

Brown, Carleton, ed. (1924). *Religious Lyrics of the XIVth Century*. Oxford: Clarendon Press.

Brown, Carleton, ed. (1939). *Religious Lyrics of the XVth Century*. Oxford: Clarendon Press.

Clark, J.P.H. and Taylor, C., eds. (1987). *Walter Hilton's Latin Writings*. 2 vols. Salzburg: Institut für Anglistik und Amerikanistik, Universität Salzburg.

Erbe, Theodor, ed. (1905). *Mirk's Festial*. EETS ES 96. London: Kegan Paul, Trench, Trübner & Co.

Farmer, Hugh, ed. (1961). *The Monk of Farne: The Meditations of a Fourteenth-Century Monk, Translated by a Benedictine of Stanbrook*. London: Darton, Longman & Todd.

Fowler, J.T., ed. (1903). *Rites of Durham*. Surtees Society 107. London: Andrews & Co.

Fox, Denton, ed. (1981). *The Poems of Robert Henryson*. Oxford: Clarendon Press.

Garrett, R.M., ed. (1909). '*De arte lacrimandi*'. *Anglia*, 32, 269–94.

Glasscoe, Marion, ed. (1993). *Julian of Norwich: A Revelation of Love*. Revd edn. Exeter: University of Exeter Press.

Gray, Douglas, ed. (1975). *A Selection of Religious Lyrics*. Oxford: Oxford University Press.

Green, R.P.H., trans. (1997). *St. Augustine: On Christian Teaching.* Oxford: Clarendon Press.

Greene, R.L., ed. (1977). *The Early English Carols.* 2nd edn. Oxford: Clarendon Press.

Hanna, Ralph, III, ed. (1974). *The Awntyrs off Arthure at the Terne Wathelyn.* Manchester: Manchester University Press.

Henry, Avril, ed. (1987). *Biblia Pauperum: A Facsimile and Edition.* Aldershot: Scolar Press.

Hodgson, Phyllis, ed. (1944). *The Cloud of Unknowing and The Book of Privy Counselling.* EETS OS 218. London: Oxford University Press.

Horstmann, Carl, ed. (1885). 'Prosalegenden: Die Legenden des MS. Douce 114'. *Archiv,* 8, 102–96.

Horstmann, Carl, ed. (1892). *Minor Poems of the Vernon Manuscript Part I.* EETS OS 98. London: Kegan Paul, Trench, Trübner & Co.

James, M.R., ed. and trans. (1919). *Henry VI: A Reprint of John Blacman's Memoir.* Cambridge: Cambridge University Press.

MacCracken, Henry Noble, ed. (1911). *The Minor Poems of John Lydgate.* EETS ES 107. London: Kegan Paul, Trench, Trübner & Co.

Morenzoni, Franco, ed. (1988). *Thomas of Chobham: Summa de arte praedicandi.* Corpus Christianorum, Continuatio Mediævalis 82. Turnhout: Brepols.

Ogilvie-Thomson, S.J., ed. (1988). *Richard Rolle: Prose and Verse from MS Longleat 29.* EETS OS 293. Oxford: Oxford University Press.

Pantin, W.A. (1976). 'Instructions for a Devout and Literate Layman'. In J.J.G. Alexander and M.T. Gibson, eds., *Medieval Learning and Literature: Essays Presented to Richard William Hunt* (pp. 398–422). Oxford: Clarendon Press.

Raby, F.J.E., ed. (1959). *The Oxford Book of Medieval Latin Verse.* Oxford: Clarendon Press.

Sargent, Michael G., ed. (2004). *Nicholas Love: The Mirror of the Blessed Life of Jesus Christ.* Exeter: University of Exeter Press.

Schmidt, A.V.C., ed. (1987). *William Langland: The Vision of Piers Plowman – A Complete Edition of the B-Text.* 2nd edn. London: J.M. Dent.

Spector, Stephen, ed. (1991). *The N-Town Play.* EETS SS 11–12. Oxford: Oxford University Press.

Stevens, Martin and Cawley, A.C., eds. (1994). *The Towneley Plays.* EETS SS 13–14. Oxford: Oxford University Press.

Turville-Petre, Thorlac, ed. (1989). *Alliterative Poetry of the Later Middle Ages: An Anthology.* London: Routledge.

Vinaver, Eugène, ed. (1990). *The Works of Sir Thomas Malory.* 3rd edn, revd P.J.C. Field. 3 vols. Oxford: Clarendon Press.

Windeatt, Barry, ed. (2000). *The Book of Margery Kempe.* Harlow: Longman.

Secondary sources and suggestions for further reading

Anderson, M.D. (1971). *History and Imagery in British Churches.* London: J. Murray.

Kamerick, Kathleen (2002). *Popular Piety and Art in the Late Middle Ages: Image Worship and Idolatry in England 1350–1500.* New York: Palgrave.

King, David (2006). *The Medieval Stained Glass of St. Peter Mancroft Norwich*. Oxford: Oxford University Press.

Marks, Richard (2004). *Image and Devotion in Late Medieval England*. Stroud: Sutton.

Michael, M.A. (2004). *Stained Glass of Canterbury Cathedral*. London: Scala.

Van Os, Henk (1994). *The Art of Devotion in the Late Middle Ages in Europe 1300–1500* (Michael Hoyle, trans.). London: Merrell Holberton.

Woodforde, Christopher (1950). *The Norwich School of Glass Painting in the Fifteenth Century*. Oxford: Oxford University Press.

Woolf, Rosemary (1968). *The English Religious Lyric in the Middle Ages*. Oxford: Clarendon Press.

Chapter 2

Religious Belief

Marilyn Corrie

During the medieval period, a single institutionalized Church oversaw the spiritual welfare of most of the men and women in Western Europe: it was only at the Reformation that Christians in Western Europe came to be offered a choice of institutionalized faiths. Viewed from this perspective, the period appears one in which Christians were exposed to a single source of religious truth. In fact, inside the 'ark' of the Church, they were exposed to many such sources: the Bible, which told them the history of their faith and the moral tenets to which they should adhere; the interpretations, or 'exegesis', of the Bible that had been produced, in Latin, by the Fathers of the Church, and that continued to be produced by scholars in the medieval period itself; the doctrines formulated by the head of the Church, the Pope, and his prelates; perhaps God himself, who might communicate directly, if often obscurely, with a chosen individual. In the first 'passus' of his great late fourteenth-century dream vision poem *Piers Plowman*, William Langland famously has the personified figure of Holy Church tell the dreamer-narrator that the best way to save his soul is through Truth: '"Whan alle tresors arn tried," quod she, "Treuthe is the beste"' (ed. Schmidt 1987: I.85). But what Holy Church means by 'Treuthe', equally famously, is many things: God, Scripture, the virtue of honesty (for example).

Sometimes, the lessons that these multiple sources of religious truth taught were passed on intact by the men, and occasionally women, who wrote creatively in the medieval period. Langland, for instance, tethers the arguments and pronouncements that are voiced by the various figures who fill the different passus of *Piers* to the statements of Scripture, and occasionally to those of patristic authors. But medieval literature – including Langland's poem – also regularly engages with Christian teaching, in a variety of ways. It dramatizes the efforts, and often struggles, of people to understand that teaching both intellectually and emotionally; sometimes it shows them querying its truth. The ways in which medieval literature, and specifically Middle English literature, engages with religious teaching in the period are the subject of this chapter.

There is an important exception to the picture that I have just sketched, however, because for most of the fifteenth century literature produced in England tends less than previously in the Middle Ages to debate what the Church told people was true. Texts produced by members of the clergy in the fifteenth century communicate the Church's doctrines to the laity with urgency; texts produced by lay people themselves – who were increasingly joining the ranks of the literate in the fifteenth century – can be seen to endorse those doctrines. The tussling with doctrine that is a feature of medieval literature all but vanishes from literature that was produced in England in the fifteenth century (Watson 1995), as the chapter will also discuss.

A striking expression of the change in the relationship between literature and religious teaching that is apparent in fifteenth-century English texts is contained in a work that was produced towards the beginning of the century, Nicholas Love's *Mirror of the Blessed Life of Jesus Christ*, to which Barry Windeatt has already referred. Following the Latin source of his text, the *Meditationes vitae Christi* ('Meditations on the Life of Christ') traditionally ascribed to 'Pseudo-Bonaventure', Love describes how St Cecilia treated the material that forms the subject of his work:

> Amonge oþer vertuese commendynges [commendations] of þe holy virgine *Cecile* it is writen þat she bare alwey þe gospel of criste hidde in her breste . . . And when she hade so fully alle þe manere of his life ouer gon, she began aȝayne. And so with a likyng & swete taste gostly [spiritually] chewyng in þat manere þe gospel of crist she set & bare it euer in þe priuyte [interior] of her breste.
>
> (ed. Sargent 2004: 11)

The idea of 'chewyng' the story of Christ's life recalls the monastic practice of ruminating on Scripture – *ruminatio* – that occupied a sizeable part of monks' time in the Middle Ages (Leclercq 1978: 90); the practice reached its apotheosis in the work of the twelfth-century scholar

Petrus Comestor, also known as Petrus Manducator – Peter 'the Eater' or 'the Digester' – who had consumed the whole of Scripture, and regurgitated it in his Latin compendium of sacred history the *Historia scholastica* (Smalley 1969: 206). But in the proem to the *Mirror*, Love uses another 'eating' metaphor, derived from St Paul's words in I Corinthians 3:1–2, that suggests that his work is intended for people who are unable to chew anything: the 'fructuouse [fruitful] matere' and 'pleyn sentence [meaning]' that the text contains, he writes, mean that it is 'souereynly edifiyng to symple creatures þe whiche as childryn hauen nede to be fedde with mylke of lyȝte doctryne & not with sadde mete [serious food] of grete clargye & of h[ye] contemplacion' (ed. Sargent 2004: 10). Love turns the audience for his text into infants, who must swallow its 'doctryne' whole because the more substantial food of the 'grete clargye' and of people who have devoted themselves to contemplating God is not appropriate for them (compare Copeland 2001, especially 72–5). In fifteenth-century England chewing religious teaching becomes permissible only for those people who had enjoyed an advanced clerical and spiritual training, and it is proscribed to those who had not.

The Teaching of Scripture

For most of the Middle Ages, the Bible remained in its 'Vulgate' Latin form; direct exposure to its lessons, therefore, was the prerogative of those who had been educated to read and understand the Latin language (who included many people who chose, nevertheless, to write in English). Priests were supposed to be competent in Latin, since they had to read from the Vulgate during the Mass and the other liturgical service of the Church, the Office, at which the respective 'canonical hours' were marked. One component of the Bible that was especially ingrained in the consciousness of both priests and other Latinate people was the Psalms, since they were read from in both the Mass and the Office (see further Kuczynski 1995).

The non-Latinate, or 'lewed', were exposed to Scripture only indirectly. This might be through translation: from early in the medieval period, certain books, and parts of books, of the Bible were turned into the vernacular (Bonnard 1884). In the late fourteenth century – unacceptably to the Church, which risked losing its monopoly on the teaching of Scripture – the whole of the Bible was translated into English by followers of the Oxford theologian John Wyclif, who, like the

Reformers of the sixteenth century, wanted all Christians to have direct access to God's Word (see also Helen Cooper's essay later in this volume). Snatches of the Vulgate are likely to have been translated when clerics preached to the laity, although their sermons were almost always written down in Latin (Wenzel 2005); excerpts were also translated in vernacular instructional texts, including the early thirteenth-century guide for female recluses *Ancrene Wisse* (where the words of Scripture are sometimes tweaked and elaborated on in translation). Scripture was paraphrased in the vernacular too, in texts such as the orthographically unique late twelfth-century *Ormulum*, the work of the priest Orm, and the later *Cursor Mundi* ('The Cursor of the World' – that is, the text 'runs over' the history of the world).

The Bible was taught to the non-Latinate visually as well, through the iconography of sculpture, wood carvings and stained glass windows in churches and chapels; or through the illustrations in books, whether luxury manuscripts like the fourteenth-century Holkham picture bible (London, British Library, MS Additional 47682) or, at the other end of the bibliographical spectrum, the late-medieval printed 'block-book' versions of the *Biblia pauperum*, the 'bible of the poor', which juxtaposed illustrations of Old Testament events and protagonists with illustrations of the events and protagonists that they foreshadowed in the New Testament (De Hamel 2001: 142, 158–64). And people might be exposed to Scripture through dramatizations of its contents, through the mystery cycles that were performed in prosperous towns towards the end of the Middle Ages, or sometimes via 'one-off' playlets. One of the most remarkable of these plays, *Le Mystère d'Adam*, which is generally thought to have been composed in the Anglo-Norman dialect of French spoken and written in England, dates from the mid-twelfth century. Juxtaposing the story of the Fall of mankind with Cain's murder of Abel, the unknown playwright elaborates on Scripture by imagining the agony that its protagonists must have experienced as a result of their transgressions. Nobody's agony, unsurprisingly, is greater than Adam's:

> Allas! pechor, que ai jo fait?
> Or sui mort sanz nul retrait.
> . . .
> En emfer si avrai ma vie.
> Dont me vendra iloc aïe?
> Dont me vendra iloec socors?
> Ki me trara d'ités dolors?
> (ed. Aebischer 1963: lines 315–38)

[Alas! Sinner, what have I done? Now there is no escape from the death
I must face. . . . My life will be in hell. From where will help come to me
there? How will I be rescued there? Who will free me from such misery?]

Adam's recognition of his identity as a sinner revises Eve's previous
claim that she has attained clear-sightedness by eating the fruit: 'Or
sunt mes oil tant cler veant / Jo semble Deu le tuit puissant' (lines
307–8) ('My eyes see so clearly – I am like omnipotent God'). Eve's
self-deception – also the first instance of female deception of a man –
is superseded by the truth, that Adam will die and, paradoxically, continue his life in hell. And yet what are rhetorical questions for Adam
are questions that, for the Christian audience, have answers: Adam
will be rescued from hell by Christ, who died on the tree of the Cross
to redeem Adam's act of eating from the Tree of Knowledge. Typology
is written into *Le Mystère d'Adam* as consummately as it was into the
later mystery cycles.

For the Latinate and the non-Latinate, the distinction between the
teaching of Scripture and the teaching of other texts was not always
as clear as the sixteenth-century Reformers insisted that it must be.
For one thing, the literate read the Vulgate in manuscripts that
surrounded its text with glosses and commentaries; while these served
to 'display' Scripture, they were also given authority by association
with it (Ghosh 2001). For another, elaborations of the Christian story
that were not 'in' the Vulgate were often accorded a comparable authority to material that was. Accounts of the lives of post-biblical saints
and martyrs sometimes took the place of readings from Scripture in
the Office (Heffernan 2005). The vernacular retellings of sections of
Scripture in the *Cursor Mundi* coexist with a rendering of the apocryphal story of the upbringing of the Virgin Mary. Occasionally, apocryphal New Testament material was incorporated into copies of the
Vulgate itself: scholars have unearthed manuscripts in which the four
canonical Gospels of Matthew, Mark, Luke and John are followed by
the apocryphal Gospel of Nicodemus, the source of the legend of Christ's
Harrowing of Hell (Fowler 1976: 10). Despite the best efforts of the
Reformers to distinguish Scripture from the accretions that it had
acquired during the Middle Ages, some of them remained stuck to it.
It is often pointed out that there is no biblical sanction for the notion
that Christ was attended by an ox and an ass in the stable in
Bethlehem – the detail was popularized by the apocryphal New
Testament Gospel of 'Pseudo-Matthew' – but it is still a familiar part
of iconography and hymnology surrounding the Nativity.

Chewing on Scripture

The attempts of the playwright of *Le Mystère d'Adam* to imagine what
the protagonists of Scripture must have *felt* are replicated in Middle
English literature; to sensibilities shaped by Protestant emphasis on the
'difference' and specialness of the individuals who feature in the Bible
– an emphasis complemented by the archaic language used in the
Authorized Version of the Bible, which entrenches the historical distance between the biblical protagonists and the reader – this is one of
the most striking features of medieval treatments of Scripture. The poet
of *Patience*, in the same manuscript as *Sir Gawain and the Green Knight*
and *Pearl*, not only imagines what Jonah must have felt when God
told him to go to Nineveh to warn its inhabitants of its imminent
destruction, had him swallowed by a whale when he tried to escape
doing so, and then destroyed the woodbine that gave him shelter: he
also imagines what God must have felt when Jonah proved a reluctant prophet (Putter 1996: 139–46). In *Cleanness*, the other poem in
the manuscript, the poet retells a variety of scriptural narratives:
Christ's parable of the wedding feast, reported by the Gospels of
Matthew (22:1–14) and Luke (14:16–24); the fall from heaven of Lucifer
and the other angels who rebelled against God; and then – more expan-
sively – the stories of Noah's Flood and the destruction of Sodom and
Gomorrah from Genesis (with elaborations on the story of the Flood
from the *Cursor Mundi*), and the story of Belshazzar's feast, which is
pieced together from material in Daniel, II Chronicles and Jeremiah.
What all of these stories have in common, according to the narrator,
is the fact that they illustrate how God punishes 'fylthe' viciously: one
should, then, make sure that one cleanses oneself of one's own
spiritual taints through the sacrament of penance, a manifestation of
God's mercy that was not available to the people whom he punished
in the Bible:

> ȝis, þat Mayster is mercyable, þaȝ þou be man fenny,
> And al tomarred in myre whyl þou on molde lyuyes;
> Þou may schyne þurȝ schryfte, þaȝ þou haf schome serued,
> And pure þe wiþ penaunce tyl þou a perle worþe.
> (ed. Andrew and Waldron 2002: lines 1113–17)

[Yes, that master is merciful, even if you are soiled, and all dirtied with
filth while you live on earth; you can shine through confession, even
if you have devoted yourself to shame, and purify yourself with
penance until you become a pearl.]

And yet the censorious tone of the narrator is undercut by flashes of empathy for the sinners whom he simultaneously condemns. In his account of the parable of the wedding feast, for example, he interpolates into Scripture to imagine the mortification that the guest who attended the feast wearing inappropriate clothes must have felt when the host singled him out for his misdemeanour:

> Þat oþer burne watz abayst of his broþe wordez,
> And hurkelez doun with his hede, þe vrþe he biholdez;
> He watz so scoumfit of his scylle, lest he skaþe hent,
> Þat he ne wyst on worde what he warp schulde.
>
> (lines 149–52)

[That other man was ashamed at his angry words, and casts down his head; he beholds the earth. He was so scared out of his wits, in case he came to harm, that he could not find a single word to say.]

In Matthew's Gospel the social standing of the ill-attired guest is not specified; but the poet of *Cleanness* – perhaps through the influence of exegetical writing on the parable – identifies him as a labourer, his clothes 'fyled with werkkez' ('stained through his labours') (line 136) and, as the host unsparingly points out, '"ratted"' ('ragged') (line 144) (the version of the parable in Luke's Gospel ends without the host condemning any of the guests, although the guests here comprise the poor and the sick). One consequence of imagining the guest to be a poor man, we might think, is that he has no option *but* to attend the feast in dirty clothes – a fact that seems to query the justice of his fate, as the *Gawain*-poet seems implicitly to query the justice of what happens to his protagonists in his other works.

There is continuity between the way in which the *Gawain*-poet engages emotionally with the experiences of figures in the Bible and the ways in which other authors, especially men belonging to the Franciscan order of friars, meditated on the experiences of Christ and his mother, the Virgin, at the Crucifixion. Friars such as John of Grimestone and William Herebert in the fourteenth century composed and collected lyrics in which the words of Christ on the Cross were recreated, sometimes in conjunction with the Virgin's words to him as she surveyed his tortured body (ed. Brown 1924: nos 12–25, 55–76; compare Wenzel 1986: 101–73). The aim was to make the faithful engage emotionally, in turn, with the Crucifixion story – to 'affect' them so that they felt love for Christ and the Virgin, especially because they saw them as fellow, suffering human beings. The

Meditationes vitae Christi – also a Franciscan work – and Love's *Mirror* grow out of this tradition; commending the whole panoply of 'diuerse ymaginacions' of scenes and events from the life of Christ that the *Mirror* contains, Love comments that through it, 'a symple soule þat kan not þenke bot bodyes or bodily þinges mowe haue somwhat [can have something] accordynge vnto is affeccion [feeling] where wiþ he maye fede & stire his deuocion' (ed. Sargent 2004: 10). But the *Mirror* and its source aim to rouse the 'affeccion' of the simple in a much more ambitious and copious way than other writing in the same vein.

Some people extended the practice of exegesis of the Vulgate into imaginative writing, engaging especially with passages of figurative language in Scripture, which particularly called out for explanation. Psalm 84:11 in the Vulgate, 'Misericordia et veritas obviaverunt sibi; justitia et pax osculatae sunt' ('Mercy and truth have met each other; righteousness and peace have kissed'), was developed into the allegory of the Four Daughters of God, personifications of the vengeful and the merciful impulses in God's being, who were reconciled when the fate of mankind after the Fall was decided through the Incarnation; in the first half of the thirteenth century, Robert Grosseteste, bishop of Lincoln and – unusually for the Middle Ages – scholar of Greek, incorporated the allegory into his larger allegory of the Redemption, *Le Château d'amour* ('The Castle of Love') (Traver 1907: 29–40; compare Sajavaara, ed., 1967). In the twelfth century, an observation shared by Matthew 24:43 and Luke 12:39 – 'Si sciret paterfamilias qua hora fur uenturus esset, vigilaret utique et non sineret perfodi domum suam' ('If the father of the family knew at what time a thief were to come, he would watch out for him and not allow his house to be broken into') – was developed into a Latin homily, *De custodia interioris hominis* ('On the Custody of Man's Soul'), which tells of the need for human reason to be vigilant in order to protect the soul from perdition. Translated and adapted into Middle English as the early thirteenth-century prose text *Sawles Warde*, the homily seems to have been redirected to a female audience, perhaps the same as the one for whom *Ancrene Wisse* was written; against the usual stereotyping of their gender, the text thus suggests that women are just as capable of regulating themselves through reason as men are (Salih 2001: 56).

For the unknown playwright of the opening pageant of the York mystery cycle, the identification of God as 'the Word' in the Gospel of John seems to have been particularly compelling. God inaugurates the cycle by making a speech that teems with rhetoric and verbal

complexity, the antithesis of the plain, colourless speech that charac-
terizes Milton's God in *Paradise Lost*:

> I am gracyus and grete, God withoutyn begynnyng,
>   I am maker vnmade, all mighte es in me;
> I am lyfe and way vnto welth-wynnyng,   the attainment of joy
>   I am formaste and fyrste, als I byd sall it be.
>   My blyssyng o ble sall be blendyng,   countenance; blinding
>   And heldand, fro harme to be hydande,   protecting; concealing
>   My body in blys ay abydande,
>   Vnendande, withoutyn any endyng.
>
>   (ed. Beadle 1982: 49, lines 1–8)

Heavy alliteration is used throughout the pageant, but God speaks using
anaphora as well. He reiterates what seems to be the same idea in
varied terms ('foremost and first', 'Unending, without any ending'),
as if asking the audience to meditate on whether what he means *is*
exactly the same in each case. It is not easy to decode what God is
saying – especially in an oral context – as his language is dense and
riddling: a projection of his inscrutability to men. The York playwright
seems to engage with the idea of God as the Word by turning him
into a poet: he is 'maker' not just in the sense of 'creator', but also in
the more technical meaning of the term in Middle English, a fash-
ioner of creative verse (compare, for example, Schmidt 1987: 144–6).
But this says as much about the playwright's conception of poetry as
it does about his conception of God: divinity is best expressed through
lyricism of the kind that God's speech displays.

Chewing on Visions

For some men, and especially women, in the Middle Ages, the medi-
ation of divine teaching through Scripture was supplemented by
teaching direct from God, transmitted to them through visions. When
they wrote about this teaching, as they often did, they frequently
simply conveyed it to their readers, as people sometimes conveyed the
lessons of Scripture – or had it conveyed by individuals who had the
ability to write that they themselves lacked. The Latin account of
the revelations of the thirteenth-century German visionary Mechtild
of Hackeborn that was written later in the century by another female
visionary, Gertrude the Great, relates how at the Nativity, Mechtild

saw the shining image of an infant cleave to her breast; after she had worshipped the child, she saw herself carry him to her fellow nuns, and then saw him suck from the nuns' breasts – a vision that simultaneously places the nuns in the same role as the Virgin and inverts the ubiquitous medieval idea of Christians feeding on Christ. The fifteenth-century English translation of Gertrude's text, known as *The Book of Ghostly Grace*, which was owned by Richard III and his wife, Anne of Warwick, offers a welcome, if not entirely predictable, interpretation of its meaning:

> In this tyme sche hadde knawynge, as God wolde, that hytt schulde be full acceptable to oure lorde God that menne schulde make joye togedders with a meke ande holye beleve of that Nativite, ande make hitt hye ande worthie with all worscheppes ande praysynges that thaye mowe [can]. . . .
>
> (ed. Barratt 1992: 55)

Mechtild's vision might be thought to show her fulfilling the same function as a priest who handles the sacramental bread in the ceremony of the Mass, since the Church affirmed that this was Christ's body (see further below) – but the text stops its readers from entertaining this idea, directing them to a somewhat underwhelming piece of teaching instead.

Such writing serves as a foil for the work of Julian of Norwich, the recipient of a series of 'shewings' in 1373, as Barry Windeatt has already discussed. As early as the shorter account of the shewings, which is usually thought to have been written soon after they were granted to Julian, she elaborates on what her visions taught her directly, subjecting them to a process comparable to the exegesis of Scripture, explaining their meaning both to herself and to any readers of her account. Sometimes this is done through the use of metaphor, as in her interpretation of the significance of what she saw in her first vision, blood trickling from beneath the crown of thorns worn by Christ on a crucifix. Julian understood from this vision that Christ loves human beings and is the means of their salvation, and in her text she expands on this inference, identifying the comfort that Christ provides with the protection offered by a close-fitting garment:

> I sawe that he es to us alle thynge that is goode and comfortabylle to oure helpe. He es oure clethynge [clothing], for loove wappes [wraps]

us and wyndes us, halses [embraces] us and alle beteches [guides] [us], hynges [hangs] aboute us for tendyr loove, that he maye nevere leve us. And so in this syght Y sawe sothelye [truly] that he ys alle thynge that ys goode, as to myne understandynge.

(ed. Windeatt 1994: 185)

The shorter account of her shewings also repeatedly reveals Julian's concerns to forge a compatible relationship between the teaching that she has received from God and the teaching of the Church. She argues, for instance, that when God revealed to her that '"alle manere of thynge schalle be wele"', this does not mean that anybody in this life can see *how* everything will be well, and so her shewing does not contravene what the Church says:

It is Goddys wille that we witte [know] that alle schalle be wele in generalle; botte it is nought Goddys wille that we schulde witte it nowe, botte as it langes [is appropriate] to us for the tyme, and that is the techynge of haly kyrke.

(ed. Windeatt 1994: 201)

Julian's statements of deference to the Church's teachings have been read as self-protective assertions of the orthodoxy of her faith at a time when the Church was becoming seriously concerned about hetero-doxy (Watson 1993); but they might just as well be read as 'straight' expressions of her unquestioning acceptance of the Church's guidance, and her worries that what she has inferred from her visions might in some way be in conflict with this.

The relationship between the revelations that were made to her and the Church's teachings is something that Julian continues to contemplate in the longer version of her text, written nearly twenty years after the shorter version, and marked by the conviction that God's purpose in giving her the visions was that they might be passed on to her fellow Christians (chapter 8). The longer account of her shewings demon-strates Julian's efforts to assimilate what God taught her to the teach-ing of Scripture too. Her vision of a lord and his poorly dressed servant who falls when he rushes to do as his lord has asked him (chapter 51; compare Barry Windeatt's essay above), itself seemingly shaped in part by the same parable of the wedding feast as interested the poet of *Cleanness,* is mapped by Julian on to the stories of both the Fall and the Redemption: she comes eventually to identify the servant with Adam and Christ. But the longer account of the shewings also shows Julian chewing on the teaching that *she* has previously offered in her shorter text. This is the case, for example, in the effusive expression of her ideas about the goodness of God that follows her description of her first vision in the longer text:

> . . . it is the same grace that the soule sekith, and evir shall, till we know verily that hath us all in himselfe beclosyd; . . . for as the body is cladde in the cloth, and the flesh in the skyne, and the bonys in the flesh, and the herte in the bouke [trunk of the body], so arn we, soule and body, cladde in the goodnes of God and inclosyd. . . .
>
> (ed. Glasscoe 1993: 9)

Here Julian plays with the metaphor that she used in the shorter text, developing her comparison of God's 'clothing' of his creatures with the physical clothing worn by the body and filling in the implications of the idea that he – or rather, by this stage, the more abstract notion of his goodness – clothes us. In a text that famously includes the image of Jesus feeding us as 'our pretious moder', Julian chews on more than just the meaning of her visions: she chews on the full significance of the concepts that she has chosen to convey that meaning.

Engaging with the Teachings of the Church

The teaching of the Church by Julian's day might vary from place to place and from preacher to preacher; but it had certain core components. Since 1215, the date of the seminal meeting of the prelates of the Church known as the Fourth Lateran Council, it had taught that all Christians had to receive the sacrament of the Eucharist at least once a year (at Easter); they had to believe that the bread, or 'Host', that was used in this sacrament changed into the body and the blood of Christ when the priest said the words of consecration over it. The faithful had to confess their sins at least once a year to their parish priest, and perform any penance for those sins that the priest imposed. Penance could take many forms: fasting or praying, for instance, or, if the sin that had been committed was a grave one, pilgrimage. Individuals might also have savings in their spiritual bank with which they could pay off the debt that their sins had incurred: the Church offered indulgences for certain deeds, including 'taking the cross' to fight the infidel in the Holy Land, or completing certain pilgrimages. If one's sins were not fully atoned for, the faithful were taught, those sins would be punished after death, either in hell (from which one would never be released) or in purgatory, from which, according to some authorities at least, one might eventually be allowed access to heaven (compare Duffy 1992: 343–8).

Since 1281, when Constitutions drawn up by the Archbishop of Canterbury, John Pecham, were promulgated, the Church had taught Christians in England that they had to know the fourteen articles of the faith, the Ten Commandments, the seven sacraments of the Church, the seven works of mercy that Christians should perform towards their fellow Christians (in fact fourteen works of mercy, since there were seven 'bodily' and seven 'ghostly', or spiritual, works), the seven virtues that they should practise and the seven deadly sins that they should avoid; they also had to know the prayers beginning 'Pater Noster' ('Our Father') and 'Ave Maria' ('Hail, Mary'), and the profession of their faith contained in the Apostles' Creed. The principal channel of all this instruction was the priest, especially the priest of the parish in which an individual lived: the Fourth Lateran Council had instructed bishops to create networks of priests to deliver its programme of spiritual education to everybody. Priests were sometimes aided in their task by manuals in Latin or the vernacular, such as the *Instructions for Parish Priests* compiled in English late in the fourteenth century, or early in the fifteenth, by the Shropshire canon regular John Mirk (ed. Kristensson 1974). But the basics of the faith were also mediated by – and elaborated on in – treatises, including the extraordinary early fifteenth-century prose work *Dives and Pauper*, in which the ramifications of the Ten Commandments are discussed in a conversation between a generic rich man and a poor man (ed. Barnum 1976–2004). Vernacular texts also mediated instruction to people who wanted to follow a more ambitious programme of spiritual instruction, either by dedicating themselves to God completely (following the 'contemplative life') or by clearing some time to contemplate God while they remained in the world (the 'mixed life'). Walter Hilton catered for members of the former group in his late fourteenth-century *Scale of Perfection*, and for members of the latter in his treatise *On the Mixed Life* (ed. Bestul 2000; Ogilvie-Thomson 1986).

Even as Julian was expressing deference to the teachings of the Church, other people in England were interrogating them, and not least Langland, who, within his wider critique of the individuals who were supposed to convey the Church's teachings, raises concerns about the nature of those teachings themselves. Langland's concerns about the Church's doctrines are evident as early as the Prologue of *Piers*, in which the dreamer's vision of the 'fair feeld ful of folk' discloses problems in the idea of pilgrimage, which, the dreamer perceives, allows people to sin with impunity subsequently:

> Pilgrymes and palmeres plighten hem togidere   vowed
> For to seken Seint Jame and seintes at Rome;
> Wenten forth in hire wey with many wise tales,   their
> And hadden leve to lyen al hire lif after.
>   (ed. Schmidt 1987: Prologue, lines 46–9)

Langland's response to this doctrine is a bold one: he re-imagines it, transforming the ritual pilgrimage into the spiritual pilgrimage to Truth that Piers directs in Passus V of the B-text onwards – a pilgrimage that does not oblige one to leave home, that substitutes labour for travel, and that promises to lead the pilgrim both to the virtue of truth and the source of all truth, God.

As the B-text goes on, the dreamer evolves into a more obedient son of the Church; and yet Langland continues to query what the Church teaches, by juxtaposing its doctrines with teaching gleaned from other sources, especially biblical and patristic ones. In Passus XII, in the course of his quest for a definition of what it is to do well (and how one can do better and best), the dreamer converses with the figure of Ymaginatif, a personification of the imaginative faculty in the human soul, who rebukes the dreamer for criticizing the personified Clergy previously (in Passus X). Ymaginatif defends the learning of the clergy (although he also suggests that '"Kynde Wit"' – natural intelligence – can teach people things that members of the clergy do not know). But his defence of '"clergie"' comes to a halt when the dreamer points out one element of clerical teaching – that an individual cannot be saved if he is not a member of the Christian Church, another doctrine that had been codified in the ordinances of the Fourth Lateran Council:

> 'Alle thise clerkes,' quod I tho, 'that on Crist leven   then; believe
> Seyen in hir sermons that neither Sarsens ne Jewes   Saracens
> Ne no creature of Cristes liknesse withouten Cristendom
>   worth saved.'   will be
>   (XII.275–7)

Ymaginatif disputes this doctrine by alluding to the evidence of Scripture. The First Epistle of Peter (4:18) says that the just man will be saved (if scarcely), and so if one is just, Ymaginatif infers, one will be saved whether one is a Christian or not:

> '*Contra*!' quod Ymaginatif thoo, and comsed for to loure,
> And seide, '*Salvabitur vix iustus in die iudicii*;
> *Ergo – salvabitur*!' quod he. . . .
>
> (XII.278–80)

['Not so!' Ymaginatif said then, and began to frown, and said, 'The just man shall scarcely be saved on the Day of Judgement; therefore – he *shall* be saved!' he said. . . .]

What Ymaginatif says here is not necessarily 'correct': although he uses Scripture – implicitly a superior authority to the authority of clerics, or 'clerkes' – as the basis for his point, that point is, itself, derived from his own, potentially fallible interpretation of Scripture. But the poem still points to problems that may inhere in what the Church teaches Christians, and those problems evidently trouble Langland (compare Adams 1988: 99–101).

Piers Plowman also presents what the Church teaches as just one doctrine among many other doctrines that seem equally plausible. In Passus X, Clergy suggests to the dreamer that 'Dowel' consists (unsurprisingly) in faith in the Church and in knowledge of the articles of the faith (X.231–40). Nobody disputes what Clergy says. But then the other figures whom the dreamer consults, including personifications of human faculties such as Thought and Wit, have different opinions about what Dowel is, and those are not disqualified either. God, the poem suggests, can be pleased in a variety of ways, not just one. The more Langland thinks about the multiplicity of definitions of Dowel with which the dreamer is confronted, the more he seems to move away from Clergy's definition. The equation of Dowel with charity (that is, love of God and of one's fellow men) that is repeatedly offered to the dreamer – by Ymaginatif amongst other figures – seems finally to overwhelm all other definitions (compare Smith 1966). In Passus XIII, Clergy comes to accept it himself (line 124) and in Passus XV, the idea is transmuted into the dreamer's climactic vision of the Tree of Charity, which is tended by Piers Plowman. If not fallacious, Clergy's opinion about what Dowel comprises is not, the poem seems to suggest, the ultimate opinion on the matter.

The Teachings of the Church and Writing in England in the Fifteenth Century

As Langland was chewing on some of the Church's doctrines, other people in England were spitting many more of them out. Wyclif and his followers, known as 'Lollards' – 'mumblers' – by their detractors, rejected absolutely the doctrine of the transubstantiation of the Host in the Eucharist. They also rejected the claim that sinners could be forgiven for their transgressions only if they confessed them to a priest: all that was necessary for God to forgive a sinner, Lollards insisted, was that the sinner be contrite for his or her sins. Some Lollards rejected not just the sacrament of penance but the other sacraments of the Church as well. The confession of one fifteenth-century Lollard, Hawisia Moone of Loddon in East Anglia, records that she believed that the sacrament of matrimony was superfluous because a man's and a woman's consent to love each other was all that was needed, and that extreme unction – the sacrament that, the Church taught, the dying had to receive in order to be admitted to heaven – was equally redundant because 'it sufficeth euery man at hys last ende oonly to haue mende [mind] of God' (ed. Hudson 1978: 35). Like other Lollard beliefs, Moone's queried both the power of the priesthood and the necessity of many of the functions that the priesthood performed.

The alternative doctrines that Lollardy offered to the doctrines of the orthodox Church led both Church and state to take increasingly repressive measures against the movement. In 1401, Parliament made adherence to Wyclif's teachings punishable by death (by passing the statute *De heretico comburendo* – 'Of the Burning of Heretics'), and in 1407, the Archbishop of Canterbury, Thomas Arundel, drew up a series of Constitutions to prevent the further spread of heterodox opinions. Parish priests were to preach in their churches only on those matters that pertained to the syllabus of the basics of the faith; neither preachers nor teachers of children were to teach ideas about the articles of the faith or the sacraments that were contrary to what the Church had determined. It was also forbidden to preach or teach against such practices as the worshipping of images – a further target of Lollard polemic – as well as to discuss clerical vices before the laity (like Langland, Lollardy criticized those too). From now on, Scripture was not to be translated into English or any other language, in case its sense was distorted in the process. The distinction between the 'grete clargye' and the rest of the faithful that Love supports in the proem to his *Mirror of the Blessed Life of Jesus Christ* was to be preserved in these ways. Love's *Mirror* served, in fact, as a complement to Arundel's Constitutions: it was examined and approved for publication by the Archbishop in 1410, the year after the Constitutions were promulgated.

The widespread disappearance of engagement with orthodox doctrines in writing produced in the wake of the promulgation of the

Constitutions coexists with force-feeding of those doctrines by the professional religious, not infrequently in conjunction with explicit refutations of Lollard ideas. Nicholas Love, who was the prior of the Carthusian monastic foundation of Mount Grace in Yorkshire, appended to his *Mirror* a treatise about the sacrament of the Eucharist that vehemently assured its readers of the reality of the transubstantiation of the Host – in the sacrament Jesus is 'verreyly [truly] & bodily present wiþ vs vnder an oþere forme bot soþely [truly] in his owne proper substance verrey god & man' (ed. Sargent 2004: 224). He then 'proved' his point by alluding to a series of miracles in which the 'Real Presence' had been made visible to both the exceptionally holy and the disbelieving. These miracles, Love observed, showed how 'þe disciples of Anticrist þat bene clepede [called] Lollardes' have 'putte many men in to errour of þis blessede sacrament' (236). Love represents the Host as food that has unique properties: it is the ultimate nourishment, given by Christ to the faithful in order that they might be sustained forever (225). But it is tasteless to those who do not believe in the miracle that takes place in it:

> . . . þe fals lollardes, þe whech hauen neiþer trewe drede nor parfite loue of oure lorde Jesus, . . . fele not þe gostly swetnesse of þis heuenly mete of his precious body, ne þe likyng mynde of hees merueiles [pleasant memorial to his marvels] shewede in þat blessede sacrament.
>
> (237)

In other writing, endorsements of orthodox doctrine are made without explicit reference to the history of challenges to that doctrine in England. And yet such endorsements seem more pointed because of this – as is the case in the very late medieval 'morality' play *Everyman*. *Everyman* tells the story of its eponymous protagonist's conversion from a life displeasing to God to one that allows his soul, at the end of the play, to be received into 'the hevenly spere [sphere]' by an angel. Confession and penance are shown to be crucial elements in Everyman's salvation: after he has been abandoned, like the prisoner figure in Boethius' *De consolatione philosophiae*, by all the earthly things in which he placed his faith – his friends, personified in the gushingly supportive but ultimately insincere figure of Fellowship; his relations, personified in Kindred and Cousin; and his Goods – he is led by his own internal faculty of Knowledge to 'Shryfte, mother of Salvacyon' and he then scourges himself, a process that allows the power of his good deeds to be revived. The essential role of the priesthood that administers both the sacrament of penance and the other sacraments of the Church is proclaimed floridly by a personification of another of Everyman's own faculties, Five Wits:

> The pryest byndeth and unbyndeth all bandes   bonds (of sin)
> Bothe in erth and in Heven.
> Thou mynysters all the Sacrementes seven;
> Though we kysse thy fete, thou were worthy,
> Thou arte surgyon that cureth synne deedly.
> No remedy we fynde under God,
> But all onely Pryesthode.
>
>   (ed. Davidson, Walsh and Broos 2007: lines 740–6)

The speech is an unambiguous corrective to anybody who either rejected the necessity of the sacraments or disputed the power of priests. At the same time, however, one's five wits are easily deceived. For Knowledge, the encomium of the priesthood that Five Wits has offered calls for modification. He agrees that what Five Wits has said is true 'if pryestes be good', but not all of them *are* good:

> Synfull pryestes gyveth the synners example bad.
> Theyr chyldren sytteth by other mennes fires, I have herde,
> And some haunteth womens company
> With unclene lyfe, as lustes of lechery.
> These be with synne made blynde.
>
>   (lines 759–64)

Everyman thus combines its regurgitation of orthodox doctrine with criticism of the priesthood that directly contravenes the commands of Arundel's Constitutions. It does so just before criticism of the priesthood united with rejection of many of the Church's teachings to precipitate the Reformation.

We do not know the identity of the person who translated *Everyman* into English from the original Dutch version of the play, *Elckerlijc*. But we do know that the author of *Le Morte Darthur* (completed 1469 or 1470), Sir Thomas Malory, was a layman, a knight of the gentry class, and so an example of those 'symple creatures' outside the ranks of the 'grete clargye' to whom Love, reinforcing Arundel's campaign, aimed to minister. With its interest in the chivalric exploits of Arthurian knighthood, the *Morte*, we might think, is untouched by the dogma that the Church in fifteenth-century England expected people like Malory to swallow. And yet Malory's 'Tale of the Sankgreal' might be said to complement that dogma, in that it shows how Sir Lancelot, who is initially a failure on the Grail Quest, proceeds to obtain a partial vision of the Grail after he confesses his sins to a priest and does penance for them. Because Lancelot's vision is *only* a partial one, we might think that he remains a failure on the Grail Quest, and that is how he is presented in the French text on which Malory based his tale, *La Queste del Saint Graal*. But this is not how the *Morte* asks its readers to view him. At the end of 'The Tale of the Sankgreal', Sir Bors returns to Camelot and tells Arthur of 'the hyghe aventures' that those knights who have been successful on the Grail Quest have attained. Lancelot, along with Sir Perceval, Sir Galahad and Bors himself, is one of those knights (ed. Vinaver 1990: 1036). It has often been argued that for Malory Lancelot's moral failings are redeemed by his chivalric prowess – but is it his prowess that redeems him, or his willingness to submit himself to the sacrament of penance? We might compare a moment in the concluding tale of the work, 'The Most Piteous Tale of the Morte Arthur Saunz Guerdon', in which Malory notes that, just before he dies, '"smytten upon the olde wounde"' that Lancelot has inflicted on him, Sir Gawayne receives the Eucharist at Arthur's insistence: Arthur 'made sir Gawayne to resceyve hys sacrament' (1232). The detail is not in either of Malory's two sources for this tale, the French *Mort le roi Artu* ('Death of King Arthur') and the English *Stanzaic Morte Arthur*. In interpolating it, is Malory recognizing the necessity of reception of the sacrament for salvation of the soul?

The endorsements of orthodox doctrine that we might read into the *Morte* in these episodes might be compared with the affirmation of the Real Presence in the Eucharist that forms the culmination of Malory's story of the Grail Quest. In the castle of Corbenic, Galahad, Perceval and Bors watch as Joseph, the first bishop of Christendom, celebrates Mass. At the elevation of the Host, or 'obley', 'a vigoure [figure] in lyknesse of a chylde' plunges into the bread. After the bread has been placed in the Grail, which Joseph is using as the communion chalice, 'a man . . . that had all the sygnes of the Passion of Jesu Cryste bledynge all opynly' emerges from it (1029–30). The culmination of the Grail Quest is a Eucharistic miracle comparable to the miracles that Nicholas Love describes in his treatise on the sacrament. Malory carried this episode over from *La Queste del Saint Graal*; but other affirmations of the Real Presence in his 'Tale of the Sankgreal' are not present in the *Queste* (Riddy 1987: 132–4). A sick knight to whom the Grail appears begs, '"Fayre swete Lorde whych ys here within the holy vessell, take hede unto me, that I may be hole of thys malody!"' (894). Lancelot fails to rouse himself from his 'half wakyng and half slepynge' state at the same time, and he is subsequently condemned by a hermit,

> 'for youre presumpcion to take uppon you in dedely synne for to be in Hys presence, where Hys fleyssh and Hys blood was, which caused you ye myght nat se hyt with youre worldely yen [eyes]'.

(896)

In the *Queste* the Grail is used as the receptacle of the Eucharist only at the culmination of the Grail Quest; but in the *Morte* Arthur's knights identify it with the receptacle of the sacrament throughout 'The Tale of the Sankgreal', and when they do so they reiterate the doctrine that the sacrament contains the Real Presence of Christ.

The *Morte*, then, seems to extend the ways in which the *Queste* complements orthodox teaching: it might be said that at moments such as the ones that I have discussed it chews on its source material, raising the profile of the orthodox doctrine that this already promotes. The unquestioning acceptance of doctrine that the *Morte* seems to display at these moments, however, distinguishes it from many of the great works of English literature that were produced earlier in the Middle Ages. The responses to doctrine that are written into these earlier works represent an important corrective to modern readings of medieval literature that assume that its authors necessarily swallowed what they were taught, with neither difficulty nor objection (compare, for example, Robertson 1962). As this essay has suggested, people in the Middle Ages frequently ruminated on religious teaching, finding it both palatable and unpalatable – and it is in the writings that they have bequeathed to us that the process of their digestion of that teaching is made visible.

References

Primary texts

Aebischer, Paul, ed. (1963). *Le Mystère d'Adam (Ordo representacionis Ade)*. Geneva: Droz.

Andrew, Malcolm and Waldron, Ronald, eds. (2002). *The Poems of the Pearl Manuscript: Pearl, Cleanness, Patience, Sir Gawain and the Green Knight*. 4th edn. Exeter: Exeter University Press.

Barnum, Priscilla Heath, ed. (1976–2004). *Dives and Pauper*. Vol. I, Pt. 1: EETS OS 275; Vol. I, Pt. 2: EETS OS 280; Vol. II: EETS OS 323. London and Oxford: Oxford University Press.

Barratt, Alexandra, ed. (1992). *Women's Writing in Middle English*. London: Longman.

Beadle, Richard, ed. (1982). *The York Plays*. London: Edward Arnold.

Bestul, Thomas H., ed. (2000). *Walter Hilton: The Scale of Perfection*. Kalamazoo: Medieval Institute Publications.

Brown, Carleton, ed. (1924). *Religious Lyrics of the XIVth Century*. Oxford: Clarendon Press.

Davidson, Clifford, Walsh, Martin W. and Broos, Ton J., eds. (2007). *Everyman and Its Dutch Original, Elckerlijc*. Kalamazoo: Medieval Institute Publications.

Glasscoe, Marion, ed. (1993). *Julian of Norwich: A Revelation of Love*. Revd edn. Exeter: University of Exeter Press.

Hudson, Anne, ed. (1978). *Selections from English Wycliffite Writings*. Cambridge: Cambridge University Press.

Kristensson, Gillis, ed. (1974). *John Mirk's Instructions for Parish Priests*. Lund: CWK Gleerup.

Ogilvie-Thomson, S.J., ed. (1986). *Walter Hilton's Mixed Life*. Salzburg Studies in English Literature, Elizabethan and Renaissance Studies 92:15. Salzburg: Institut für Anglistik und Amerikanistik, Universität Salzburg.

Sajavaara, Kari, ed. (1967). *The Middle English Translations of Robert Grosseteste's Château d'amour*. Mémoires de la Société Néophilologique de Helsinki 32. Helsinki: Société Néophilologique.

Sargent, Michael G., ed. (2004). *Nicholas Love: The Mirror of the Blessed Life of Jesus Christ*. Exeter: University of Exeter Press.

Schmidt, A.V.C., ed. (1987). *William Langland: The Vision of Piers Plowman – A Complete Edition of the B-Text*. 2nd edn. London: J.M. Dent.

Vinaver, Eugène, ed. (1990). *The Works of Sir Thomas Malory*. 3rd edn, revd P.J.C. Field. 3 vols. Oxford: Clarendon Press.

Windeatt, Barry, ed. (1994). *English Mystics of the Middle Ages*. Cambridge: Cambridge University Press.

Secondary sources and suggestions for further reading

Adams, Robert (1988). 'Langland's Theology'. In John A. Alford, ed., *A Companion to Piers Plowman* (pp. 87–114). Berkeley: University of California Press.

Bonnard, Jean (1884). *Les Traductions de la Bible en vers français au moyen âge*. Paris: H. Champion.

Copeland, Rita (2001). *Pedagogy, Intellectuals, and Dissent in the Later Middle Ages: Lollardy and Ideas of Learning*. Cambridge Studies in Medieval Literature 44. Cambridge: Cambridge University Press.

De Hamel, Christopher (2001). *The Book: A History of the Bible*. London: Phaidon.

Duffy, Eamon (1992). *The Stripping of the Altars: Traditional Religion in England c. 1400–c. 1580*. New Haven: Yale University Press.

Fowler, David C. (1976). *The Bible in Early English Literature*. Seattle: University of Washington Press.

Ghosh, Kantik (2001). *The Wycliffite Heresy*. Cambridge Studies in Medieval Literature 45. Cambridge: Cambridge University Press.

Heffernan, Thomas J. (2005). 'The Liturgy and the Literature of Saints' Lives'. In Thomas J. Heffernan and E. Ann Matter, eds., *The Liturgy of the Medieval Church* (pp. 65–94). 2nd edn. Kalamazoo: Medieval Institute Publications.

Kuczynski, Michael P. (1995). *Prophetic Song: The Psalms as Moral Discourse in Late Medieval England*. Philadelphia: University of Pennsylvania Press.

Leclercq, Jean (1978). *The Love of Learning and the Desire for God: A Study of Monastic Culture* (Catharine Misrahi, trans.). 2nd edn, revd. London: SPCK.

Putter, Ad (1996). *An Introduction to the Gawain-Poet*. London: Longman.

Riddy, Felicity (1987). *Sir Thomas Malory*. Medieval and Renaissance Authors 9. Leiden: E.J. Brill.

Robertson, D.W., Jr. (1962). *A Preface to Chaucer: Studies in Medieval Perspectives*. Princeton: Princeton University Press.

Salih, Sarah (2001). *Versions of Virginity in Late Medieval England*. Cambridge: D.S. Brewer.

Schmidt, A.V.C. (1987). *The Clerkly Maker: Langland's Poetic Art*. Piers Plowman Studies 4. Cambridge: D.S. Brewer.

Smalley, Beryl (1969). 'The Bible in the Medieval Schools'. In G.W.H. Lampe, ed., *The Cambridge History of the Bible Volume 2: The West from the Fathers to the Reformation* (pp. 197–220). Cambridge: Cambridge University Press.

Smith, Ben H. (1966). *Traditional Imagery of Charity in Piers Plowman*. The Hague: Mouton.

Traver, Hope (1907). *The Four Daughters of God: A Study of the Versions of this Allegory with Special Reference to Those in Latin, French, and English*. Bryn Mawr College Monographs 6. Bryn Mawr: Bryn Mawr College.

Watson, Nicholas (1993). 'The Composition of Julian of Norwich's *Revelation of Divine Love*'. *Speculum*, 68, 637–83.

Watson, Nicholas (1995). 'Censorship and Cultural Change in Late-Medieval England: Vernacular Theology, the Oxford Translation Debate, and Arundel's Constitutions of 1409'. *Speculum*, 70, 822–64.

Wenzel, Siegfried (1986). *Preachers, Poets, and the Early English Lyric*. Princeton: Princeton University Press.

Wenzel, Siegfried (2005). *Latin Sermon Collections from Later Medieval England: Orthodox Preaching in the Age of Wyclif*. Cambridge Studies in Medieval Literature 53. Cambridge: Cambridge University Press.

Chapter 3

Women and Literature

Catherine Sanok

The representation of women in medieval literature is an old topic – as old as medieval literature itself. Geoffrey Chaucer, for example, raises the issue in the Prologue to *The Legend of Good Women*, in which the God of Love angrily confronts the poet because, for one thing, he has written the story of an unfaithful woman, Criseyde. In his assessment of Geoffrey's poetry, the God of Love follows the protocols of antifeminist literature, in which a woman is either a very rare example of perfect virtue or one of many examples of feminine vice. As a woman who breaks her vows of love, Criseyde can only be the latter, the God of Love assumes, and her story may therefore discourage others from loving. To atone for this 'heresy' against the religion of Love, the poet must compose a 'legendary', a collection of saints' lives, telling the stories of 'good women' who exemplify faithfulness. Presented as companion texts, *Troilus and Criseyde* and *The Legend of Good Women* form a literary 'diptych' offering diametrically opposed representations of women (Blumenfeld-Kosinski 1994). Chaucer's is not the only such pairing: he probably knew Jean le Fèvre's fourteenth-century French translation of the Latin antifeminist *Lamentations of Matheolus* and the poem Jean wrote to atone for it, the *Livre de Leesce* ('Book of Happiness'). Chaucer in turn influences his fifteenth-century successor Thomas Hoccleve, who claims in his *Dialogue with a Friend* that his tale of the Roman emperor Jereslaus's wife was reparation for his ambivalent *Letter of Cupid* (Percival 1998: 106–7, 153). Playful lyrics explore the same dynamic: in one, verses proclaiming the excellence of women are undone by a Latin refrain that declares 'Cuius contrarium verum est' ('the opposite of this is true'). These works are literary elaborations of the familiar virgin/whore dichotomy, rooted in the religious precedents of Eve and Mary. As medieval lyrics and sermons often remark, the words that hail the latter as the mother of God – Ave – invert the name of the woman, Eva, responsible for introducing sin into the world. The construction of women as good or bad, virgin or whore, Mary or Eve is so reductive that it is hard to imagine what interest it might hold for a poet like Chaucer. This chapter considers why the binary representation of women proved so productive for medieval writers and so interesting to their readers.

Medieval antifeminism is the foundation for many misogynist commonplaces that still have currency. Women were derided as talkative, over-sexed, manipulative, changeable, unlearned but cunning, insubordinate, greedy and proud. The greatest attention, especially in comic traditions, was paid to their speech and their sexuality: women were held to be equally incontinent with secrets and with sex. The idealization of women in the Middle Ages generally inverts the terms of antifeminist satire: women are praised for their chastity, obedience and reserve. We may reject as misogynist the emphasis on sexual purity as readily as we do the emphasis on sexual appetite, perhaps even more readily. For this reason it is especially useful to distinguish between antifeminism and misogyny. Antifeminism names a medieval discourse, ranging across several genres, that represents women as mad, bad and dangerous to know. Misogyny is a broader evaluative term for representations of women, overtly negative or positive, that we can recognize as limiting or devaluing women's ethical, political, social or spiritual agency. Excoriating a woman for her sexual appetite is part of a tradition of antifeminist stereotype; praising another for her virginity is part of a misogynist equation of a woman's ethical status with her sexuality.

The ideas about female sexuality in medieval antifeminism derive, as scholars have long recognized, from theories about the physiology of sexual difference that were inherited from Aristotle and Galen (Bullough 1973; Blamires 1992: 38–42). Medieval writers derived from Aristotle an understanding of the female body as an inferior instantiation of the male body, as well as a distinction between female matter and male seed, which confers form on the matter. Competing ideas came from the Galenic tradition, which posited both male and female seed, but argued for male superiority, manifest in men's greater heat.

According to Galen, women's relatively cold nature prevents their generative organs from attaining full development: they remain internal during gestation instead of emerging outside the body, as men's do. Male and female genitals are thus complementary, as are their natures, even as female deficiencies account for women's sexual appetite: being cold and wet, they are naturally attracted to male heat. The preoccupation with female sexuality in Middle English literature, however, is not simply a reflection of scientific discourses. It is also a central way in which texts investigate networks of human relations. This is most obviously the case in the context of marriage, but it is even true of virginity, which is significant primarily as an expression of a vow to God, not, as we shall see, as a physical state of not having had sex. Indeed, virginity is very frequently represented as a kind of spiritual marriage, consummated only in death.

Marriage was, in medieval political theory, both a metonym of and a metaphor for social hierarchy: that is, both the smallest unit of social order and an image of it. So, for example, the 1352 Statute of Treason, which was developed in response to a petition by the Commons to limit the crimes to which the charge of treason could be applied, nevertheless includes a wife's murder of her husband under its aegis. As Paul Strohm has argued, behind this definition of treason is a belief that husbands 'participate analogically and symbolically in the regality of the king' (Strohm 1992: 125). The frequent use of political metaphors in the context of love suggests the cultural centrality of this analogy. In Hoccleve's *Letter of Cupid*, unfaithful (male) lovers are described as 'traitors' and their betrayal as 'treason'. Hoccleve then expands the metaphor through a more explicit equation of political and sexual faithlessness:

> Al thogh þat men by sleighte & sotiltee
> A cely symple and ignorant womman   foolish
> Betraye is no wondir, syn the Citee
> Of Troie, as þat the storie telle can,
> Betrayed was thurgh the deceit of man,
> And set a-fyre and al doun ouerthrowe
> And finally destroyed, as men knowe.

> Betrayen men nat Remes grete and kynges?
> What wight is þat can shape a remedie   person is there who
> Ageynes false and hid purposid thynges?
> Who can the craft tho castes to espye   tricks; discern
> But man, whos wil ay reedy is t'applie   to apply himself

To thyng þat sovneth into hy falshede?   has to do with
Wommen be waar of mennes sleighte, I rede.   advise
(ed. Fenster and Erler 1990: 180)

Hoccleve's naïve voice here reads the story of Troy and other accounts of treason as cautionary tales for women: men's known proclivity for political deceit points to the likelihood that they will be unfaithful to their lovers. This bathetic reading of classical literature trivializes the supposed concerns of women by inverting and elaborating a familiar conceit in which a sexual relationship serves as an image of a larger community and the volatility of love figures the fragility of social order.

This conceit was especially important in late-medieval England, which was marked by political crisis and social change (see Helen Barr's essay later in this volume). In John Gower's *Confessio Amantis*, for example, the poet's lament for the degraded social world he inhabits is addressed through the 'lover's confession', the searching penitential ritual that will correct his posture of love. And in a prophetic poem once attributed to Chaucer, lechery is the fourth sign of the destruction of England, here referred to by its mythic name, Albion:

Whan feyth failleth in prestes sawes,   teachings
And lordes hestes ar holden for lawes,   commands
And robbery is holden purchas,   acquisition
And lechery is holden solas,
Than shal the lond of Albyon
Be brought to grete confusion.
(ed. Forni 2005: 130)

Sexual morality is here made parallel with religious, political and economic order, and its perversion, like the perversion of this order, is both a cause and sign of social crisis. Indeed, sexuality is given prominence as the last in this list, the ultimate mark of moral and social 'confusion' – a term that denotes destruction in Middle English, not merely disorder.

Change and Constancy

The analogy linking sexual relations and social order in Middle English literature intersects with antifeminist stereotypes of women as 'slydynge' – as figures for instability and mutability, and therefore for change and historical process. The goddess Fortuna is the allegorical figure for this. As the whimsical and merciless force responsible for political change, Fortuna embodies historical contingency. The same cultural paradigm admits of both moralized and non-moralized versions. In Malory's *Morte Darthur*, Guinevere's adulterous relationship with Lancelot is a prime cause of the destruction of the Arthurian world. Chaucer's *Troilus and Criseyde*, on the other hand, embraces a correlative, but not causal, relation between female infidelity and political instability: Criseyde's faithlessness does not cause the fall of Troy, but parallels it. Although the poem's narrator works hard to present Troilus as the personification of the city, Criseyde is by far the closer image of the besieged Troy. The courtly rhetoric used throughout the poem imagines her seduction as a kind of military assault, and her changing affections – she is famously 'slydynge of corage' (IV.825) – presage the change that the city itself will undergo. But they do not cause it. Indeed, the poem's focus on Criseyde's infidelity – rather than Helen's – complicates a fantasy of moral causality that implicates women in temporal loss and decline.

If antifeminist stereotypes about women's unruliness are figures for other dangers that jeopardize political community, idealizations of women's virginity or marital fidelity provide a key image and model of stability. The faithful observance of the marriage vow guarantees social order, just as its breach marks the threats against it. Narratives of constancy in Middle English literature generally – though not exclusively – focus on women, just as narratives of infidelity do. This is surely in part because sexuality is so central to women's moral status in the Middle Ages, but it is also because in this tradition women's constancy opposes *male* instability – the instability of male behaviour and masculine institutions. Thus Alceste, who according to legend was so constant in her love for her husband that she was willing to die for him, is paired with the volatile God of Love in the Prologue to *The Legend of Good Women*. Love is hot-tempered and vulnerable to flattering courtiers and his own temper: his tyrannical behaviour is both a personal failing and a political threat. As the figure who mitigates Love's hasty judgement, Alceste represents a model of emotional restraint who also ensures just rule in Love's court. Her pre-eminence among women is a consequence of her constancy, as even her iconography suggests: her allegorical symbol, the daisy, is a figure for stability as well as responsiveness. The narrator hastens to see the daisy 'unclose / Agayn the sonne, that roos as red as rose' (F-Prologue, lines 110–12): it opens in response to the sun but does not move from its place, and so also seems to anchor the sun, just as Alceste establishes the ethical limits of masculine power and aggression.

The emphasis on feminine constancy here, and in much Middle English literature, both promises political stability and marks its absence. Hence the many stories of women's constancy framed by anxiety about the instability of masculine institutions. In *The Canterbury Tales*, *The Clerk's Tale*, *The Physician's Tale*, *The Tale of Melibee* and *The Man of Law's Tale* all address this theme. The *Confessio Amantis*, which opens with an anxious account of the decay of the social world, tells some of the same stories: above all, the tale of Constance, whose very name references the virtue that she personifies and whose story recounts a woman's steadfast devotion to God and to her husband in the face of extraordinary trials. Women come to occupy the position of constancy in the late-medieval cultural imagination, and their stability is frequently defined against intemperate male behaviour and corrupt masculine institutions.

The 'legends' that Geoffrey writes at Alceste's command in *The Legend of Good Women* are a case in point: just as Alceste's equanimity rebukes Love's tyranny, so the constant love of good women catalogued in the legends is a pretext for stories about the moral and political failings of men and the institutions they represent. In the first legend, Cleopatra is an exemplar of fidelity in love – she chooses death willingly, like Alceste, as fulfilment of her 'covenaunt' with Antony (line 688) – while Antony himself is first introduced as a 'Rebel unto the toun of Rome' (line 591). Chaucer employs a different strategy in *The Physician's Tale*, the story of Virginia, who dies to protect her virginity in the face of a corrupt court that condemns her to sexual slavery. Although Livy and Boccaccio present the story primarily as an exemplum of political vice, the Physician – especially in his long moralizing aside to governesses and parents of young girls – presents the story as an exemplum of sexual virtue. The substitution suggests that the emphasis on feminine chastity in Middle English literature often has as its unconscious the instability of masculine political order.

Patience and Protest

In the face of such instability, how should one act? This is a crucial question for vernacular texts. Medieval literature was deeply influenced by both a Boethian insistence on the meaninglessness and unreality of worldly concerns, and an Augustinian idea that worldly existence is a kind of exile. But these powerful models of rejecting the world – and thus any active engagement in its reformation – were opposed by equally powerful countermodels, most importantly in representations of Christ. Although many texts foreground Christ's role as a divine exemplar for patience – in its strict etymological sense of suffering (compare Latin *patientia*) – some writers, such as William Langland, emphasize Christ's role as reformer and represent social commitment as central to his message. *Piers Plowman*, in fact, explores the confrontation of these two perspectives on Christian ethics. But the conflict pervades even texts that do not examine it explicitly. Indeed, we might say that a core preoccupation of late-medieval narrative culture is the tension between patience and protest, that is, between the ideal of suffering and the responsibility to initiate change.

Female characters are a privileged – though far from unique – vehicle for exploring this tension: gender codes held up higher expectations for patience from women and a more generalized endorsement of their capacity for suffering. The founding text of those codes – the account of Eve in Genesis – makes suffering in childbirth women's lot. And women are supposed to be subordinate to men and so also to bear patiently their authority. Antifeminist literature, on the other hand, elaborated a pervasive stereotype of women who protest against these norms: who complain or manipulate or demand sovereignty. At the risk of oversimplifying Chaucer's very complex project in *The Canterbury Tales* and his rich investigations of the representation of women, we can see the female characters here as explorations of these two possibilities: Virginia, Constance and Griselda, the focus of *The Clerk's Tale*, are exemplars of patience; the Wife of Bath is medieval literature's most memorable figure of feminine protest.

What do the 'patience' stories tell us? *The Clerk's Tale* is probably the hardest case: Griselda can be read as a paragon or a monster. After the peasant Griselda vows, on her marriage to Walter, the Marquis of Saluzzo, to subordinate her will to his, Walter takes first their daughter and then their son from her, on the pretext that his people object to them as his political heirs, and he leads Griselda to believe that they have been killed. In fulfilling an extreme form of an expected feminine role – submission to her husband – Griselda violates other aspects of that role: her role as mother. On the most basic level, the tale is an exploration of the fissures in gender ideology, a limit case in which patience becomes monstrous. But it is also a fantasy that even this extreme form of feminine patience is not monstrous, for the children do not die after all. If only we knew – or when we know –

the whole story we see that it is simply a test. Griselda's story confirms the epistemological grounds for a patient relationship to the social world. Her experience substantiates the Boethian insistence that the world of appearances is deceiving; that a God's-eye view would show something quite different from what looks like capricious Fortune on the ground. Importantly, the reader occupies precisely this omniscient position: privy, like God, to Walter's plot, we know all along that he is merely testing her, not murdering her children. The shock of Griselda's acquiescence in their deaths is always already tempered by the knowledge that they are safe.

The tale is, in the first instance, a lesson for women about their subordinate status: patient submission to male authority is richly rewarded here. But if the tale's resolution confirms a key tenet of medieval gender codes, the horror of its unfolding challenges that tenet. Griselda remains a woman who – believing that her children will be killed – allows them to be taken from her without protest. Chaucer opens up a reading that attends to the cost of an ideology of patience, as a gendered norm, for women. He does this, not least, in his suggestion that Griselda's behaviour is unnatural. 'Wel myghte a mooder thanne han cryd "allas!"' (*The Canterbury Tales*, IV.563), the Clerk interjects after recounting how Griselda takes leave of her daughter; but Griselda does not cry out. This tale of a woman's abdication of moral agency paradoxically creates and confirms that agency – by no means a given in the Middle Ages – by imagining what it would mean to give it up as Griselda does.

If, through Griselda, Chaucer confirms women's moral agency by imagining its absence, through the Wife of Bath he imagines a woman's energetic embrace of agency, only to question the possibility of truly challenging powerful gender codes. Through the Wife, Chaucer explores how vulnerable dominant discourses are to subversion, revealing how readily antifeminist commonplaces are appropriated as arguments by the other side. The Wife repeats antifeminist commonplaces about women's sexuality, their manipulative and acquisitive nature, and their raw need for power and social approval, turning these into a defence and demonstration of women's ability to act. The corollary of this, however, is that the Wife's rejection of both idealized gender codes and antifeminist stereotypes (represented by her mutilation of the 'book of wikked wyves' from which her fifth husband, Jankyn, reads to her) is not, and cannot be, total. This is not only because it simply revalues those stereotypes but also – and more importantly – because it confirms some of the premises of medieval misogyny, especially that sexuality is the primary arena for women's social identity and action. The Wife of Bath's Prologue is at once a bracing response to medieval antifeminism and a shattering exposé of the inefficacy of protest.

Between Griselda's extreme passivity and the Wife's outspoken protest we might place Cecilia, the virgin martyr whose legend is told by the Second Nun. Saints are prime exemplars of patience; they suffer in imitation of Christ's Passion. But their willing submission to death is a rejection – not an acceptance – of political and social authority. In saints' lives, patience is a form of protest. The two are conflated, especially, in Cecilia's preaching: when she remains alive after three attempts to cut off her head, Cecilia turns her house into a church and instructs others in Christian belief. Preaching was categorically proscribed to medieval women; Cecilia's teaching is, therefore, the final act in a series that defies standard gender expectations, including her rejection of her husband's sexual advances and her contempt for the authority of the judge Almachius who interrogates her. In her challenge to such expectations, Cecilia is very like other female saints, especially virgin martyrs, celebrated in medieval legendaries and sermon cycles, except that while Cecilia accedes at a minimum to her family's demand that she marry, most virgin martyrs reject altogether marriage and the forms of male authority that structure it as an institution. St Margaret of Antioch refuses the advances of the prefect Olibrius. Her refusal is no surprise: Olibrius is lascivious and arrogant. But St Agnes refuses even a love-struck prince whose earnestness is not questioned. In the long fifteenth-century verse version of her legend by the Augustinian friar John Capgrave, Katherine of Alexandria prefers to rule in her own right as queen rather than subject herself and her political authority to a male consort.

Of course, virgin martyrs do not act from principled resistance to patriarchy or to compulsory heterosexuality. Rather, they choose spiritual authority and spiritual marriage over earthly institutions. Their resistance to social norms is warranted by the dedication of their virginity to their heavenly spouse, as the miraculous invulnerability of their virgin bodies attests. Despite the relentless assaults of her persecutors, the virgin martyr is unharmed or speedily healed, the integrity of her body miraculously preserved and made manifest. If these stories provide a model of energetic resistance to male authority, they also – like most other medieval genres – define women's spirituality and morality primarily in terms of sexuality. Recent scholarship has laboured to understand the cultural work of narratives that make women suffer extreme physical violence but also celebrate them for refusing the political and social protocols of their day, so categorically that they die for their beliefs. Surely this complicated exploration of the relationship between patience and protest accounts in large part for the hold these figures had on medieval literary culture.

Virgins and Wives

Virgins, as Sarah Salih has argued, troubled the very category of 'woman'. Women were condemned to suffer in childbirth, as noted above, but virgins escape the punishment due their sex. Salih suggests that virgins were sometimes understood as a 'third sex' in the Middle Ages, not fully female but also not male (Salih 2001: 25). This is one way to understand the virgin's special prerogatives. But if virgins did not always fit comfortably in the category of woman, they were often conspicuously feminized through attention to their beauty and in the nuptial language used to describe their vocation. Virginity is a form of ascesis, part of a programme of self-denial, with overtones of both disciplining the flesh and penitential suffering – that is to say, a highly ritualized form of patience. But it is also patience in a sense closer to the modern one, for the virgin did not so much reject marriage as wait for its ultimate form: spiritual marriage to the Godhead. Virgin martyr narratives suggest the joyful union of the saint and her God at the end, as a voice calls her to join him at the end of her life. So in an early Middle English legend of St Katherine, the girl's final prayer before her execution is answered by a voice from heaven that says, 'Cum mi leoue leofmon, cum nu min iweddet, leouest an wummon' (ed. d'Ardenne and Dobson 1981: 52) ('Come my dear lover, come now my spouse, dearest of women!'). The bridal language of virgin martyr narratives reminds us, as Simon Gaunt notes, that virginity is not the absence of sexuality: it is a form of sexuality (Gaunt 1995: 186). Medieval narrative representations of virginity are fully aware of this, and they exhibit what many modern readers find an unsettling crossing of asceticism and eroticism.

The legend of St Katherine quoted above, along with the legends of St Margaret and St Juliana, forms part of a small collection of works intended for anchoresses, religious women who had taken a vow of enclosure. The language of spiritual eroticism that we find in the Katherine legend echoes more elaborate representations in other anchoritic texts, such as the practical and spiritual handbook for anchoresses *Ancrene Wisse*, and *Þe Wohunge of Ure Lauerd* ('The Wooing of Our Lord'), an extended meditation on Christ as divine lover. The *Wohunge* begins with the language of the biblical Song of Songs:

> Iesu swete iesu . mi druð . mi derling . mi drihtin . mi healend mi huniter . mi haliwei . Swetter is munegunge of þe þen mildeu o muðe . Hwa ne mei luue þi luueli leor? Hwat herte is swa hard þat ne mei to melte iþe munegunge of þe? Ah hwa ne mej luue þe luueliche iesu?
>
> (ed. Thompson 1958: 20)

> [Jesus, sweet Jesus, my dear, my darling, my Lord, my Saviour, my honey-drop, my balm, sweeter is the memory of you than honey in the mouth. Who cannot love your lovely face? What heart is so hard that it cannot melt in the memory of you? Ah, who cannot love you, lovely Jesus?]
>
> (trans. Savage and Watson 1991: 248)

The prayer eventually modulates into a careful explanation of the many ways in which Christ is superior to earthly men: if a man is loved for his possessions, how much richer is Christ, ruler of heaven; if a man is loved for generosity, how much more generous is the Saviour who gave his life, and so on. But the frank substitution of divine for earthly bridegroom emphasizes the erotic nature of the anchoress's devotion, as do flashes of physicality that add point to the allegory: the speaker pauses for a moment to think of Jesus' 'flesch hwit under schrud' ('body white under clothing'). As the prayer turns to a meditation on the Passion, the body of the divine beloved receives still greater attention, first as object of violence – 'þu wes for mi luue wið cnotti swepes swungen swa þat ti luueliche lich mihte beo totorn 7 torent . 7 al þi blisfule bodi streamed on a Girre blod (33) ('you were beaten with knotted whips for my love, so that your lovely body could be all torn and rent; and all your blessed body flowed with one bloody stream' (254)) – and then as evidence of love – 'A swete iesu þu oppnes me þin herte for to cnawe witerliche 7 in to reden trewe luue lettres . for þer I mai openlich seo hu muchel þu me luuedes' (35) ('Ah! sweet Jesus, you open your heart to me, so that I may know it inwardly, and read inside it true love-letters; for there I may see openly how much you loved me' (255)). The equation of suffering and love here allows the anchoress to imagine her own vocation as a literally 'pas-sionate' union with God: 'Mi bodi henge wið þi bodi neiled o rode . sperred querfaste wiðinne fowr wahes' (36) ('Let my body hang with your body, nailed on the cross, fastened from side to side within four walls' (256)). The prayer's refrain, 'leue þat te luue of þe beo al mi likinge' ('grant that love of you be all my pleasure'), links the ecstatic love language of the opening passage to the eroticized violence of the Passion sequence, defining physical suffering, including the privations of the anchorhold, as a form of erotic pleasure.

The sensual imagination of this prayer is disciplined somewhat in the more fully narrative version of the courtly allegory found in *Ancrene Wisse*. Book 7 of the text includes a story with 'a wrihe for-bisne' ('a hidden allegory') (ed. and trans. Millett and Wogan-Browne 1990: 112–13): a lady, besieged in her castle by powerful enemies, nevertheless refuses the courtship of a strong and beautiful king. The allegory is carefully elucidated: the lady is the soul besieged by the devil; the king is Christ; the joust in which his body/shield is pierced is the Passion. In this parable, Christ's sacrifice is not an atonement for original sin, but an inducement to love: 'to schawin hire open-liche hu inwardliche he luuede hire, ant to ofdrahen hire heorte' ('to show her openly how deeply he loved her, and to attract her heart') (116–17). Rather than cleansing the lady-soul of past sin, Christ's joust-sacrifice obligates her in the future. The allegory here trades not in the spiritual eroticism of *Þe Wohunge of Ure Lauerd* but in the notion of love service, and it encourages not passionate identification with Christ but guilty recognition of the limits of that identification. Griselda's suffering is finally 'enough,' but the lady's never can be.

Directed towards God, desire is good for virgins. But spiritual mar-riage is not the only kind that is endorsed in Middle English narra-tive culture. Although there is a strong tradition of anti-matrimonial satire, deriving largely from Latin clerical culture, late-medieval England witnessed a new positive valuation of secular marriage. As recent critics have emphasized, one project of fifteenth-century liter-ary culture was to reconcile spiritual and social values. Tensions between the social and economic priorities of the merchant class and the devotional traditions they were eager to embrace produced new forms of 'social praxis' that resolved, or at least obscured, these ten-sions by creating fictions of their compatibility (Ashley 1998; Coletti 2001). A crucial way in which texts imagine that their reading publics might 'achieve spiritual validation while remaining an active member of mercantile society' is to re-imagine marriage (Ashley 1998: 374).

The early fifteenth-century *Storie of Asneth* is a good example. Asneth is the daughter of Potiphar, a priest and prince of Pharaoh's kingdom. She is fair and chaste and devoted to the Egyptian gods whose images adorn the tower in which she dwells. Her father wants to marry

her to Joseph, but she indignantly refuses on the grounds that he is
a stranger, a slave, a shepherd, and she worthy to marry a king's son.
But as she watches Joseph approach her father's house on Pharaoh's
errand, she is struck with desire. Her spirits fail and her body trem-
bles as she remarks his nobility; she is equally overcome by his
beauty, asking herself:

> 'Who was ever gete of a man so fair, so fresh of
>   face?   engendered
> Or what womman myhte conceive and bere so moche light?
> Of most wrecched now I am; forfeted I have hys grace,
> When I dispurned hym to my fadir with wordis of
>   unright.'   disparaged
>   (ed. Peck 1991: lines 201–4)

For love of Joseph, she imposes on herself an eight-day fast and for-
sakes the idols she had held in reverence. Her conversion makes her
a fit wife for Joseph: her prayers are answered by an angel who promises
that she will be Joseph's spouse 'in worlde withoute end' (line 460).
Asneth herself specifies that his beauty baited her, like a fish, desire
for Joseph leading her to God:

> 'For as the fyssh by the hook ys take by distresse,
> So ys beauté drow me to hym by vertuus provydence,   his
> And ladde me to Almighty God with gret gentynesse,
> And did me taste of the drynke of the eternal sapience.'
>   (lines 710–13)

Here, physical desire is the necessary mediating force transforming idolatry into devotion. The story uses the easy inversions of the good and
bad woman – when Joseph first sees Asneth looking at him from her
window he fears she is licentious – to imagine a spiritual analogue,
the ready conversion of pagan to Christian. Importantly, these bin-
aries elide a third category, Judaism: Joseph's religion and his God are
rendered in Christian terms. The possibility of conversion in turn recu-
perates feminine desire as spiritually efficacious: the story, that is, is
about marital ethics as well as the superiority of Christianity, and especially about the legitimacy of desire as part of devotional life. It provides both a lesson for laywomen and confirmation of the spiritual
value of their marriages, represented as an arena for moral agency and
growth. The single extant manuscript of this story gives rare specific
evidence for the sort of women who might learn these lessons (Peck,

ed., 1991). The names Margaret and Beatrice are inscribed on the book's first page and family heraldry identifies them as members of the Lynne family, daughters of a wealthy London merchant. The manuscript was written, in part, by John Shirley, a well-known participant in London's book economy and Margaret's husband. Beatrice's husband, Avery Cornburgh, is mentioned by name in the book as well. Well-off laywomen like these are encouraged by the story to enjoy their husbands' prestige, their good looks and fine clothes, all as part of spiritually edifying desire.

Such women were not only interested in narratives of marriage, however. They consumed virgin martyr legends as avidly as vowed religious women did. The collection of female saints' lives, given the modern title *The Legends of Holy Women*, by Osbern Bokenham – like his contemporary John Capgrave an Augustinian friar – includes several virgin martyr legends dedicated to laywomen: Bokenham's life of St Katherine is addressed to Katherine Denston and Katherine Howard, his life of St Agatha to one Agatha Flegge. The collection testifies to a significant overlap between lay and religious women's reading: the single extant manuscript, which altogether names six laywomen as patrons, was copied for a house of nuns. Moral handbooks like the fifteenth-century *Book of the Knight of La Tour-Landry*, translated from a French text that the eponymous knight wrote for his daughters, give us some sense of how laywomen read virgin martyr legends like the ones in Bokenham's collection: it exhorts its readers to be faithful to their husbands by referring to St Katherine and other virgin martyrs who 'had leuer [preferably] be martered rather thanne they wolde do that foule synne' (ed. Wright 1906: 83). If nuns and anchoresses were encouraged to imagine their virginity as a kind of marriage, laywomen were encouraged to imagine marriage as a kind of chastity. Women's sexuality marks a surprising intersection between spiritual and secular domains, even as – and perhaps because – it is also the primary sign of the difference between those domains.

Woman and Women

We should not be surprised by this overlap between the categories of virgin and wife, religious women and laywomen, because late-medieval literary culture worked hard to construct 'women' as a coherent category, one that collapsed synchronic differences – differences in social identity as well as sexual status – and historical ones:

differences separating, say, classical women from late-medieval ones. It did so, in part, through the understanding of narrative as exemplary, as when *The Book of the Knight of La Tour-Landry* represents early Christian virgin martyrs as models for late-medieval laywomen. 'Woman' as a category is also produced in medieval literary culture through the strategies of antifeminism and its antithesis, defences of women. Both, as was discussed briefly above, assume that the behaviour of a woman, or perhaps a catalogue of several women, can establish the moral profile of the sex as a whole. In this way, medieval defences of women accept the logic of antifeminism, since in countering antifeminist stereotype with examples of good women, they assume and confirm that 'woman' is an ethically meaningful category.

Medieval literature also sometimes constructs 'men' as an ethically meaningful category, especially in relation to women: men are supposed to establish and maintain their authority over women of their social station. But it more frequently distinguished between them, recognizing the very different ethical expectations for the first three estates: men who rule, men who pray and men who work. Perhaps for this reason, the bad behaviour of one man is rarely understood as paradigmatic of his sex, as the behaviour of one woman is. Walter is a moral monster, but he does not prompt questions about whether men in general are moral monsters in the same way that Griselda prompts questions for the Clerk and the Host about contemporary women's capacity for patience. At the end of his tale, the Clerk asserts that women are no longer capable of Griselda's extreme patience, but Harry Bailly nevertheless wishes that his wife – who is neither a peasant nor the wife of a marquis – could hear the story. Women are treated as a single category: the fourth estate embraces them all, without much attention to the differences between them.

The Wife of Bath's Tale provides one of the most complex explorations of the tension between individual identity and categorization as a woman. This is most obviously so in the task set the knight as a test and punishment for raping a girl: that he discover what women desire most. The question itself essentializes women; it assumes they form a coherent community defined by a shared desire. The knight's adventure at first challenges this assumption: it turns out that women want many different things – riches, honour, fine clothing, good sex. 'Women' do not want anything; they each want something different:

He seketh every hous and every place
Where as he hopeth for to fynde grace
To lerne what thyng wommen loven moost,
But he ne koude arryven in no coost
Wher as hy myghte fynde in this mateere
Two creatures accordynge in-feere.   in agreement
(*The Canterbury Tales*, III.919–24)

This lesson is, however, replaced by another, if only – and conspicuously – through magic. The plot ultimately confirms the assumption that individual women can be subsumed under the category of Woman, most obviously in the single answer that wins the knight his freedom and proves that they form a coherent category after all – women desire sovereignty over their husbands. More subtly, the tale also posits a series of substitutions that equate one woman with another. In medieval practice an accusation of rape might be resolved by marriage to the victim, but here the knight is forced to marry the old hag who has provided him with his answer. This substitution of the old woman for the raped girl – who disappears from the story altogether – anticipates a substitution that is given much more narrative attention: the substitution of the beautiful maiden for the old hag in the knight's marriage bed. The hag's pillow sermon famously challenges the category of gentility, insisting that this is a matter of ' "vertuous lyvyng" ' rather than ' "old richesse" '. But her magical transformation works to reconfirm another category of identity, womanhood. Indeed, in its argument against distinctions based on social rank, the pillow sermon is thematically congruent with the way in which the plot of the tale itself erases differences between women. A woman's class does not matter, the tale suggests, not so much because nobility is not dependent on birth, but, more significantly, because her sex supersedes other categories of identity.

I should emphasize that the reading I have sketched here follows the logic of the plot and not the way this logic is complicated by the voice of the Wife. A reading that followed the psychological portrait developed across the Wife's Prologue and her tale might emphasize the way in which the multiple answers to the knight's question all seem to come from her; it is not so much that women want many different things but that the Wife herself does. Such a reading might also note that the answer the knight finally gives is patently inadequate. The court in which he declares that women want sovereignty over their husbands is composed of maidens and widows as well as wives: his answer cannot account for their desires. This awkwardness is stark evidence that medieval gender codes have impoverished the Wife's understanding of human possibility. These alternative readings are witness to the complex exploration of the relationship between the category and the individual in the Wife of Bath's performance itself – the uneasy border she occupies as a character caught between an allegorical mode and, to use a later term, a 'humanist' one.

The woman/women problem registers in more comic terms in the twelfth-century *lais* of Marie de France. In the *lai* that opens the collection, *Guigemar*, the eponymous hero and his beloved are separated when her husband discovers them. Before they part, they mark each other with love tokens: the lady ties a knot in Guigemar's shirt and he binds her thighs with a belt. When they encounter one another again, the lady easily recognizes Guigemar, but he is not sure the woman before him is his beloved because, as the narrator slyly observes, 'Les femmes se ressemblent beaucoup' (trans. Harf-Lancner 1990: line 779) ('Women look very much alike'). Her beauty reduces her to a generic woman, rather than distinguishing her from others; hence the need for the belt as the sign and confirmation of her identity. Marie here plays with a narrative analogue of misogyny: the antifeminist conflation of women into a single category becomes a complication of the plot. Guigemar needs a token, an external symbol of an individual, historically particular, woman, because *as a woman* she lacks individuality or singular identity.

Identity and Community

In its larger argument, *Guigemar* rehearses a structure that many scholars recognize as central to romance: the formation of the knight's identity through the experience of love. Knighthood is represented as a form of brotherhood, and Arthurian romance, in particular, in the myth of the Round Table, insists on the knights' shared identity. But this communal identity is challenged by the singular love of the knight for a lady, which distinguishes him from the others, just as the knight in battle – his own identity obscured by his armour – is identified by his lady's sleeve. Romance, especially in early formulations like those of Chrétien de Troyes, is about the individualizing force of love, in tension with both the communal life of knights and the fraternal bonds that join them. Chrétien, again and again, stages heterosexual bonds as a threat to this brotherhood and as constitutive of the knight's singular identity.

Because a knight's identity is formed in, and represented by, his erotic commitments, the knight's unsettled sexuality in *Guigemar* is untenable. Uninterested in love, Guigemar happens upon a hind (a female deer) with antlers (distinctive features of a male deer). When he tries to kill the animal, Guigemar is wounded in the thigh by his own spear and the hind tells him that he will only be cured through love. When the lady grants her love, his body is restored to wholeness, a physical symbol of the complete and mature chivalric identity he acquires through heterosexual desire. A knight cannot love 'women'; he must love and be loved by a particular woman. Yet Guigemar cannot recognize or grant the individuality of the woman he loves because doing so would expose how derivative his own identity is. Given how pervasive the romance plot was in medieval culture, we might recognize the totalizing representation of women, whether in romance idealization or antifeminist stereotype, as a response to the heterosexualized fantasy of individual identity. If erotic bonds make one an individual, then men gain their identity through women. As a sign of someone else's identity, women, on the other hand, lack their own.

We might return to the chivalric allegory in *Ancrene Wisse* from this perspective. Literature about virginity has often been seen as a complement to romance: virgin martyr legends, as Brigitte Cazelles has argued, echo romance in the way they idealize women (Cazelles 1991). But they also often significantly revise romance constructions of identity, in which the female beloved stands as the necessary but problematic source of male identity. Christopher Cannon has argued that the literature of anchoritic enclosure, and *Ancrene Wisse* in particular, helps to create, imagine and consolidate an idea of a self with an inside and an outside, by giving it an architecture and by developing a theory of the body and its senses as the necessary, if regrettable, portal to the spiritual 'inside' (Cannon 2003). If in romance women stand as the private alternative to public identity and as a sign of the knight's individuality, anchoritic literature gives women themselves an interior self – a private identity of their own. And it does so, in part, by means of the erotic language through which their religious vocation is understood. The allegory in *Ancrene Wisse* seems to replicate romance; at issue, however, is not the knight's ability to love, as it is in *Guigemar*, but the lady's. Meditations like *Þe Wohunge of Ure Lauerd*, as we saw, cultivate this ability. In anchoritic literature as in romance, the beloved object confers and confirms the identity of the lover, but here the lover is the lady devoted to her God.

Like *Ancrene Wisse*, *Pearl* accepts the dynamic of romance, in which love confers individual identity. Unlike *Ancrene Wisse*, however, it also follows romance in that it represents this identity in tension with communal identity – with the crucial difference that the community is Christian rather than chivalric. The dreamer is confused by the Pearl-maiden's new status as one of the 144,000 Brides of Christ – a privilege beyond his expectations. She tries to teach him that the categories of social identity do not apply in heaven, and – a harder lesson still – that she is no longer his Pearl. But he persists, and when he tries to reach her, she is lost to him again. *Pearl*, then, like *Guigemar*, represents women as unknowable to men: it too is a narrative of loss and rediscovery, and again the reunion with the beloved is tainted with a sharp new awareness of the elusiveness of her identity, which the male lover cannot fully grasp or master. *Pearl* extends this trope to a pastoral lesson about the differences between secular and sacred life: the dreamer's commitments to earthbound social, generational and intellectual hierarchies are rejected by the Pearl-maiden, who shows how they are undone by the idea of Christian community. In antifeminist texts, a woman's rejection of social protocols makes her a threat to society; here it makes her the embodiment of spiritual perfection. And while the dreamer's desire for the girl individualizes him, as it might in romance, the Pearl-maiden rejects precisely this, since she does not belong to him after all or any more. In contrast to the chivalric allegory in *Ancrene Wisse*, in *Pearl* the holy woman's love of Christ does not confer her own private identity but refuses private identity altogether, in favour of the collective identity of Christian communion.

Women Readers and Women Writers

The perennial temptation of historical criticism is to see progress, rather than simply change. In literary criticism, this often takes the form of claims of increasing complication or sophistication. But early Middle English representations of women are as complex as later ones, as we have seen in our brief look at the early thirteenth-century anchoritic texts. By the late fourteenth century, however, the expanding range of vernacular texts and a broader acknowledgement of women's participation in literary culture do shape literary meaning to a different extent, if not in a wholly new way. Fifteenth-century poets like John Lydgate and Osbern Bokenham frequently address their female readers or include specific reference to their female patrons in their poems, making reception by women part of the literary meaning, and not just social history, of a text. So too poems in a female voice – from courtly allegories like *The Assembly of Ladies* (ed. Pearsall 1962) to the lyrics found in the manuscript compiled by the Findern family (Cambridge, Cambridge University Library, MS Ff.1.6) – insist that the question of women's authority and experience be addressed. And women's participation in public drama, like the Candlemas play preserved in Oxford, Bodleian Library, MS Digby 133, opens up new questions about the relationship between women's social lives and the representation of women (Gibson 1996).

The female audience becomes part of the fiction of the text when it is invoked either through the text's generic address to women or its naming of a historical woman as patron. John Lydgate's fifteenth-century *Life of St Margaret* does both, with a broad invocation of 'Noble princesses and ladyes of estate, / And gentilwomen lower of degré' (ed. Reames 2003: lines 519–20) and a specific identification of Anne Mortimer, Countess of March, as the poem's patron (lines 69–74). So, too, reference to a woman owner in the colophon of a manuscript, or even in a testament that specifies to whom her more lavish codices are to be bequeathed, makes a female audience visible. The considerable evidence that recent scholarship has discovered of women's book ownership and patronage should therefore be part of our assessment of the representation of women in literary culture (see, for example, Meale 1993).

Part of this project involves tracing the relationship between women's growing participation in literary culture and strategies of representation. Karen Winstead, for example, has found that fifteenth-century saints' lives like Lydgate's respond to the concerns of their female readers through a new emphasis on the saint's manners and the devotional practices that would be appropriate to a late-medieval laywoman (Winstead 1997: 112–46). But even when the strategies of representation do not change, the meaning of a narrative tradition may do so as it becomes affiliated with a new audience. Our own understanding of *The Legend of Good Women*, for example, with its laudatory portraits of figures like Cleopatra and Medea, may depend very much on whether we imagine it as addressed to Richard II's queen Anne, as the 'F' version of the poem is, or to a literate male audience (one able, that is, to read Latin) familiar with classical texts. The first encourages a straightforward reading of the legends as celebrations of women's faithfulness; the second opens an ironic reading of them as a devastating indictment of how very few good women the poet could find in all his books. An awareness of how a text's social affiliations might shape its meaning accounts for the frequent address to an audience – and increasingly to a specifically female audience – in late-medieval literature.

If the female reader is an important part of late-medieval fictions, as well as historical fact, so is the female writer, as Jennifer Summit has taught us. Summit argues that the English literary tradition was founded on the figure of the 'lost woman writer', a fantasy of loss that helped to consolidate the incipient idea of tradition and the authority of male writers (Summit 2000). Some of these lost women writers have, of course, been recovered, most notably Margery Kempe, whose writing was known only through a small collection of extracts until the 1930s, when the full manuscript of her remarkable book was rediscovered. Together with the work of Julian of Norwich, *The Book of Margery Kempe* allows us to take women's own self-presentation as authors into account in our understanding of the representation of women in Middle English literary culture. In particular, we can recognize their deployment of tropes of feminine dependence or inferiority as a paradoxical strategy of authority. Kempe's emphasis on her use of a scribe is a means of establishing the authority of her text and its formal resemblance to saints' lives, which were recorded through similar witnesses. Julian adopts the pose of the unlearned woman, a simple conduit for 'shewings' from God, yet from these she develops her audacious and sophisticated theology.

As we might expect, both writers also ring changes on conventional representations of women – in the tenderness of the maternal Christ in Julian's shewings, for example, or in Kempe's fusion of the troublesome wife and holy woman in one character. But what is more striking by far is the way that Julian's shewings and *The Book of Margery Kempe* both operate on a representational level that resists the category of 'woman'. Julian's theology is universalist, grounded in Christ's participation in a shared humanity that makes sex and other kinds of difference meaningless. Margery Kempe is, in sharp contrast, relentlessly particularized, both through the wealth of local historical detail that place her *Book* in the genre of autobiography (before it existed as such) and through the character's claims to a privileged relationship with God. We might see these texts' most profound response to masculine literary traditions in the category shifts that they effect, preferring human community on the one hand, and a single individual on the other, to 'women' as a literary topic.

References

Primary texts

Blamires, Alcuin, ed. (1992). *Woman Defamed and Woman Defended*. Oxford: Clarendon Press.

D'Ardenne, S.R.T.O. and Dobson, E.J., eds. (1981). *Seinte Katerine*. EETS SS 7. Oxford: Oxford University Press.

Fenster, Thelma and Erler, Mary, eds. (1990). *Poems of Cupid, God of Love*. Leiden: Brill.

Forni, Kathleen, ed. (2005). *Chaucerian Apocrypha*. Kalamazoo: Medieval Institute Publications.

Harf-Lancner, Laurence, trans., and Warnke, Karl, ed. (1990). *Lais de Marie de France*. Paris: Lettres Gothiques.

Millett, Bella and Wogan-Browne, Jocelyn, eds. and trans. (1990). *Medieval English Prose for Women*. Oxford: Clarendon Press.

Pearsall, D.A., ed. (1962). *The Floure and the Leafe and The Assembly of Ladies*. London: Thomas Nelson.

Peck, Russell, ed. (1991). *Heroic Women from the Old Testament in Middle English Verse*. Kalamazoo: Medieval Institute Publications.

Reames, Sherry, ed. (2003). *Middle English Legends of Women Saints*. Kalamazoo: Medieval Institute Publications.

Savage, Anne and Watson, Nicholas, eds. and trans. (1991). *Anchoritic Spirituality: Ancrene Wisse and Associated Works*. New York: Paulist Press.

Serjeantson, Mary, ed. (1938). *Legendys of Hooly Wummen by Osbern Bokenham*. EETS OS 206. London: Oxford University Press.

Thompson, W. Meredith, ed. (1958). *Þe Wohunge of Ure Lauerd*. EETS OS 241. London: Oxford University Press.

Wright, Thomas, ed. (1906). *Book of the Knight of La Tour-Landry*. Revd edn. EETS OS 33. London: N. Trübner.

Secondary sources and suggestions for further reading

Ashley, Kathleen (1998). 'Historicizing Margery: The *Book of Margery Kempe* as Social Text'. *Journal of Medieval and Early Modern Studies*, 28, 371–88.

Blumenfeld-Kosinski, Renate (1994). 'Jean le Fèvre's *Livre de Leesce*: Praise or Blame of Women?' *Speculum*, 69, 705–25.

Bullough, Vern (1973). 'Medieval Medical and Scientific Attitudes toward Women'. *Viator*, 4, 485–501.

Cannon, Christopher (2003). 'Enclosure'. In Carolyn Dinshaw and David Wallace, eds., *The Cambridge Companion to Medieval Women's Writing* (pp. 109–23). Cambridge: Cambridge University Press.

Cazelles, Brigitte (1991). *The Lady as Saint*. University Park: Pennsylvania State University Press.

Coletti, Theresa (2001). '*Paupertas est donum Dei*: Hagiography, Lay Religion, and the Economics of Salvation in the Digby *Mary Magdalene*'. *Speculum*, 76, 337–78.

Dinshaw, Carolyn (1989). *Chaucer's Sexual Poetics*. Madison: University of Wisconsin Press.

Gaunt, Simon (1995). *Gender and Genre in Medieval French Literature*. Cambridge: Cambridge University Press.

Gibson, Gail McMurray (1996). 'Blessing from Sun and Moon: Churching as Women's Theater'. In Barbara Hanawalt and David Wallace, eds., *Bodies and Disciplines: Intersections of Literature and History in Fifteenth-Century England* (pp. 139–54). Minneapolis: University of Minnesota Press.

Meale, Carol (1993). 'Alle the bokes that I haue of latyn, englisch, and frensch: Laywomen and their Books in Late Medieval England'. In Meale, ed., *Women and Literature in Britain, 1150–1500* (pp. 128–58). Cambridge: Cambridge University Press.

Percival, Florence (1998). *Chaucer's Legendary Good Women*. Cambridge: Cambridge University Press.

Salih, Sarah (2001). *Versions of Virginity in Late Medieval England*. Woodbridge: D.S. Brewer.

Staley, Lynn (1994). *Margery Kempe's Dissenting Fictions*. University Park: Pennsylvania State University Press.

Strohm, Paul (1992). *Hochon's Arrow: The Social Imagination of Fourteenth-Century Texts*. Princeton: Princeton University Press.

Summit, Jennifer (2000). *Lost Property: The Woman Writer and English Literary History, 1380–1589*. Chicago: University of Chicago Press.

Winstead, Karen (1997). *Virgin Martyrs: Legends of Sainthood in Late Medieval England*. Ithaca: Cornell University Press.

Wogan-Browne, Jocelyn (2001). *Saints' Lives and Women's Literary Culture*. Oxford: Oxford University Press.

Chapter 4

The Past

Andrew Galloway

A Culture of History

From the coming of the Normans in 1066 – or, a more significant starting point, a generation later, when the fuller transformation of Anglo-Saxon culture by a more entirely Norman administrative world had set in – a more or less central preoccupation with the past and its stories, 'true' or not, and framed and pointed for a number of purposes, becomes evident in English writing. This preoccupation is found throughout the increasing deluge and complex variety of English writing right up to the arrival of the Welsh Tudors who became the rulers of England in 1485 – or, again perhaps a more decisive moment, when the second king of that line seized sovereignty of the English Church in the 1530s, demolishing the religious properties and rituals that had maintained centuries of medieval Catholic Christianity.

This obsession with the past in the period is not surprising in a culture based on a religion for which, as Barry Windeatt has already shown, history was pregnant with meaning. The fullness of this meaning was unfolded only through history, from the negotiations in the Bible between God and humanity in the Pentateuch, to the stories of Israel's kings and prophets that showed the struggles of the chosen people against their enemies, and themselves. Twelfth-century Anglo-Norman chroniclers, heirs to a culture that had been repeatedly conquered, could add many parallels and continuations to this biblical foundation, as when Henry of Huntingdon in the 1130s shaped

English history around an Exodus-like account of five plagues, or when the sins and civil wars in the biblical Book of Kings, especially the story of David and his successors, were echoed in the elaborate history of the pre-Saxon British kings – including the first full account of King Arthur – that Geoffrey of Monmouth 'discovered' and translated into Latin in 1138 from a source that is conveniently lost.

Religion was not the only wellspring for a new obsession with the past after the Conquest: virtually all principles of authority and order adverted to history and tradition, even – or especially – during periods of major changes or challenges. This is evident in bookish lineages of monastic rights and liberties, which appeared especially in later medieval England when monks were most criticized by friars, Lollards and rebellious peasants; colourful long rolls displaying the 'trees' or pumpkin-vines of noble or royal families appeared, similarly, just when inheritance claims were most dubious. Even an ancient sword might be brought out, as happened in 1280 when the English king, Edward I, suddenly demanded written charters showing the evidence by which all nobility claimed their land (see Clanchy 1993: 35–43). The past was continuously, if sometimes all too malleably, part of present uses and meanings. From the early thirteenth century on, prayers for the dead were included in the Mass, demonstrating the ongoing maintenance of the larger mixed community of the living and the dead that is characteristic of medieval Christian society generally. The sixteenth-century Reformers of the English Church found, however, that many local parishioners had taken to inserting among the prayers for the local dead the names of enemies still alive – who were thus wished into their graves by these pious words: a manipulation of history that the Reformers picked out for special contempt (Bossy 1983: 45–6). In fact, the practice is condemned in the medieval *Dives and Pauper* too (ed. Barnum 1976–2004: Vol. I, Pt. 1, 159; Vol. II, 67).

In medieval writings as well, the past is not treated in ways that are familiar from our world. Even prose Latin chroniclers (usually Benedictine monks) who laboured the most to collect and ponder history, laying the foundations for the modern posture of historical writing – as the rigorous pursuit of 'truth' about the past – do not maintain such a posture in our terms or for our reasons. The massively influential, early eighth-century Latin chronicler Bede – still our best source for many aspects of early-medieval Northumbrian England – conveys, as he repeatedly insists in his *Ecclesiastical History* and his prose *Life of St Cuthbert*, only stories that have been maintained by sufficiently pious witnesses. In the twelfth century, new emphases on written documentation emerge among Latin chroniclers (as documents also more fully define property claims, royal administration and trade). But their uses of documentary authority are also not necessarily consistent with 'modern' historical standards, forms and goals. Geoffrey of Monmouth, for instance, creates his elaborate pre-Saxon history of Britain by filling in some convenient gaps in Bede by means of his access to and translation of a 'certain very ancient book written in the British language', which allows him to present nearly full-born the story of King Arthur and his conquests. Geoffrey's work, in a terse pseudo-classical Latin prose like that of Sallust or Livy, and preserved in copies that often look like those of the works of classical historians that were produced in the period, shows enough contact with the writings of the sixth-century British historian Gildas to substantiate his assertion; but it also recycles narrative elements from stories readily available in quite different genres, such as the legend of St Ursula and the eleven thousand virgins, which reappears in Geoffrey's account of the British king Conan's effort to send British women to Brittany. Yet Geoffrey's *Historia regum Britanniae* ('History of the Kings of Britain') is the most influential chronicle of the Middle Ages; it henceforth infuses nearly all prose Latin chroniclers' works as well as countless vernacular poems, in French and English alike (see further Helen Cooper's essay in this volume).

It is generally useful to think of stories in this period about 'the past' not simply as seeking to reveal the past as an end in itself (which in fact it never entirely is), but also as a kind of 'language' of law, moral theology, social rights or other pointed claim in some sense useful for the present (naming living enemies in prayers for the dead is just a blunt instance). Geoffrey's stories, for example, assert the ancient civility of the pre-Saxon British at a time when Anglo-Norman chroniclers characterized them as barbarous. They also assert the innate 'rights' of a people to be free from other peoples: a claim with some importance during the early stages of the Anglo-Norman conquest of Geoffrey's Wales. Historical stories can be used for a variety of purposes, and what is most striking from this period forward is how numerous these purposes were, and how great the range of materials emerging to serve them. This is particularly visible in Middle English writing, which, demoted to low social prestige after the Norman Conquest, naturally tended to narrative and homily rather than theology, science and government, spheres that, as Jeremy Smith discusses below, English began to occupy only late in the period. Generally blocked from other domains throughout this span, English writers cultivated history as the basis for their most important developments, including what increasingly came to be considered a new kind of writing: 'poesye'.

Past and Present

If all genres are considered, the vast array of writings about the past from Geoffrey's twelfth century on, in Latin, French and Middle English, can be loosely categorized into several basic historical 'matters': biblical (including the extra-biblical expansions of 'salvation history' exemplified in mystery plays); classical (from writings about Troy to ones about Thebes or Alexander the Great); and 'medieval' (including texts about Arthur and Charlemagne, but also ones more broadly about Britain or England, in verse more often than prose). French written in England presents especially elaborate re-handlings of history by self-conscious poetic versifiers. The mid-twelfth century saw, along with Arthur's arrival in history and literature, a burst of French poetry (much of it sponsored in Henry II's court) exploring the distant classical past. This was a period of brief optimism about the Crusades, and of rapid expansion of the English 'nation' to include not just Normandy but also a wide continental expanse from Brittany to Aquitaine, bordering on Aragon and Navarre to the south and including Scotland in the north. The exotic realms of the past offered a broad historical legitimacy to the new imperial ambitions. A trilogy of long and rich Anglo-Norman historical romances showed the way: the *Roman de Thèbes* of around 1150 (ed. Mora-Lebrun 1995), the *Roman d'Enéas* of around 1160 (ed. Petit 1997), and Benoît de Sainte-Maure's vast *Roman de Troie* of around 1165 (ed. Constans 1904–12). The last of these began an especially rich lineage of historical writings, in part because of the claim (echoed by Geoffrey of Monmouth and throughout English medieval literature) that the fall of Troy led not only to the exile of Æneas to found Rome but also the exile of his great-grandson Brutus to found Britain: a place that was, implicitly, equally mighty.

If these three great 'antique historical poems' opened paths into the past, they were quite willing to inject contemporary courtly concerns into their visions of that past, using it to explore love and human choices in a way that suggests connections between the ancient world and the present moment. Thus the author of the *Roman d'Enéas* creates a love-relation between Enéas and his wife-to-be Lavine at the future site of

Rome. Just as Chaucer's Criseyde, seated at a window, will moment-
ously fall in love with Troilus over two centuries later, so in the twelfth-
century French translation and reinvention of Virgil's ancient poem,
the *Æneid*, Lavine glances out the window at Enéas and is 'saisi'
('seized'), leading her to a passionate inner struggle, and debate,
between hatred of Enéas and a history-changing love for him:

> 'Ffolle Lavine, qu'as tu dit?
> Amors me destraint moult por lui.
> Et tu l'eschive, si le fui!
> Ne puis trouver en mon coraje.
> Ja en ers tu hier sauvage.
> Or m'a Amor toute dontee.'
>   (ed. Petit 1997: lines 8196–202)

['Foolish Lavine, what have you said? Love for him holds me tightly.
But you can escape him/it, you can flee! I can't find it in my heart to
do so. But lo, yesterday you were hostile to him. But now Love has
given me entirely away.']

Lavine's tension between 'love' and 'duty' is reconciled by her politically necessary marriage with Enéas at the end of the poem. In contrast, Virgil's *Æneid* stops before the marriage, and even omits any direct
contact between Æneas and Lavinia. For Virgil, Lavinia is simply the
prize of war between men. Virgil thus avoids founding Rome on entrap-
ping erotic love; indeed, he shows how the passion binding Æneas to
Dido at Carthage in the first quarter of the *Æneid* nearly destroys Æneas
and prevents any Roman destiny, as well as leading Dido to suicide.
The twelfth-century French rewriter of this story, addressing courtly
readers and patrons who might fancy themselves the heirs of Trojans,
balances the tragic story of Dido as a victim of empire with a more
happily consummated one of Lavine as a co-creator of empire. The
change would have had clear relevance during the marriage of Henry
II to Eleanor of Aquitaine, since Eleanor helped to create and govern
England's 'first empire'. It also showed how history could be imagined as an interplay between erotic choices and their consequences,
by which women's private passions for the first time were shown as
crucial to political history.

The first long historical poem in Middle English, Laȝamon's *Brut* from
the early thirteenth century, owes its vitality and complexity to these
new resources of interpersonal historical imagination, but tinges them
with darker ironies, immediately dramatic and more broadly historical.

Written during or shortly after King John's troubled reign, when Henry II's empire was lost, Laȝamon translates Wace's French version of Geoffrey of Monmouth's *Historia regum Britanniae*, but further enriches the story with a continuous sense of tension between separate and often dissonant perspectives on history, including further transactions between present and past. Laȝamon mentions, for instance, that King Arthur comes from 'Bruttainne' (the Middle English word for 'Brittany' as well as 'Britain'): a detail not found in his Arthurian source that makes a clear nod to the deceased young Arthur of Brittany, the son of King John's dead older brother Richard I. John had imprisoned and apparently murdered the thirteen-year-old Arthur of Brittany to deny his claims to the throne (Allen 1998).

Laȝamon uses the rhetorical resources of Latin as well as Anglo-Saxon epic poetry adroitly to enrich the perspectives available within history. His Arthur, for instance, indulges in elaborate similes, found nowhere in his source, that show the king concerned with his own literary afterlife, even ahead of immediate political success. Thus he decides to release his trapped enemy, Emperor Childric, not (as in Geoffrey of Monmouth and Wace) in a misguided instance of generosity, but instead to ensure that glorious stories will be told about him:

> '. . . swa heo scullen wræcchen . to heoren scipen liðen.
> sæilien ouer sæ . to sele heore londe.
> & þer wirð-liche . wunien on riche.
> and tellen tidende . of Arðure kinge.
> hu ich heom habbe i-freoied . for mines fader saule
> & for mine freo-dome . ifrouered þa wræcchen.'
> Her wes Arður þe king . aðelen bidæled.
> nes þer nan swa rehȝ mon . þe him durste ræden.
> (ed. Brook and Leslie 1963–78: lines 10422–9)

['. . . so they must journey as wretches to their ships, to sail over the sea to their own splendid land, and dwell there honourably in their kingdom, and tell tidings about Arthur the king, how I have freed them for my father's soul, and for my own freedom [or: because of my own generosity] I have helped the wretches.' Here Arthur the king was deprived of good judgment; there was no man so rash as to dare to advise him.]

Laȝamon has added Arthur's aspiration for future poetic fame to Wace's text, as he has added the dramatically silent presence of a cowed but (correctly) pessimistic audience of courtiers. By this means, characters' conflicting views on history are seen to be crucial to events; yet however lyrically powerful those characters' historical imaginings, Laȝamon suggests, they are ultimately defeated by circumstances that overwhelm any one human being's visions and intentions. Writing only a century and a half after the Norman Conquest, using a poetic style that is in fact quite different from the 'classical' style of alliterative Old English epic poetry to which it superficially gestures, Laȝamon manipulates his single main source, Wace, to emphasize diverse perspectives lurking in every past moment, comparable to the diverse English, French and Latin sources that Laȝamon claims in his prologue he has 'pressed into one' to create his poem (see Galloway 2006). Only Laȝamon's lack of broad structural manipulation, and the steadily linear chronology of his plot, keep modern scholars from regarding his work as a major epic poem.

The most complex thwarting of our kinds of distinction between 'history' and 'literature' are in romances, which, after their début in French in the mid-twelfth century, begin appearing in English by the later thirteenth century. These accounts of heroic figures and their adventures often feature historical personages, sometimes presenting clear support of contemporary aristocratic lineages whose living representatives offered the surest means of literary patronage. This is the case, for example, with the romance of *Gui de Warewic*, which seems to have been composed to glorify the ancestry of the thirteenth-century earls of Warwick; its hero, a member of the court of the tenth-century Anglo-Saxon king Athelstan, becomes a pilgrim (although he is still a warrior) and then a penitent hermit who is at length assumed into heaven. Translated from French into several English versions, *Gui de Warewic* was followed by other, less pious romances about Athelstan and his court. These probably all responded to twelfth-century Latin chroniclers' interest in the period of the Battle of Brunanburh, which was commemorated in a now-famous Old English historical poem that the Anglo-Norman chroniclers, at a time when they could still partly understand Old English, found bubbling up from the prose lines of *The Anglo-Saxon Chronicle* in, as the archdeacon Henry of Huntingdon says, 'a kind of song, using strange words and figures of speech' (trans. Greenway 1996: 311). Transmitting such instances of lost Anglo-Saxon rough-hewn grandeur and barbaric mystery in Latin (as Henry of Huntingdon strove to do) could only increase, and pass down to later medieval England, the sense that pre-Norman England was an alien place indeed. The romances in French and English that look back to Anglo-Saxon England convey this general historical perception as fully as any Latin chronicles and annals, while finding in that lost world new ways to frame contemporary issues (see Rouse 2005).

Romances about more recent English history also speak to the present, as the Crusades-set poem *Richard Cœur de Lyon* suggests. This text – probably based on a version in French, but preserved only in a vivid Middle English narrative from the early fourteenth century that has been translated for 'Lewed men' who 'cune Ffrensch non' ('know no French') (ed. Brünner 1913: line 23) – presents the English king Richard I as wondrously 'lewed' himself. Richard delights in violence and terror, serving the cooked heads of Saracens to his heathen guests, and savouring with a keen appetite the pork-like flavour of one Saracen 'ʒonge and ffat' whom he devours personally (line 3087). The romance may mirror tales of cannibalism from the real Crusades, but more likely it serves the function of claiming that kings are even more heartily crude than the people of common lineage and social position who probably constituted the audience for English rather than French romances in this period (see further Helen Cooper's essay in this volume). Richard in this romance is a man of the people, and he shames the effetely courtly and French Duke of Burgundy, who refuses to dirty his hands in building a city wall as Richard does because, as the duke says, '"My fadyr nas mason ne carpentere"' (lines 5955–6044).

Another superheroic but also 'common' English king appears in the adroit late thirteenth-century English version of the story of Havelok the Dane, a king who figures in some historical narratives of the early kings of England (such as the twelfth-century verse history of England by the Anglo-Norman writer Gaimar: see Smithers, ed., 1987). According to the vivid early fourteenth-century verse chronicle of Robert Mannyng, Havelok's exploits were still popularly associated at that date with various parts of the landscape of Lincolnshire (see Galloway 2002: 271). Havelok, an unrecognized royal heir, has to work as an urban labourer, who gains his living in a kitchen and among a throng of porters, and out-competes those advertising their skills by pushing them all aside ('He shof hem alle upon an hyl' (line 893)). Once king, he makes a kitchen scullion, his most loyal friend, into the Earl of Cornwall (lines 2901–12). Again, the king of England is imagined as intimately part of the common social world – and as joined with this against the French-speaking world of imperious and distant governance that the real king of England occupied.

More directly contemporary accounts of English history often use what we would consider 'legendary' bases even for highly detailed and political narratives that are, in other respects, 'reliable'. The most self-consciously 'historical' of such works, the prose *Brut*, which is extant in French and English versions, surviving in hundreds of copies (French ed. and trans. Marvin 2006; English ed. Brie 1906–8), presents increasingly detailed though still brief political and social narratives, organized by each king's reign; its more recent narratives are sometimes our best source for 'data', including those concerning the Good Parliament of 1376 and the Peasants' Revolt of 1381, which are described in unparalleled detail in the Anglo-Norman version of the *Brut* from northern England called the 'Anonimalle' chronicle, or the story of the execution of the aristocratic heretic, Sir John Oldcastle, in 1412, which is related in the fifteenth-century English versions (ed. Brie 1906–8: 386). Yet even the *Brut* opens in many of its copies, French and English, with the account of King Diocletian of Syria sending his thirty-three daughters who have just murdered their thirty-three new husbands off to the uninhabited island of Britain, where they copulate with demons and produce a new race of giants. This story's 'truth value' derives from its explanation of the giants in Britain described by Geoffrey of Monmouth, and perhaps from its parallels to the story of the Nephilim in Genesis 6:4, as well as its implication that women, including those responsible for first populating Britain, are rebellious of old, an issue that haunts most English historical literature (see further below).

The Individual in History

As all this makes clear, our definition of medieval 'literary creativity' must usually accommodate an exchange of some kind or kinds with history. At a minimum, this appears in some complex uses and transformations of the authoritative stories that were fashioned by the ancient *auctores* (see Jane Griffiths' essay later in this volume; compare also Helen Cooper's essay). But the engagement with the past in Middle English literature also involves an array of issues that might better be considered 'philosophy of history', such as the intricate relations between private experience and larger historical developments: an issue already broached by Laȝamon, but tackled more insistently in Middle English texts of the late fourteenth century. In Chaucer's epic (or epic romance), *Troilus and Criseyde*, written in the mid-1380s, Troilus' and Criseyde's intimate feelings and thoughts are made immediately part of the wider social world by the deftly intrusive machinations of Pandarus, but they are also made part of the sweep of history by the linkage between Criseyde's departure from Troy and the entry into the city of Antenor – the Trojan who betrayed his own people – for whom she serves as a means of exchange. The same might be said of the interplay in Langland's *Piers Plowman* between the difficult journey of the individual Will and the sequence of teachers and visions that offer the questing dreamer many kinds of tradition, to be pondered, broken down, and somehow made meaningful. Or again, in Gower's *Confessio Amantis*, Amans encounters a long succession of historical narratives from his 'confessor' Genius, and both struggle to draw from them cogent ethical and psychological points from which the individual can learn. Later fourteenth-century English writing presents an increasing distinction between literary extractions from history – including what is sometimes termed 'poesye' (a word that first appears in English at this time) – and narratives claiming to evoke and serve the past directly. A new aspiration in English writing to negotiate more powerfully with history, and to attain some position outside it in a more 'timeless' realm of craft and monumental poetry, seems evident. The shift is one of complex reorientation around new conceptual and discursive centres rather than any abrupt transformation; still, it marks a real change in the relations of English literature to historical vision.

The shift can be exquisitely subtle. The opening of the late fourteenth-century alliterative poem *Sir Gawain and the Green Knight*, for instance, presents its story as if it were a small elaboration of a familiar historical trajectory leading to the founding of Britain:

> Siþen þe sege and þe assaut watz sesed at Troye,
> Þe borʒ brittened and brent to brondez and askez,
> Þe tulk þat þe trammes of tresoun þer wroʒt
> Watz tried for his tricherie, þe trewest on erth.
> Hit watz Ennias þe athel and his highe kynde,
> Þat siþen depreced prouinces, and patrounes bicome
> Welneʒe of al þe wele in þe west iles . . .
>
>   (ed. Andrew and Waldron 2002: lines 1–7)

[After the siege and the assault had ceased at Troy, the city destroyed and burned to brands and ashes, the man who hatched the plots of treason there was well known for his treachery, the truest [or: the most certain] on earth. It was the noble Æneas and his high-born kindred, who afterwards laid waste provinces and became lords of almost all the wealth in the western isles . . .]

This may not be recognizable 'history' to us (or to readers of the accounts of the fall of Troy in Virgil or Livy), but it closely follows histories in the tradition to which Laȝamon's *Brut* belongs, as well as the prose Latin *De destructione Troiae* ('On the Destruction of Troy') by the thirteenth-century Italian writer Guido de Columnis, which itself relied on Benoît de Sainte-Maure's *Roman de Troie*. Here Æneas is a traitor to the Trojans, who forced him into exile because of his betrayal of Helen of Troy and Troy itself. The form of the opening of *Sir Gawain* is, moreover, modelled on the similar historical recapitulation in the *Roman d'Enéas*:

> Quant Menelax ot Troie assise,
> onc n'en tourna tres qu'il l'ot prise,
> gasta la terre et tout le regne
> pour la venjance de sa femme.
> La cité prist par traïson,
> tot craventa, tours et donjon,
> arst le paÿs, destruist les murs:
> nuls n'i estoit dedenz seürs.
> (ed. Petit 1997: lines 1–8)

[When Menelaus had besieged Troy, he did not turn away until he had taken it, devastated the land and all the kingdom in vengeance for his wife; he took the city by treason, levelled everything, towers and keeps, burned the land, demolished the walls: nothing remained secure within it.]

Yet for all of its initial connections to standard 'historical lineages' of Britain (which are recalled in nearly identical words in its final stanza), *Sir Gawain* makes it clear that its elaboration of a minor episode in one knight's life does not simply tuck invisibly into the account of England's nation-making that 'everyone' routinely knows. For Sir Gawain learns a curious lesson: everything known to history is revealed to be deceptive, including his own reputation, with which he is continually confronted. Gawain returns to court bearing the green girdle that he previously accepted as a means of self-protection and of gift-exchange as a badge of deep shame – as an epitome of his own unsettling transformations, after he has learned that his own sense of knightly identity and the 'trouthe' for which he is known are thoroughly malleable.

But even this is not the end of the questioning of the stable realities of history in the poem: at Gawain's return, the court takes up the girdle as a universal badge of honour, a celebratory fashion-statement. Larger social and historical contexts are juxtaposed with private experience and individual intention and seem to render those finally

irrelevant – a lesson that ironically suggests that no triumphant historical trajectory such as the one limned at the beginning of the poem
can do justice to the disenchanted, private universes of unsettled identities like Sir Gawain's:

> Vche burne of þe broþerhede, a bauderyk schulde haue,
> A bende abelef hym aboute, of a bryȝt grene . . .
> For þat watz acorded þe renoun of þe Rounde Table . . .
> (lines 2516–19)

> [Each member of the brotherhood was to have a baldric, a band dia-
> gonally about him, of a bright green . . . for that was decreed the
> renown of the Round Table . . .]

From Gawain's point of view, and ours as readers, nothing con-
firmed by public history is comfortingly secure in its meanings: the
repetition of the opening lines about Britain's history at the end is thus
deeply and significantly ironic. Private selves are deeper and more real
than the collective public realms familiar from historical discourse –
yet those public realms are also the sum creations of such selves. The
poem teaches that insides are bigger than outsides, yet also that interpersonal relations as well as longer historical developments shape identity and self-image far more than Sir Gawain would want. Even his
posture as a 'penitent knight' is not in his control to maintain, since
the court wants to celebrate him. The poem's thin blade of irony that
seems not to decapitate what it severs is the quintessence of an
emerging claim for the status of English writing as 'literature': as a
mode that stands back from the past yet is deeply involved with it,
drawing on a vast quantity of historical narratives but increasingly often
struggling to assert an authority somehow independent from history.

Women and the Idea of History in Late-Medieval Literature

Yet history's powers, or excuses, persist, even for the most self-
consciously 'literary' English authors. In Chaucer and the English courtly
writers who followed him in the fifteenth century, one of history's
most constantly repeated lessons – deriving ultimately from Christian
legend, but with the point of this often sharpened further – is that
women, as Catherine Sanok's essay has already suggested, are potent
figures needing various kinds of discipline or abnegation. This idea,

while framed in a jocular or ironic way in works written for women as well as men, directly builds on the focus on women's historical importance emerging in the twelfth-century French and Latin works noted above, but it carries a new emphasis in the claims of late-medieval English writers about poetic authority. Such writers' concerns with the issue of individual errant choices in, and responses to, history find focus on women's inner experience especially, and rarely with any final endorsement of the souls of these daughters of Eve. Chaucer's most intent student of women's history, the Wife of Bath, vehemently rejects the dull lesson of endless stories that claim that historical women are the root of 'variance' and lack of 'trouthe' – yet, as the epitome of 'variance' and lack of 'trouthe' herself, she is offered in terms that reinforce it. If, as suggested above, the historical *Roman d'Enéas* and other twelfth-century products of Anglo-Norman culture first used women's subjectivity as a beacon for all subjectivity within the complex patterns of history, the later medieval absorption of such traditions often implies the need to constrain women's subjectivity, while using it to explore further the value to narrative of 'personalized' historical perspective. The idea that subjectivity is a potent force within visions of the past and historical trajectories, that is, finds its first expression through women; they, in turn, remain, and indeed increasingly become, the focus of its severest penalties and blame.

Chaucer's artful handling of this, in his many histories of tragic women, is to decry the unfair centring of blame on them and to position himself as 'all womanis frend' (as the sixteenth-century Scottish poet Gavin Douglas puts it in his translation of Virgil's *Æneid*, the *Eneados*; ed. Coldwell 1957: line 449); simultaneously, however, Chaucer assembles all the ingredients for their guilt. In a triumph of vivid imagination of the past, Chaucer's narratives explore with extraordinary detail historical (or ostensibly historical) women's consciousness, especially their struggles to achieve full consciousness of their own identities; yet their struggling self-questioning often leads them to fulfil, like the Wife of Bath, the trait of 'variance' or moral 'instability' for which they remain the icons. Chaucer's Criseyde is as famous and influential an instance as the Wife, presented as both an eloquent re-reader of history and a paradoxical fulfilment of what she tries on and rejects in the received images of herself that she ponders – her reputation, for example, as a woman who has done other women '"deshonour"' (*The Canterbury Tales*, V.1066). Most of Chaucer's eloquent historical or quasi-historical women offered his poetic followers opportunities for exploring with great subtlety individual consciousnesses in history, and for condemning no less fully women's seemingly inevitable moral lapses.

John Lydgate, for instance, more than most of Chaucer's fifteenth-century male devotees, found ways to use the historical women that Chaucer had pondered to demonstrate the ethical foibles of personal subjectivity in historical settings. A Benedictine monk but also Chaucer's closest reader and the most ambitious courtly poet of the fifteenth century, Lydgate found numerous opportunities to pretend to defend women while directing severe blame on to them in his two monumental historical poems: *The Troy Book* (ed. Bergen 1906–35), written around 1412–20, a vast, sometimes rambling expansion of Guido de Columnis; and *The Fall of Princes* (ed. Bergen 1923–7), of the 1430s, a massive collection of the downfalls of great rulers followed by brief considerations of the stories' morals, in which both a very feminine Fortune and actual women are given major roles in the blame.

In *The Troy Book*, Lydgate archly ponders how he might 'shrive' ('confess' or 'absolve') his source Guido for the misogyny that he has displayed (I.2116–36), in a clear repetition of Chaucer's claims in *Troilus and Criseyde* that he is struggling against his fictional source 'Lollius', whose story dictates that Criseyde must be unfaithful (see, for example, the *prohemium* to Book IV of *Troilus*). The emotional identifications and competitions in these intertextual historical relations run deep, and the role of misogyny in Middle English works striving for literary 'monumentality' is worth pondering closely. Both Chaucer and Lydgate often adopt overtly submissive yet rebelliously minded roles before their commanding French and Latin sources, which they would, they both claim, betray if they could. This suggests some complex identification with their portrayals of women in history, who, like these ambitious poets themselves, can pursue some authority of their own only indirectly, by subtly negotiating with the oppressive traditions imposed on them. Yet writing in a language that real women could and did read, and offering female characters as their most verbally eloquent, persuasive and sympathetic figures, Chaucer and his followers nonetheless implicitly denounce such feminine voices and minds at crucial moments in their re-creations of the past. Perhaps this offered them a means of positing a level of 'authority' or 'poesye' by a complicated identification with, yet rejection of, the women who seemed to epitomize human involvement in the secular, historical world. In these terms, the notorious ending of *Troilus*, where the narrator renounces both the faithless Criseyde and all the 'wrecched world' of the 'corsed' pagan history that he has so sensitively explored, is simply a more overt epitome of these pressures than usual (see Dinshaw 1989: 28–64). Here the 'language' of history could be made to express at least a hope for transcendence from history, and for some authoritative ideal of poetic immortality.

Lydgate especially ends up making women's errantly independent minds the target of his criticism of human 'variance' in the vast panoply of history that he unfolds throughout his career. Telling the story of Jason's betrayal of Medea (following Guido and in turn Benoît, who position that story as the prelude to the story of Troy), Lydgate outdoes Chaucer, and may indeed be here (as often) in deliberate direct intertextual response to, or competition with, him, in showing Medea's barely self-conscious ulterior motives. Chaucer's perspective on her is withering enough; in his 'defence' of such 'good women', *The Legend of Good Women* (*c.* 1385), he conveys Medea's dogged argument to Jason for why he should love her, supposedly a demonstration of 'hire trouthe and . . . hire kyndenesse' (which Jason then villainously spurns). Her speech, however, includes a long set of clues indicating her naïve belief that she can barter for someone's permanent and total love if she simply gives him something he badly needs at the moment, namely protection:

Tho gan this Medea to hym declare	Then began
The peril of this cas from poynt to poynt,	
And of his batayle, and in what disjoynt	predicament
He mot stonde, of which no creature	
Save only she ne myghte his lyf assure.	
And shortly to the poynt ryght for to go,	
They been acorded ful bytwixe hem two	
That Jason shal hire wedde, as trewe knyght;	
And terme set to come sone at nyght	
Unto hire chamber and make there his oth	
Upon the goddes, that he for lef or loth	for any reason
Ne sholde nevere hire false, nyght ne day,	
To ben hire husbonde whil he lyve may,	
As she that from his deth hym saved here.	Since it was she who
	(lines 1629–42)

Chaucer's indirect discourse quietly, but with devastating clarity, presents Medea's naïve hopefulness beneath her offer of life-saving tools in exchange for Jason's undying love. She triumphantly concludes her offer with a concise summary of the terms of her proposed exchange, as if presenting simple equivalents, a fair and reasonable bargain. She is a less sophisticated version of the bartering lady of the castle in *Sir*

Gawain and the Green Knight, who, with more calculation, convinces Sir Gawain to accept the putatively protective green girdle, yet who is spurned by Sir Gawain no less than Medea is spurned by Jason – and then vilified when Gawain bursts out with a vicious diatribe against deceptive women throughout history, as if this were history's most basic lesson (ed. Andrew and Waldron 2002: lines 2414–28).

Lydgate's Medea outdoes Chaucer's in revealing ulterior motives pressing through eloquent formal language, in this case her urgent sexual desire for Jason, which loads the terms of her flattery of this handsome stranger at her father's court:

'For þinges two myn herte sore meve,	move sorely
Þis is to seyne, loue and gentillesse,	This is to say; nobility
What þat I mene clerly to expresse	
To ȝoure persone, and no þing to concele	
Or we parte, liche as ȝe schal fele.	Before
For me semeth, first of curtesye,	out of
In sothefastnes, and of genterye,	truthfulness; out of good manners
Þat to straungeris euery maner wyȝt	kind of person
Is bounde and holde of verray due riȝt	
To make chere, and trewly as for me,	
Be-cause, Iason, þat I in ȝow se	
So moche manhod, & so gret worþinesse,	
I wil not feyne with al my besynesse	industry
To helpe and forther in al þat may ȝou like'.	

(ed. Bergen 1906–35: I.2314–27)

'Manhod' takes on a bodily presence here that it normally lacks in Middle English, as does the seemingly innocent claim of a pressing social need for Medea 'to make chere' to Jason. Her negotiations with him lead unwaveringly to sex: once Medea has obtained Jason's vow of faith, she uses that to demand that they follow good medieval canon law, which declared that a promise for marriage in words of the future would be clinched and fulfilled by a sexual act. As Medea manœuvres toward this goal, she shows even more clearly that sex is what most preoccupies her mind, providing a pornographic subtext to her allusions to canon law's sacramental obligations:

'Iason', quod sche, 'þan I schal ordeyne	
A mene weye þat we bothe tweyne	common
May efte ageyn at leyser mete sone,	
For to parforme al þat is to done	
In þis mater, liche to oure entent,	in conformity with our plan

Wher schal be made a fynal sacrament
Of oure desire, þat no man schal vnbynde,
Þouȝ now þer-to we may no leyser fynde.'   Though we can find no
                                              leisure for it now
                                                   (I.2657–64)

This, however, was not the only way that English writing built
a tradition of its own historical vision in the late Middle Ages. A different view of history, and, arguably, a less misogynist tradition,
developed in fifteenth-century English historical Christian drama, in
the mystery cycles that were performed at the feast of Corpus Christi.
These plays, which were already being written and produced in
numerous towns by the late fourteenth century, wove into the majestic history of salvation from Creation to Doomsday an immediate and
humane endorsement of the present urban community, along with a
remarkable capacity for farce, familial tragedy, political commentary,
and theology.

In the Corpus Christi drama, the roles of Mary and other women in
sacred history achieve highly validated status, and not simply because
their identities transcend regular humanity. Rather, they receive a degree
of sensitive rather than ultimately damning representation precisely
because of their quotidian nature, which is treated without the pressures of irony and, perhaps, without the striving for high poetic
individual prestige that fuels the explorations (and ultimate condemnations) of women's eloquent tongues and independent minds in courtly
historical poetry.

Because of this, it is ironic that the substantial tradition of religious
historical drama was doomed to end with the Reformation, which out-
lawed it along with the institutions and rituals of the medieval
Church, while the more ironic and misogynist poetic courtly historical tradition, with Chaucer as its figurehead and English literature's
'father', survived and flourished (see David Matthews' essay at the end
of this volume). The character of a culture is revealed by what it chooses
to inherit and define as 'tradition', and this is as clear in the
Renaissance, which seized on Chaucer the sympathetic but witty love
poet, as it was after the Norman Conquest, which seized on the 'bar-
barity' of the Anglo-Saxons who had just been conquered, a view that
English writers themselves only gradually redeemed.

What the fifteenth-century drama of the Corpus Christi plays
inherited was a rich tradition of Latin liturgical drama along with a
host of secular literary forms and motifs; what it chose to exploit from

this inheritance, however, was quite new. The Latin liturgical drama insists on presenting differences between history, and life, past and present that could only be bridged by the priests and monks who regularly summoned the Eucharist into life, and, for example, the season of Easter feasting after the penance of Lent. In contrast, the urban Corpus Christi drama insists on the continuities between history present and past, and between language sacred and everyday – precisely the kind of mixing of spheres of history that the religious and literary reformers in the Renaissance most disparaged.

The large and rich range of these plays precludes offering any one instance as exemplary; but a glimpse of this final medieval form of English literary treatments of the past might be obtained through one of the smallest plays among all the cycles, *The Salutation of Elizabeth* (based on Luke 1:39–56) from the mystery cycle that was performed at Wakefield (ed. Bevington 1975: 368–71). This brief play (ninety lines) is remarkable in that nothing happens. Instead, it is a play of potentiality, especially the potential of everyday life and speech to yield the sacred. Mary, pregnant with Jesus, casually encounters and speaks to Elizabeth, who is old but also miraculously pregnant, with the future John the Baptist; Elizabeth greets Mary with words used for the widely known prayer 'Ave Maria' ('Hail, Mary').

In the prayer, the greeting to Mary is followed by the celebratory observation that she is 'full of grace' – 'the Lord be with you, blessed be you among women, and blessed be the fruit of your womb Jesus . . .'. The genius of the Wakefield play is that these potent words emerge naturally among the common speech-acts of greeting that any two fifteenth-century townswomen might use. The women discuss their own conditions and ask about their relatives, then portions of the prayer are sprinkled throughout Elizabeth's loving but everyday talk, while the language of the women, with similar naturalness, follows the elegant stanza form of most of the Wakefield plays:

ELEZABETH.   Full lang shall I the better be,
That I may speke my fill with thee,
My dere kins-woman,
To witt how thy freyndys fare   know
In thy countré where thay are;
Therof tell me thou can,
And how thou farys, my dere derling.

MARY.   Well, dame, gramercy your asking . . .   thank you very
much for asking

. . .
Dame, God that all may
Yeld you that ye say,   may God who can do everything reward
                          you for what you say
And blis you therfore.   give you joy for it

Elizabeth.   Blissed be thou of all women,
And the fruite that I well ken   know
Within the wombe of thee . . .
                          (ed. Bevington 1975: lines 13–33)

The risk of such a 'natural' strategy for presenting so historically potent
a set of words is that it may seem to degrade and literalize the sacred;
and it is in just such terms that the cycle drama was criticized by the
Lollards and, later, the Protestant Reformers. The greatness of this strategy, however, is that it brings the powers of everyday language up to
a level of sacred history. If the 'Ave' can emerge in reply to common
greetings, then any common words have the potential to generate sacred
speech, of equivalent authority, sanctity and historical efficacy. The
invisible transformation of the humble, bourgeois present by such means
is a uniquely powerful instance of historical imagination, one deserv-
ing as much credit as anything preserved from the vast and vital accom-
plishments of medieval transactions with the past.

References

Primary texts

Andrew, Malcolm and Waldron, Ronald, eds. (2002). *The Poems of the Pearl
    Manuscript: Pearl, Cleanness, Patience, Sir Gawain and the Green Knight.* 4th edn.
    Exeter: University of Exeter Press.
Barnum, Priscilla Heath, ed. (1976–2004). *Dives and Pauper.* Vol. I, Pt. 1: EETS
    OS 275; Vol. I, Pt. 2: EETS OS 280; Vol. II: EETS OS 323. London and Oxford:
    Oxford University Press.
Bergen, Henry, ed. (1906–35). *Lydgate's Troy Book.* EETS ES 97, 103, 106, 126.
    London: Kegan Paul, Trench, Trübner & Co.
Bergen, Henry, ed. (1924–7). *Lydgate's Fall of Princes.* EETS ES 121–4.
    London: Kegan Paul, Trench, Trübner & Co.
Bevington, David, ed. (1975). *Medieval Drama.* Boston: Houghton Mifflin.
Brie, F.W.D., ed. (1906–8). *The Brut or the Chronicles of England.* EETS OS 131,
    136. London: Kegan Paul, Trench, Trübner & Co.
Brook, G.L. and Leslie, R.F., eds. (1963–78). *Laȝamon: Brut.* EETS OS 250, 277.
    London: Oxford University Press.

Brünner, Karl, ed. (1913). *Der mittelenglische Versroman über Richard Löwenherz: kritische Ausgabe.* Wiener Beiträge zur englischen Philologie 42. Vienna: Wilhelm Braumüller.

Coldwell, David F.C., ed. (1957–64). *Virgil's Æneid Translated into Scottish Verse by Gavin Douglas.* Scottish Text Society 25, 27, 28, 30. Edinburgh: William Blackwood.

Constans, Léopold, ed. (1904–12). *Le roman de Troie par Benoît de Sainte-Maure.* Paris: Firmin-Didot.

Greenway, Diana, ed. and trans. (1996). *Henry, Archdeacon of Huntingdon: Historia anglorum – The History of the English People.* Oxford: Clarendon Press.

Marvin, Julia, ed. and trans. (2006). *The Oldest Anglo-Norman Prose Brut Chronicle.* Woodbridge: Boydell Press.

Mora-Lebrun, Francine, ed. (1995). *Le roman de Thèbes.* Paris: Livre de Poche.

Petit, Aimé, ed. (1997). *Le roman d'Enéas.* Paris: Livre de Poche.

Smithers, G.V., ed. (1987). *Havelok.* Oxford: Clarendon Press.

Secondary sources and suggestions for further reading

Allen, Rosamund (1998). '*Eorles* and *Beornes*: Contextualizing Lawman's *Brut'.* *Arthuriana,* 8.3, 4–22.

Bossy, John (1983). 'The Mass as a Social Institution, 1200–1700'. *Past and Present,* 100, 29–61.

Clanchy, M.T. (1993). *From Memory to Written Record: England 1066–1307.* 2nd edn. Oxford: Blackwell.

Dinshaw, Carolyn (1989). *Chaucer's Sexual Poetics.* Madison: University of Wisconsin Press.

Faith, R. (1984). 'The "Great Rumour" of 1377 and Peasant Ideology'. In R.H. Hilton and T.H. Aston, eds., *The English Rising of 1381* (pp. 43–73). Cambridge: Cambridge University Press.

Galloway, Andrew (2002). 'Writing History in England'. In David Wallace, ed., *The Cambridge History of Medieval English Literature* (pp. 255–83). Cambridge: Cambridge University Press.

Galloway, Andrew (2006). 'Layamon's Gift'. *Publications of the Modern Language Association,* 121, 717–34.

Rouse, Robert (2005). *The Idea of Anglo-Saxon England in Middle English Romance.* Cambridge: D.S. Brewer.

Part II

The Production of Middle English Literature

Chapter 5

Production and Dissemination

Alexandra Gillespie

At the end of his *Troilus and Criseyde*, written in the mid-1380s, Geoffrey Chaucer writes:

> Go, litel bok, go, litel myn tragedye,
> Ther God thi makere yet, er that he dye,
> So sende myght to make in som comedye!
> . . .
> But subgit be to alle poesye;
> And kis the steppes where as thow seest pace
> Virgile, Ovide, Omer, Lucan, and Stace.
> . . .
> [And] prey I God that non myswrite the. . . .
> (V.1786–92)

Chaucer's 'litel bok' is, firstly, the literary text itself, which will catch God's forgiving attention, he hopes, or at least follow in the footsteps of its famous literary forebears. The 'bok' thus seems rather formless and timeless, except that the 'makere' of this text is not divine, but human, and his poem must therefore be the product of lived experience and a specific context for literary production. In the 1380s, Chaucer was a London bureaucrat, alive to the Christian belief that the profit of literary work is the 'comedye' of heavenly reward. But Chaucer was also alive in the world, writing accounts as an official at the wharves – and hoping for, or receiving, patronage for his writings, as he probably had in the 1360s and 1370s in the household of Edward III and retinue of John of Gaunt. The gifts of patrons were the only *worldly* profit that writers of medieval texts could expect.

In his famous *envoy* to *Troilus*, however, Chaucer not only describes his literary work as a 'bok': he also describes the form in which posterity will know that text, the mechanism for its transmission, written or miswritten. It is sent into the world *as* a 'bok'. The word 'bok' had a wide semantic range in Middle English. It could mean any composition in words, spoken aloud or written. It could also mean folded pages, a bound codex, or some other text-bearing object. Both these senses may be employed by Chaucer in order to keep his idea of *Troilus* hazy, staving off that moment when his 'litel bok', the text, takes the form of a 'bok'-as-object, and then goes somewhere he cannot follow.

Chaucer's famous 'go, litel bok' stanza thus suggests some of the concerns of Daniel Wakelin's chapter later in this volume, on the material forms of medieval texts. But it also suggests the broad scope of the present chapter, which will make three main points. First, medieval texts were produced in some particular form so that they could be made available to specific listeners or readers. They were made by individuals with the skills, time and access to the materials needed to produce them in that form. Texts were thus produced and disseminated in specific historical contexts.

The second point in this chapter is that those contexts were too complex to be neatly categorized, and were subject to change throughout the medieval period. Chaucer's stanza in *Troilus* is a useful example, in that the author stands in the middle of a transition that inflects his ideas about his 'litel bok' – a transition that underpins this essay. On the one side of the change is a culture – its roots in the Anglo-Saxon period – in which most texts and books were produced and disseminated in religious contexts or in aristocratic households for noble patrons. A great many of these texts were not in English but in Latin or, after the Norman conquest of 1066, Anglo-Norman French (see further Jeremy Smith's essay in this volume). On the other side of the change marked by Chaucer's career is a new and different culture of textual production. In this culture, English was increasingly a preferred language for composition, even in traditionally French courtly settings. A growing metropolitan bureaucracy created a new class of professional writers, who sometimes wrote imaginative texts in English as well as official documents. The increasingly literate and sometimes unsanctioned interests of the English laity, including those of middling rank (gentry and merchants) whose numbers swelled over this period, created different levels and kinds of demand for religious and secular reading material. Lastly, texts were being composed and written down in settings in which book production – and so textual dissemination – was an increasingly organized, commercial and innovative business. At the end of the period we think of as medieval something decidedly modern arrived in England: William Caxton with his printing press, in 1476 – and for the first time literary texts were copied not just for patrons or personal use but speculatively, for sale.

The broad transition just described should not be regarded as straightforward. At the end of the Middle Ages, Caxton, England's first printer, had old-fashioned aristocratic patrons as well as a press; he supplied books to a royal court where most texts were still read in French and Latin, because those languages had currency in England even in the late fifteenth century. Quite early in the period considered here, texts were produced by the religious in Middle English, and for lay readers. While it is important to note historical patterns, the most useful point is that the sites for medieval textual production were multiple and overlapping, and the boundaries between them permeable and shifting. Middle English literary works belonged not to a static or homogeneous culture, but a heterogeneous and changing one.

The third and final point of the chapter is that, having been made for this changeful society, and having been made in some material form, literary texts were themselves open to change. They were heard by different audiences or passed from one reader to another. They were, sometimes, just as Chaucer dreads in the line that follows his 'go, litel bok' stanza, transmitted beyond their authors' intention, miswritten, misunderstood, or at least understood *differently* at every encounter. Medieval literary culture was partly produced by these processes of dissemination – by scribes and reciters, readers and listeners, as well as by famous authors.

Methods and Means of Textual Production and Dissemination

The popular image of the minstrel-poet, travelling from one inn to another, or singing for his supper at the command of some wealthy patron, is not without foundation. Voice and performance and the skills associated with the use of these 'technologies' for textual production were important in the Middle Ages. The royal courtiers described in Edward IV's 1471 household book were 'acustumed, wynter and

somer, in after nonys and in euenynges, to drawe to lordez chambrez
..., there to kepe honest company... in talking of cronycles of
kinges ... or in pypyng, or harpyng, synging, other [or] actez mar-
ciablez [chivalric deeds]' and there are references in the records of
thirteenth- and fourteenth-century English kings to payments made
to minstrels (Wogan-Browne et al., eds., 1999: 113). At the other end
of the social scale are the tellers of tales found in the tavern of a medieval
town, such as the one that is depicted in Passus V of the B-text of
William Langland's *Piers Plowman* (*c.* 1379). There, Sloth proudly confesses that he has no idea how to say his '"Paternoster"' like a priest,
but is a fine teller of tales of Robin Hood.

In *Piers Plowman*, Langland sets one oral culture – that of oral story-
telling – against another, that of Christianity. Sloth is slothful because
the medieval devout were meant to speak their beliefs and chant parts
of the liturgy from memory. The priests who ministered to them had
some responsibility for the oral production of texts as well. Those with
university training would have been familiar with the classical *artes
memorativae* ('arts of memory') (Carruthers 1990); all would be
expected to be able to recall the teachings of Scripture, which formed
the basis for the homilies, catechisms and advice that formed their daily
work. Many Middle English sermon cycles and some pastoral dialogues
were recorded in writing; these must stand for a rich oral tradition
that has left no such trace (Spencer 1993).

The medieval 'authors' of oral texts were not necessarily authors in
the sense that we use the word – writers of original works of literature (compare the essay by Jane Griffiths below). Many medieval texts
are retellings of old stories, and it is especially difficult to distinguish
those texts that were 'original' oral compositions from those that were
performances of written texts, or to discern which texts were passed
down by speakers long before they were recorded in the written forms
in which they survive to the present day. The relationship between
memory, creativity, speaking and writing in the Middle Ages was always
a fluid one.

Flux and change are also central to an account of the technologies
and skills associated with writing itself. In the Middle Ages, the ability to read and write were wholly separate skills. A child might be
shown how to form letters at the singing or grammar schools that were
attached in some way to monasteries or other Church foundations,
including some nunneries. The role of these schools was, in part, to
edify England's religious. The religious were, in turn, to spread God's
Word, and also to help administer their monastic estates or manage

local churches. Female religious were not charged with divine ministry, but the most powerful of them had nunneries to run, and record keeping and correspondence must have been a part of their work. As a result, religious men and women constituted most of those who needed and were taught the skill of writing in medieval England (Orme 1973).

However, as the Middle Ages progressed, there were more reasons and chances for others not destined for religious vocations to handle a pen. The business of the landed and mercantile classes in England and government itself increasingly became a matter of written record. Basic skills in document production were useful to those who helped manage feudal estates or traded goods; those skills might be imparted at grammar schools or in large households, where there were often tutors on hand. By the late-medieval period, the more advanced training that was needed to produce legal writs and lawbooks required a sojourn at the Inns of Court, in the neighbourhood of the City of London, or in the royal offices in Westminster. Some of the many lawyers educated in the metropolis must have carried their learning back to the provinces, where they may have shared it, or guarded it, as the basis for their own livelihood. By the late thirteenth century, there were lay people dwelling in English towns whose surname – 'scrivener' (scribe) – indicates that they were copyists for hire (Clanchy 1993; Doyle 1990).

So there was growth in the number of people who *could* write in the Middle Ages. There was a parallel increase in the availability of surfaces on which they could write, and the speed at which they did so. Late-medieval scribes wrote in a new sort of script, a cursive lettering that could be reproduced more quickly than the 'textura' script that was found in (mostly Latin) religious books (Parkes 1979). And routinely after 1400, scribes of all kinds wrote on paper, which was much cheaper than parchment made from animal skins.

Such evidence of innovation coexists with the fact that access to writing technologies was far more restricted in the Middle Ages than it is today. It took a long time and a lot of work to make a book: even with cursive scripts, scribes could produce only four to six pages of text per day (Kwakkel 2003). Books were always luxury items – the preserve of social élites. A medium-to-large parchment book was worth the equivalent of hundreds, even thousands, of our own dollars or pounds. Even the small collations of paper leaves on which poems sometimes circulated (in what modern scholars call 'booklets') were worth a few pennies – and a few pennies was several days' wages for a medieval labourer (Bell 1936–7). Books were never produced speculatively; if such expensive objects were wanted, they had to be ordered. A great many books in Latin and French were commissioned from abroad. In the 1330s, the Bishop of Durham, Richard Bury, wrote a treatise, the *Philobiblon*, in which he describes how he sent forth money for books 'in abundance' to 'stationers and booksellers, not only within our own country, but . . . spread over the realms of France, Germany, and Italy' (trans. Thomas 1913: 62). Even if there was somebody 'within our own country' who could take on an order for a book, the commissioner might need to find a copy of the text he wanted, and then wait months as an ad hoc team, assembled from jobbing artisans, went about its arduous work (Gillespie 2007).

The conditions in which texts were given material form are important to any history of medieval textual production, because any author who wrote down his or her text for him- or herself must necessarily have been familiar with some aspects of book manufacture. Laȝamon, author of the twelfth-century Arthurian chronicle of England the *Brut* (compare Andrew Galloway's essay above), says that to make his work he took quills ('fetheren') in his fingers and applied these to 'bok-felle', book-skin or parchment (line 1). At the other end of the period, *The Book of Margery Kempe*, written in the 1430s, is known only because Kempe, sometime brewer and visionary author but never writer, arranged for her story to be copied down as she dictated it to a local priest. Having finished this act of collaborative textual production, the priest says that he wrote a preamble to Kempe's book on a 'qwayr' (ed. Windeatt: 50): a 'quire' was a technical term for a gathering of paper sheets in this period, one that might later be stitched and bound into a larger codex. In present-day Western society, where most people can write and where more books – containing more texts – are printed every year, many of them also available electronically, it is easy to forget that the production of medieval texts in written forms was *never* an unskilled or a casual activity. It was always a technologically knowing one, involving hard physical labour and requiring access to training and scarce resources.

Who, then, would choose – or was able – to write in the Middle Ages? In what circumstances was it worth putting effort into composing, performing or writing down a text? Margery and her priest provide one answer: she felt compelled to share her mystical version of Christian devotion with others to help with their own salvation. Writing and talking about God was the way her priest earned his keep. Material rewards for secular compositions were harder to come by.

There was no way, given how slow and expensive book production was, to sell multiple copies of a work at a profit to an author. Sustained literary endeavour outside of religious contexts therefore always depended on patronage. Writers – or performers – of texts might be given reward in food, lodging, or perhaps an annuity or job in a patron's gift. The first record of cash payment to any writer for an English work survives from 1439, when the monk John Lydgate was paid by the abbot of St Alban's monastery for a *Life of St Alban*. Lydgate names other patrons in his writings: Humphrey, Duke of Gloucester; various noblewomen; and the London Goldsmiths' Company among them. What these men and women had in common was surplus wealth. The Anglo-Norman poet Wace makes the point explicitly in his late twelfth-century *Roman de Rou*: a writer must attend to the concerns of those '[ki] unt les rentes e le argent / Kar pur eus sunt le liure fai' ('who have feudal rents and ready money / because for them books are made') (quoted in Lucas 1982: 223).

Medieval literary production was thus restricted – but it does not follow that the textual culture of the Middle Ages was an impoverished one. Oral literary traditions were available to all; Langland's Sloth, who forgets his prayers, nonetheless has ready access to stories he enjoys. A great many medieval people could *listen* to writing. It needed only one literate servant, one learned person in a village, to transmit a written text – whether a royal proclamation, a letter or a work of fiction – by reading it aloud. Even social élites – including the courtiers of Edward IV referred to above – appear to have preferred this mode of dissemination, the 'prelection' of texts. Some of the biggest and most expensive medieval books – the huge, twenty-two kilogram Vernon manuscript of English texts (Oxford, Bodleian Library, Eng. poet. a.1), for instance – were probably made for this sort of oral performance (Coleman 1996). And by the end of the Middle Ages – although books were never within the reach of the vast majority of the populace, whose subsistence lifestyles left no time or cash for luxuries – there *were* more written texts of all kinds about, to be read aloud from or to be read silently. They were more often in English: about ten times more Middle English literary manuscripts survive from the century after 1375 than from the century before that date. They were therefore more accessible to the middling sort of medieval person (Edwards and Pearsall 1989; Meale 1989).

That person, man or woman, was also increasingly likely to be able to read. This was not only because the number of merchants and minor landowners with time, resources and reasons to learn their letters grew;

it also followed from institutional shifts within the medieval Church. As Marilyn Corrie's essay has already discussed, in 1281, following the instructions of the earlier Fourth Lateran Council in Rome, Archbishop Pecham established a syllabus that prescribed the learning of the laity in England. Every child was to know his – or her – 'Ave Maria', 'Pater Noster' and Creed, and to understand the Ten Commandments, the sacraments, and something of his or her own salvation. And for all of that, some grasp of the alphabet was very useful (Duffy 1992: 53–87). That there is such range in the surviving corpus of medieval literary texts, in spite of the material impediments to literary production, is a reflection of this sort of cultural change. There was never just one way of obtaining, making or knowing a text in the Middle Ages.

Religious Contexts: Books in and beyond the Cloister

At the beginning of the medieval period, monasteries, which were first founded in England in the eighth century, were the most important of the various places for English textual production. Monasteries' endowed wealth enabled their literate members to turn from manual labour to *otium*, the leisured activity of the devout, and writing was one way to eschew the sin of idleness. Of all England's medieval institutions, monasteries were the only ones that were permanently situated, and therefore the only locations where it was possible to establish and maintain collections of texts – that might inspire new compositions, which in turn might survive for modern readers. Monastic 'rules' followed by the 'regular' clergy demanded that they were able to read and write. In some cases the application of these skills – the copying or study of Scripture or patristic theological texts – was mandated. From these conditions emerged a great many texts: almost *all* the new writing penned in England from the eleventh and twelfth centuries can be linked to monastic communities (Cannon 1999).

Early English monastic writing is not the stuff from which most modern accounts of medieval literature are compiled. It tends to be in Latin and to involve the chronicling of institutional myths and histories (compare Andrew Galloway's essay in this volume). Its relevance to a broad English literary culture was considerable, however. Monastic writers built textual edifices not merely to secure the authority of their foundations, but to negotiate a share of worldly power. The cloister walls were meant to be porous. Matthew of Paris, the great Benedictine monk, author and artist of the 1200s, wrote Latin texts that were available to the nobles, royal counsellors and courtiers, and clerics who visited him at St Alban's, and he also composed works in Anglo-Norman for noble women like Isabel de Warenne, Countess of Arundel. Especially after Pecham's edicts, monastic textual production often expressed the pastoral concerns of the regular clergy. Many important didactic religious treatises were composed by monks. The texts *Handlyng Synne* (1303), by Robert Mannyng, a monk of the Gilbertine order at Sempringham, Lincolnshire, and the *Ayenbite of Inwyt*, or 'Remorse of Conscience' (completed 1340), by a Benedictine monk, Michael, of Northgate in Kent, both address 'learned' clerics and the 'lewd' laity, both of whom might be helped by such monastic writing.

Thus, while the activities of the Benedictine monk Lydgate for London guilds and fifteenth-century princes (see above) might seem to represent a broadening of the literary interests of the regular clergy, in fact they serve to make a wider point. Monks, the texts they produced and their reasons for producing them had never been strictly of the cloister.

As spiritual leadership was located away from their foundations late in the Middle Ages, the interest of the regular clergy in the dissemination of their texts was intensified. After about 1200, the university colleges at Oxford and then Cambridge were founded and the fraternal and mendicant orders were also established in England in the thirteenth century. The mission of the friars was pastoral, and they were as sensitive as Matthew of Paris or Lydgate to the reach of a message contained in a well-turned text. St Francis, who founded the Franciscan order, told his followers to be *joculatores Dei* – God's minstrels. In the mid-thirteenth century, the Franciscan friar Thomas of Hales composed his Middle English *Luve Ron*, a poem on spiritual love for a young female religious. Other friars, some of them dwelling in the colleges founded by their orders at the universities, penned penitential manuals and sermon collections. Some of these were in English. The catechetical dialogue *Dives and Pauper* was composed by an unnamed friar of Longleat in about 1410, for instance, and it was then distributed widely in manuscripts. It was still in enough demand to warrant printed editions in 1493, 1496 and 1536 (Fleming 1977).

Even those religious who chose the enclosed life of the hermit or anchoress seem to have imagined spaces for their ideas beyond the walls that surrounded them. In the early thirteenth-century *Ancrene Wisse*, a male spiritual adviser to a group of anchoresses writes that they should not write letters to the outside world – which suggests that this was the sort of thing that such women could and did do. This supplies a context for Julian of Norwich's decision to record the visions she received in 1373, or that, earlier, of the mystic Richard Rolle to leave his hermit's cell to advise and write for Yorkshire laywomen. Julian says that God gifted her skill of expression and revelation because he wanted to have her vision 'knowen more than it is' (chapter 86): what was learned and experienced in a life of contemplation was worth sharing, and a text could pass from an enclosed space, even when its writer chose not to disseminate it (Millett 1996).

The medieval religious found multiple audiences and readerships for their writing in part because early codicological activity was concentrated in England around religious institutions. There were no scriptoria – designated rooms for writing – in English monasteries for most of the Middle Ages. A room was built for scribes at the abbey at St Albans, but not until about 1380. Monks typically worked in cells or the cloister. Monasteries, as well as cathedrals and large churches, employed lay book producers from local towns to make service books and tomes for library shelves. It is no coincidence that the scribes and limners who produced multiple copies of Lydgate's *Fall of Princes* and *Life of St Edmund* in the 1460s dwelled near to, and were sometimes employed by, the poet's monastic brethren at Bury St Edmunds. Nor is it surprising to find that *all* of the printing presses established outside of London in the first fifty years of printing were near or attached to religious institutions – the colleges of Oxford, but also the monasteries at St Albans, Tavistock and Canterbury. The resources of the religious made their institutions sites at which books, as well as the texts that they contained, were produced, and these were then available for circulation in much wider contexts (Doyle 1989).

Spreading God's Word was, moreover, the core business of the secular clergy – clerics who lived not under rule, but in *saeculum* ('the world'). It was they who were directly charged by Archbishop Pecham with delivery of his syllabus. Bishops held copies of his edicts and useful pastoral texts that visiting priests could copy and then carry to the far corners of England (Gillespie 1989). The need to disseminate Christian learning widely may have prompted new ways of thinking about the function of books. In the fourteenth century, a number of large religious prose tracts containing all the basic tenets of the faith and stocks of Christian stories were penned by unnamed clerics. The early fourteenth-century *Cursor Mundi* and *The Pricke of Conscience* (*c.* 1360) are rarely studied now, but they were the most widespread of vernacular texts in the Middle Ages. In places where parishioners lived miles from a local parson, such works may have served in the place of priests, as a basis for both pious household culture and personal devotion.

The involvement of secular clergy in the dissemination of texts was not always motivated by ministerial concerns. All sorts of texts – romances, treatises on arts of war, love lyrics and animal fables – turn up in manuscripts that belonged to the religious. Around 1500, for instance, a copy of Chaucer's *Canterbury Tales* that was printed by Richard Pynson in 1494 and is now in the John Rylands Library in Manchester passed from Robert Saham, priest, via his executor, a parson from Finningham, Suffolk, to a woman, Elle Lee, wife of a Bury St Edmunds squire. From there it seems to have moved to a husbandman from nearby Buxhall (Gillespie 2006: 91–2). One literate cleric's book might easily become a much wider community's reading material.

Textual production and the rendering of texts in written form was a way to establish and extend normative attitudes in the Middle Ages, as Archbishop Pecham seems to have realized. But as they circulated widely, and turned up in unexpected places, medieval texts could also constitute a threat to norms. Who knows, for instance, what Elle Lee, as a wife and gentlewoman, might have made of the transgressive remarks of the Wife of Bath about biblical interpretation? Reading is a transitory and often untraceable activity, but it is never a passive one: the dissemination of a text routinely involves its reproduction in new forms and the making of new meanings for it.

In a sense, it was this radical openness of texts that made the work of John Wyclif so controversial in late fourteenth- and fifteenth-century England. His Latin theological writings in favour of the disendowment of the monasteries and against papal authority, the cult of the saints and belief in transubstantiation were problematic enough (compare Marilyn Corrie's essay above). But Wyclif also wrote works in English for circulation outside of the scholastic circles in which he moved at Oxford, and some of these works were about the capacity of such vernacular texts to change a culture. Scripture, Wyclif argued, should be available to lay people in English, in books they could hold, read and hearken to, so that they might know God better. Wyclif's followers, who were known as Lollards, took up his cause. They promoted his beliefs and preached around England from English Scripture. Literates within Lollard circles trained unlettered fellows; standardized versions of Wyclif's writings and a vernacular Bible emerged, copied perhaps in the provincial households of Lollard knights, or by scriveners in urban shops; sympathetic priests also distributed Wycliffite material, some of it, probably, written down (Hudson 1989). One way of thinking about the vagaries of the manuscript culture described above – the fact that there was no centralized place or system for the production of books – is that while it made texts less accessible than did later print cultures, it also made the manufacture of illicit texts difficult to police.

This is not to suggest that the ecclesiastical authorities were without the means to address the problem. As has already been mentioned in this volume, in the 1380s many of Wyclif's views were declared heretical by England's bishops and then by the Pope; in 1401 it became an offence to hold some of those views, punishable by burning at the stake; and in 1409 Archbishop Thomas Arundel published his Constitutions, which banned unsanctioned works of vernacular theology, disseminated by speech or by writing, produced since Wyclif's time (Watson 1995). But in the lists of the books owned by those tried for heresy in the early fifteenth century, and in writings produced to refute Wyclif's positions, which quote his texts at length, it is clear that Lollard texts were widely available. Decades after the burnings began, the Wycliffite Bible was still the English text most often copied by English scribes: around 250 of these books are extant today.

English texts produced in or for religious contexts do not reflect a static or stable culture. They reveal the unfixed boundaries of lay and clerical worlds and deal in both orthodoxy and dissent. They retained their capacity to change, as well as reinforce, the attitudes of those who encountered them.

Secular Contexts (1): Courtly Texts and their Dissemination

Secular medieval institutions, no less than religious institutions, supplied complex conditions for textual production and unexpected channels for the movement of texts. Households were perhaps the most important of these institutions, especially in the early Middle Ages – but this chapter will also consider others that grew in importance in the period, from the guild hall to the government office.

Feudal power was centred on medieval households, but also dispersed across them. It was concentrated, first and foremost, at the royal 'courts' – a word used here to mean the household spaces inhabited by the king, his family, and those who attended them. But it was also shared, sometimes uneasily, with the English barons and noblemen who presided over their own, provincial 'courts', and went to war (or just to see the king in London) with great retinues. Feudal power was also shared with an increasing number of 'gentlemen' who had lesser landholdings; and there was a growing class of burgesses, whose mercantile activities sometimes made them very wealthy. At all these levels of medieval society, the household was the heart of social and economic activity – for masters; their wives (royal women often held their own courts); children; attendants and counsellors; tutors; local priests or household chaplains; administrators; the labourers who worked feudal lands; the merchants who supplied household needs. In Middle English, a monarch's or a great lord's court is often referred to as a 'press', meaning throng or crowd. Lesser, non-courtly households may have been less crowded, but they were still affected by the pressing and competing concerns of the English realm (Smith 2003).

The image of the household as a busy meeting place rather than a private retreat (as we perhaps think of it today) is key to understanding its function as a site for medieval literary work. At the highest levels of medieval society, texts were produced by aspirant attendants of, and visitors to, the courts of kings and aristocrats. They were made, to recall Wace, for those with 'rents', silver and perhaps a hankering for a poem or two. Chaucer's career is exemplary in this respect. He was sent to the noble household of the Countess of Ulster as a page boy, to be trained as an attendant to kings and nobles. His training worked: he served as a soldier with John of Gaunt in France. Later he served, in England as well as abroad in France, as a squire to Edward III. He probably wrote – perhaps in fashionable courtly French – some of the 'balades, roundels, virelayes' that are alluded to in the Prologue to *The Legend of Good Women* while he was in the king's or Gaunt's affinity. He received various gifts and payments from his patrons, perhaps for his literary as well as military or other services.

Chaucer's move to London in the mid-1370s – he became a customs official at the docks at that time – is sometimes depicted as a change of literary scene: from a setting in which knights and ladies whiled away the hours singing ballads to the mixed milieux of the metropolis. This is probably to misrepresent the diffuse activities of the provincial court. Some of the writers of literature in these contexts were clerics who had the task of ministering to those who gathered in great households and perhaps in the surrounding locale. An English life of St Jerome, for instance, was written by Simon Wynter, a Brigittine brother of Syon, for the Duchess of Clarence, to whom he was an adviser. Writers for noble patrons were often record keepers, working within great households as secretaries or heralds. The knight Sir John Chandos took his herald with him to the wars in France in the 1360s to record the events of battle and the affinities of those who fought. There, the herald wrote, in French, his great poem on the death of England's Black Prince and the decline of its chivalric culture. War brought other writers to the English courts: Charles d'Orléans (d. 1465), a French nobleman, composed many elegant French lyrics during his years as a hostage in the household of the Duke of Suffolk. Strangers of a different cast sometimes came to the seats of England's rulers. The French chronicler Jean Froissart visited Edward III's court in search of patronage. Humphrey, Duke of Gloucester, and protector of Henry VI, was very much in favour of Italy's new learning, *studia humanistica*, and in the 1420s and 1430s humanist thinkers as well as local *litterati* – Lydgate, or the Augustinian friar John Capgrave – sent him texts and visited his palace library at Greenwich.

The diverse composition of medieval households, especially noble and royal courts, may account for the multiple, sometimes irreconcilable, concerns of texts produced in those contexts. The *Gawain*-poet, for instance, is usually imagined as someone in a noble, even royal, employment, perhaps a chaplain. It is notable that his texts seem to query, even as they depict, the wealth and splendour of aristocratic life – the exclusion of a dirty peasant from a manorial feast in *Cleanness*; the ultimately empty worldly riches that infuse *Pearl*; the futile games and hollow laughter of *Sir Gawain and the Green Knight*.

It is likewise notable that the characteristic form for the Middle English texts linked to secular households is not the lavish presentation copy, made for a poet to gift to his lord, but the manuscript miscellany – a collection of texts gathered from exemplars as and when then came to hand (Hanna 1996). The manuscript London, British Library, Harley 2253 is a useful example. It was probably made in the 1330s, conceivably for the Mortimers, a large landholding family in the West Midlands: documents relating to the family's castle are preserved in the binding of the book, and its scribe was a copyist of land deeds for the area. But not all the miscellaneous contents of the book are apparently a product of, or even concerned with, secular aristocratic life. Alongside Anglo-Norman poems that make remarks about the taxing of landholders are English, Latin and French lyrics, including 'Dum ludis floribus', which is voiced by a lovelorn Parisian student. Lords and their ladies inhabited a space into which all sorts of texts were carried – one in which the rather erratic process of medieval book production might, or might not, have seen those texts preserved, and from which those same texts readily passed.

The role of the household as a site for the wider dissemination of texts is an important one. Books, and the texts they contained, moved from households to new readers and listeners as much as they did from monasteries. Sometimes they moved as gifts. In the early 1500s, the mother of Henry VII, Margaret Beaufort, had devotional books and her favourite sermons printed, so that they could be distributed to ladies-in-waiting, visitors to her household, and the nuns at Syon Abbey. The movement of texts was often less formal than this. As Chaucer moved from court to city, and city to province, so did his texts. His 'courtly' poems – for instance, his complaint to Richard II about his empty purse, or his *Parliament of Fowls*, which may allude to that king's betrothal – do not survive in any royal book. But there is a copy of his *Complaint to His Purse* in Cambridge, Magdalene College, MS Pepys 2006, a book owned by a family of London mercers. And the *Parliament* turns up in the Findern manuscript (Cambridge University Library, MS Ff.1.6), a compilation made by men and women in a small gentry household in Derbyshire.

The movement of medieval texts did not always follow a top-down pattern. In Findern and similar household books there are lyrics, recipes, songs and stories that were probably never reading matter for the great personages of the realm, but that passed rapidly between folk of lesser degree (Boffey and Meale 1991). The textual culture associated with secular households was thus one subject to centripetal pressure – a drawing in of the energy, activity and interests of people, including writers – but also to centrifugal forces, as poems for queens and kings found merchant-class readers, and as all manner of texts passed from one household to another.

Secular Contexts (2): Texts in Urban Spaces

The towns and cities of England were always a place of literary production – of minstrelsy in taverns, or performances and playing in market squares. In the later Middle Ages, such traditions were invigorated by the same economic and social changes that saw Chaucer's poetry pass to the compilers of the Findern miscellany – the movement of resources to those of middling rank. In this period – crucially for modern readers and scholars – urban texts were also given written form. There are surviving records of London *puys* (song competitions), ceremonials and festivals. Copies of the annual biblical plays that were put on for the feast of Corpus Christi and widely attended in such towns as York and Chester are also extant. All these literary events were organized by the parish-based craft and trade guilds and other fraternities and oligarchies that formed in urban areas at the end of the Middle Ages, as labour became increasingly specialized and as populations and competition for business grew (Barron 2005).

However, the final section of this chapter is primarily concerned with the effect of two other historical developments on medieval English literature. The first of these is linked to trade and craft specialization: the development of a commercial industry for book production. As noted above, scriveners who made part of their living from writing were already working in towns in England early in the Middle Ages, and there were also booksellers in urban centres or market fairs. But book men settled more permanently after about 1280: first in Oxford, around the university, where books were always in demand, and then in the mid-1300s in the City of London – the nation's commercial centre – and near to Westminster, where parliament and the legal courts and royal offices were located. By 1350, London's Textwriters (makers of religious books in 'textura' hands: see above); Scriveners (who specialized in copying legal documents); Limners (illustrators); and Bookbinders had formed guilds to protect their interests. Disseminating texts to London's many visitors and inhabitants had become important business.

The second change is related to the first, because demand for documentary production, and the training of those who could meet that demand, were never wholly separable in England from the bureaucracy generated by administrative and legal procedure. In the fourteenth century, that procedure was increasingly centred on both written records, as noted above, and the metropolis. In such offices as the Exchequer and the Privy Seal, and at the Court of Chancery and other courts of law (all these ostensibly linked to the king's household), men, mostly trained in the nearby Inns of Court, produced a myriad of writs, bills, proclamations and statutes by which to administer the realm. Out in the city streets, members of the Scriveners' Company were occupied in writing documents for those who needed to have their pleas heard by the king or his officers. A new bureaucracy had made for a new class of 'clerkly' writers (Hanna 2005).

Clerkly Writers, English Authors

The changes just described involved *centralization* of textual activity; they also, paradoxically, loosened textual production and dissemination from the traditional sites of monastery, church and household. They are important because they are a way to think about the work of some of the most famous producers of medieval English texts. Langland wrote at least part of his *Piers Plowman* in London and, given the documentary texture of his poem, may well have carried out clerkly duties of some sort. Chaucer was an account keeper; in the *House of Fame* he talks about totting up his 'rekenynges' at the end of the day (line 653), before getting down to the imaginative business of his dream vision. John Gower describes himself in the dress of a sergeant-at-law, a petty court official, in his *Mirour de l'Omme*, and Thomas Hoccleve was Clerk of the Privy Seal. The poet of the early fifteenth-century *Richard the Redeless* and *Mum and the Sothsegger* is a bookish sort of fellow, perhaps a legal scrivener. In the latter poem he decides he will counsel the king using a bag of official documents – a 'quayer' (ed. Barr 1993: line 1348); a 'penyworth of papir' (line 1350); 'a volume . . . of viftene leves' (line 1353); more than one 'rolle' (lines 1364, 1565); 'a paire of pamphilettz' (line 1370). Thomas Usk was a scrivener for the Goldsmiths; he may have copied out literary texts in his spare time. He wrote his own treatise, *The Testament of Love*, perhaps in 1384 while under house arrest, or in 1387, while awaiting execution for treason. It is full of echoes of Chaucer's *Troilus and Criseyde* – as if that poem, hot off Chaucer's pen, was beside him, or fresh in his mind as he wrote.

Usk's imprisonment and death, the result of his entanglement in violent London factionalism during the reign of Richard II, is a reminder that the spheres of these men's influence and activity were several, and full of risk as well as opportunity. Langland was in minor holy orders, and via its dream vision format, *Piers Plowman* directs its savage satire at worldly corruption. Langland's revision of the radical content of his text after the Peasants' Revolt of 1381 (compare Helen Barr's essay in this volume) suggests that he realized that a text that was safe one moment could become transgressive the next, and responded accordingly. Chaucer was a sometime beneficiary of courtly patronage; Hoccleve and Gower, who address poems variously to kings and princes, aspired to similar positions. Usk, following a tradition stretching back to Boethius, may have hoped that his prose tract about the mercy of mighty lords and ladies might be his 'get out of jail free' card. These authors, like all the others described in the chapter, composed texts in conditions that enabled and motivated their creativity – because writing was their daily business and the pen ever in their hand. But they also wrote *across* the multiple, constantly shifting, sometimes fractious contexts for medieval literary production.

And they wrote, finally, in the company of those who would ensure that their writings existed in far-flung forms, like those that Chaucer anticipates for his 'litel bok'. Not only was Usk on hand to copy *Troilus* (before 1387), but along the street was the shop that employed Adam Pinkhurst, a signed-up member of the London Scriveners' Company, copyist of the Hengwrt and Ellesmere manuscripts of *The Canterbury Tales*, and probably the 'Adam' Chaucer chastises in his poem to an error-prone scribe (Mooney 2006). It was possible that the likes of Adam would 'myswrite' texts. It was possible that such men – newly available in and about London to join the ad hoc teams that booksellers needed to make lavish books like the Ellesmere *Canterbury Tales* – would press texts forward in new forms to new readers, audiences and all sorts of unpredictable responses. But it was also possible that trained scribes and book producers would achieve a degree of renown for English texts that could not have been imagined before the late fourteenth century. A London clerkly author could copy his own writings. He could also see, down the street, other ways to get his 'bok' out in the world – where it might impel social change, or at least take a place in posterity alongside 'Virgile, Ovide, Omer'. Some late-medieval English writers may have produced texts not for patrons, or even God, but because, far from monastery or court, they saw a chance for those texts to 'go', range over time and space, and end up written into volumes like this one.

References

Primary texts

Barr, Helen, ed. (1993). *The Piers Plowman Tradition: A Critical Edition of Pierce the Ploughman's Crede, Richard the Redeless, Mum and the Sothsegger and The Crowned King*. London: J.M. Dent.

Brook, G.L. and Leslie, R.F., eds. (1963–78). *Laȝamon: Brut*. EETS OS 250, 277. London: Oxford University Press.

Glasscoe, Marion, ed. (1986). *Julian of Norwich: A Revelation of Love*. Revd edn. Exeter: University of Exeter Press.

Thomas, E.C., ed. and trans. (1913). *The Love of Books: The Philobiblon of Richard de Bury*. London: Chatto & Windus.

Windeatt, Barry, ed. (2000). *The Book of Margery Kempe*. Harlow: Longman.

Wogan-Browne, Jocelyn, Watson, Nicholas, Taylor, Andrew, and Evans, Ruth, eds. (1999). *The Idea of the Vernacular: An Anthology of Middle English Literary Theory 1280–1520*. Exeter: University of Exeter Press.

Secondary sources and suggestions for further reading

Barron, C.M. (2005). *London in the Later Middle Ages: Government and People 1200–1500*. Oxford: Oxford University Press.

Bell, H.E. (1936–7). 'The Price of Books in Medieval England'. *The Library*, 4th ser., 17, 312–32.

Boffey, Julia and Meale, Carol M. (1991). 'Selecting the Text: Rawlinson C.86 and Some Other Books for London Readers'. In Felicity Riddy, ed., *Regionalism in Late Medieval Manuscripts and Texts: Essays Celebrating the Publication of a Linguistic Atlas of Late Mediaeval English* (pp. 143–69). Cambridge: D.S. Brewer.

Cannon, Christopher (1999). 'Monastic Productions'. In David Wallace, ed., *The Cambridge History of Medieval English Literature* (pp. 316–48). Cambridge: Cambridge University Press.

Carruthers, Mary J. (1990). *The Book of Memory: A Study of Memory in Medieval Culture*. Cambridge: Cambridge University Press.

Cavanaugh, Susan H. (1988). *Books Privately Owned in England, 1300–1450*. Woodbridge: Boydell & Brewer.

Clanchy, M.T. (1993). *From Memory to Written Record: England 1066–1307*. 2nd edn. Oxford: Blackwell.

Coleman, Joyce (1996). *Public Reading and the Reading Public in Late Medieval England and France*. Cambridge Studies in Medieval Literature 26. Cambridge: Cambridge University Press.

De Hamel, Christopher (1994). *Scribes and Illuminators*. London: British Library.

Doyle, A.I. (1989). 'Publication by Members of the Religious Orders'. In Jeremy Griffiths and Derek Pearsall, eds., *Book Production and Publishing in Britain 1375–1475* (pp. 109–23). Cambridge: Cambridge University Press.

Doyle, A.I. (1990). 'The English Provincial Book Trade before Printing'. In Peter Isaac, ed., *Six Centuries of the Provincial English Book Trade in Britain* (pp. 13–29). Winchester: Oak Knoll.

Duffy, Eamon (1992). *The Stripping of the Altars: Traditional Religion in England c. 1400–c. 1580*. New Haven: Yale University Press.

Edwards, A.S.G. and Pearsall, Derek (1989). 'The Manuscripts of the Major English Poetic Texts'. In Jeremy Griffiths and Derek Pearsall, eds., *Book*

Production and Publishing in Britain 1375–1475 (pp. 257–78). Cambridge: Cambridge University Press.

Fleming, J.V. (1977). *An Introduction to the Franciscan Literature of the Middle Ages.* Chicago: Franciscan Herald Press.

Gillespie, Alexandra (2006). *Print Culture and the Medieval Author: Chaucer, Lydgate, and Their Books, 1473–1557.* Oxford: Oxford University Press.

Gillespie, Alexandra (2007). 'Books'. In Paul Strohm, ed., *Oxford Twenty-First Century Approaches to Literature: Middle English* (pp. 86–103). Oxford: Oxford University Press.

Gillespie, Vincent (1989). 'Vernacular Books of Religion'. In Jeremy Griffiths and Derek Pearsall, eds., *Book Production and Publishing in Britain 1375–1475* (pp. 317–44). Cambridge: Cambridge University Press.

Hanna, Ralph, III (1996). 'Miscellaneity and Vernacularity: Conditions of Literary Production in Late Medieval England'. In Stephen G. Nichols and Siegfried Wenzel, eds., *The Whole Book: Cultural Perspectives on the Medieval Miscellany* (pp. 37–51). Ann Arbor: University of Michigan Press.

Hanna, Ralph, III (2005). *London Literature, 1300–1380.* Cambridge Studies in Medieval Literature 57. Cambridge: Cambridge University Press.

Hudson, Anne (1989). 'Lollard Book Production'. In Jeremy Griffiths and Derek Pearsall, eds., *Book Production and Publishing in Britain 1375–1475* (pp. 125–42). Cambridge: Cambridge University Press.

Knapp, Ethan (2001). *The Bureaucratic Muse: Thomas Hoccleve and the Literature of Late Medieval England.* University Park: Pennsylvania State University Press.

Kwakkel, E. (2003). 'A New Type of Book for a New Type of Reader: The Emergence of Paper in Vernacular Book Production'. *The Library*, 7th ser., 4, 219–48.

Lindenbaum, Sheila (1999). 'London Texts and Literate Practice'. In David Wallace, ed., *The Cambridge History of Medieval English Literature* (pp. 284–309). Cambridge: Cambridge University Press.

Lucas, Peter J. (1982). 'The Growth and Development of English Literary Patronage in the Later Middle Ages and Early Renaissance'. *The Library*, 6th ser., 4, 219–48.

Meale, Carol M. (1989). 'Patrons, Buyers and Owners: Book Production and Social Status'. In Jeremy Griffiths and Derek Pearsall, eds., *Book Production and Publishing in Britain 1375–1475* (pp. 201–38). Cambridge: Cambridge University Press.

Millett, Bella (1996). 'Women in No Man's Land: English Recluses and the Development of Vernacular Literature in the Twelfth and Thirteenth Centuries'. In Carol M. Meale, ed., *Women and Literature in Britain, 1150–1500* (pp. 86–103). Cambridge: Cambridge University Press.

Mooney, Linne R. (2006). 'Chaucer's Scribe'. *Speculum*, 81, 97–138.

Orme, Nicholas (1973). *English Schools in the Middle Ages.* London: Methuen.

Parkes, M.B. (1979). *English Cursive Book Hands, 1250–1500.* London: Scolar Press.

Smith, D. Vance (2003). *Arts of Possession: The Middle English Household Imaginary*. Minneapolis: University of Minnesota Press.

Spencer, H.L. (1993). *English Preaching in the Late Middle Ages*. Oxford: Clarendon Press.

Steiner, Emily (2003). *Documentary Culture and the Making of Medieval English Literature*. Cambridge Studies in Medieval Literature 50. Cambridge: Cambridge University Press.

Watson, Nicholas (1995). 'Censorship and Cultural Change in Late-Medieval England: Vernacular Theology, the Oxford Translation Debate, and Arundel's Constitutions of 1409'. *Speculum*, 70, 822–64.

Chapter 6

The Author

Jane Griffiths

In 1527, the London printer Richard Pynson issued an edition of John Lydgate's compendium of stories relating the downfall of great men and women from biblical times up to the Middle Ages, *The Fall of Princes* (1430s). The book opens with a striking image (see Figure 6.1). Under the heading 'Here begynneth the boke of Iohan Bochas, discryuing [describing] the fall of pri[n]ces, princesses, and other nobles: trans-lated into Englysshe by Iohn Lydgate monke of Bury', a full-page wood-cut shows a figure seated at a writing-desk. He holds out an open book to a man in ermine-edged robes, who stands at the head of a proces-sion of nobles. The seated figure could represent Cardinal Wolsey, at that time the most powerful man in England after the king, Henry VIII: the image may, therefore, show a 'prince' contemplating the falls of the princes whose stories are related in the book that he is holding (Gillespie 2006: 170–2). But the figure could also represent the author of the text, and indeed the naming of both the original author of Lydgate's material, Giovanni Boccaccio ('Iohan Bochas'), and Lydgate himself at the head of the page might lead us to look for him in the woodcut. Seen in this way, the woodcut might be thought to recall 'presentation scenes' – images of authors presenting their com-positions to their patrons – that were common in manuscripts and other printed editions of the time. And yet presentation scenes typically show the author kneeling to offer his work to the patron. They suggest that the work ultimately owes its existence to the patron, and that the author is merely its facilitator. In the Pynson woodcut, by contrast,

Figure 6.1 Title page of Richard Pynson's 1527 edition of John Lydgate's
Fall of Princes (London, British Library, C.12.i.8, A1r; *STC* 3176).
Reproduced by permission of the British Library.

the author is placed in the seat of authority, as the figure whom his readers – as we might interpret the procession of nobles in the image to be – approach for guidance. The implication is that a certain deference is being paid to him, as the individual responsible for the work that he is shown displaying.

The attitude towards authorship that the Pynson woodcut might thus be thought to reveal is still current today. As an act of creation, authorship carries a certain cachet. The importance of the author of a text in that text's production is recognized in the customary inclusion of his or her name with the title of the work. Such conventions are the product of expectations created by early printed books like Pynson's edition of Lydgate's *Fall*. Such books, however, also suggest that these expectations already existed by the time they were produced: they seem to answer a desire in their prospective purchasers to know who the author of the text was. Identifying the author, by means of title-pages and author portraits, might even be regarded as a way of promoting the wares of printers and publishers, perhaps a commercial imperative for them (see further Brown 1995). The attitudes to authorship that early printed books like Pynson's disclose had, in fact, been current for some time by the early sixteenth century; they existed already in the exclusively manuscript culture that existed for most of the Middle Ages (compare Alexandra Gillespie's chapter above, and see also Daniel Wakelin's chapter later in this volume). A good illustration is provided by manuscripts of Lydgate's many works, which regularly use his name as a 'brand' (Gillespie 2006; Meyer-Lee 2007: 49–54).

But for much of the Middle Ages, very different attitudes towards authorship prevailed. The importance of the individual who gave a text its verbal form was appreciated much less, if at all. The distinctive ways in which people in the Middle Ages often thought about the authors of texts are the subject of this chapter. The chapter will also explore some of the ways in which that thinking came to change in England. This was the result, in large part, of the experiments of medieval English authors themselves, who tested established ideas about authorship against their own practice, and subverted them through this. There is no author of whom this is more true than Geoffrey Chaucer, whose writings the chapter will consider in some detail. In the later works of such writers as Lydgate himself and his contemporary Thomas Hoccleve, matters raised by Chaucer are taken up and explored further. Much has been written about the emergence of 'modern' ideas surrounding authorship in the late Middle Ages. And yet we might see earlier ideas about authorship lingering to the very end of the period, apparent in the anxiety with which some writers assert themselves. When the court poet John Skelton came to write his extraordinary works in the very late fifteenth century (and the early sixteenth), he showed an extreme – and notorious – interest in drawing attention to his own presence within those works. This can be seen as an act of self-exaltation – but it is self-exaltation that defines itself against the background of other, traditional ideas about an author's role.

Ideas about Authorship

The Pynson woodcut emphasizes the author's importance in the creation of his work; and yet it was a consistently recurring assumption in the Latin academic culture of the Middle Ages that authority did not reside within the person who gave a work its textual form, but in some factor external to him. One of the most prominent expressions of this idea is the claim made by many authors that they are merely a vessel for a message that originates with God; recycling the words of St Paul in Romans 15:18, the fourteenth-century preacher Robert of Basevorn, for example, wrote in his *Forma praedicandi* ('Outline of Preaching') (1322) that he 'dare not speak of any of those things which Christ works in me' (quoted in Minnis 1988: 162). Authority (*auctoritas* in Latin) was also located in the writings of previous authors that a new author might use: in established classical, patristic or scriptural sources, which were referred to in Latin academic culture as the work of *auctores* (Minnis 1988). The authority of a new writer, by implication, was only transferable from such sources: it was a mantle that could be assumed exclusively by virtue of allusion to them. The theory has its origins in academic *accessus ad auctores*: that is, prologues or introductions to the works of classical and later authors that were provided by latter-day grammarians. Yet, it was exceptionally influential even outside academic circles, key, notably, to the ways in which Chaucer, Gower and other English authors who wrote in the vernacular thought about their own status, as will become evident below.

We now tend to value a piece of writing if we think that it says something that nobody has said before; but the medieval theory that authority resides in the work of established *auctores* implies a respect for the achievements of the past, and a desire to defer to these. The idea underlies the continuity between 'olde bokes' and 'newe science [knowledge]' – like that between 'olde feldes' and 'newe corn' – that Chaucer establishes towards the beginning of *The Parliament of Fowls*:

> For out of olde feldes, as men seyth,
> Cometh al this newe corn fro yer to yere,
> And out of olde bokes, in good feyth,
> Cometh al this newe science that men lere.   learn
>
> (lines 22–5)

It is apparent too in the Prologue to Chaucer's later *Legend of Good Women* – although the deference to the 'doctrine' of previous texts that this section of the work professes is significantly undermined in at least some of the 'legends' of good women that follow, a fact that is one manifestation of Chaucer's querying of traditional ideas about the location of *auctoritas* by this stage in his writing career (see further below):

> Than mote we to bokes that we fynde,   must
> Thurgh whiche that olde thinges ben in mynde,
> And to the doctrine of these olde wyse,   wise writers
> Yeve credence, in every skilful wise,   give; way
> That tellen of these olde appreved stories,   proved true
> Of holynesse, of regnes, of victories,
> Of love, of hate, of other sundry thynges,
> Of whiche I may not maken rehersynges.
>
> (F-Prologue, lines 17–24)

Even the authority of *auctores* was not necessarily perceived to reside in the *auctores* themselves. Inspired by Aristotle's theories about causation that were rediscovered by scholars in Western Europe in the thirteenth century, the individuals who composed the *accessus ad auctores* emphasized that the *auctor* was only the *causa efficiens*, or 'efficient cause', of his work – the person who brought the text into being. Equally important roles in the creation of the work were ascribed to its 'material cause' (*causa materialis*), the literary materials that constituted the sources of the *auctor*; its 'formal cause' (*causa formalis*), the pattern imposed by the *auctor* on his materials; and its 'final cause' (*causa finalis*), the ultimate justification for the existence of the work, or the particular good that the *auctor* had intended to bring about (Minnis 1988: 28–9). Although the *auctor* derived some authority from his position as the craftsman of his work, then, the idea that the work had a *causa finalis* ultimately reduced the *auctor* to the status of a conduit of the message that it was the principal function of the text to convey. It seems also that when scholars referred to '*auctores*', what they were thinking of was not essentially the individuals who were behind the texts to which they were alluding but the texts themselves: they were, according to Alastair Minnis, 'interested in the *auctor* mainly as a source of *auctoritas* . . . The notion of the *auctor* as an agent engaged in literary activity was submerged' (Minnis 1988: 72).

The idea that the person who gave a piece of writing its textual form was of only subsidiary importance in the creation of that piece of writing is one reason why the name of the author of a text is often suppressed in medieval manuscripts: the readers and copyists of a text were often less interested in who had written it than in the message that it contained or the function that it served. The same idea accounts for the probability that many medieval authors never attached their names to their texts in the first place. This seems especially to have been the case with the many lyrics that survive to us, which were habitually composed primarily for the use and benefit of the audience that the poems would reach, not to glorify the authors themselves (Woolf 1968).

When the authors of medieval texts *do* identify themselves, they do not necessarily challenge the idea that an author was merely a channel for the material that his text contains. This is apparent, for example, from the *Chronicle* completed in 1338 by the Gilbertine monk Robert Mannyng, to whom Alexandra Gillespie has already referred. At the beginning of his work, Mannyng addresses the 'lordynges þat be now here' ('gentlemen who are now present'); he suggests that they:

> . . . listene & lere   learn
> alle þe story of Inglande
> als Robert Mannyng wryten it fand   as; found it written
> & in Inglysch has it schewed,
> not for þe lerid bot for þe lewed.   learned; unlearned
>   (ed. Sullens 1996: lines 1–6)

Such an instance of self-naming might be thought to assert that Mannyng is exalting himself as the author of the work; and yet he in fact speaks as if his own contribution to his text were negligible – he will tell the story 'als Robert Mannyng *wryten* it *fand*' (my emphasis). In the very first line of his early thirteenth-century *Brut*, the Worcestershire priest Laȝamon similarly records his own name: 'An preost was on leoden, Laȝamon was ihoten' ('There was a priest amongst the people: he was called Laȝamon'). But he nonetheless represents himself as remaining in the service of 'þa soþere word' that are contained in his text:

> Laȝamon leide þeos boc and þa leaf wende;
> he heom leofliche biheold – liþe him beo Drihten!
> Feþeren he nom mid fingren and fiede on boc-felle,
> And þa soþere word sette togadere,
> And þa þre boc þrumde to are.

[Laȝamon took these books and turned the pages; he gazed fondly at them – may God be kind to him! He took quills with his fingers and composed on parchment. He put the truer words together and condensed the three books into one.]

(ed. Brook and Leslie 1963–78: lines 24–8)

Laȝamon's encounter with his source-texts is presented in slightly more interventionist terms than Mannyng's would be later – he depicts himself as a compiler and an editor of those texts, one who selected material from them and compressed them. But, like Mannyng, he refuses the idea that he is the most important factor in the production of the *Brut*.

In *Piers Plowman*, William Langland projects his name into the text when he has his dreamer-narrator identify himself in the course of his conversation with the figure of Anima in Passus XV of the 'B-Text' of *Piers* (*c.* 1377–9): '"I have lyved in londe . . . my name is Longe Wille"' (ed. Schmidt 1987: XV.152). And yet identifying the narrator with the author of the poem seems dependent on knowing the identity of the author already (Middleton 1990; De Looze 1991); and we might think that rather than asserting that he is the author of the poem, Langland's insertion of his name into it serves above all to lend an impression of authenticity to the experiences of the poem's narrator figure. Moreover, the protagonist's Christian name, Will, is not just a Christian name, but a faculty of the human mind – something that suggests that the narrator's spiritual quest is not peculiar to him, but that he is a representative of the peregrinations of the will of all human beings. Langland's naming of himself, therefore, indicates how he is just like everybody else as much as it suggests that, as the author of *Piers Plowman*, he recognizes that he is somehow 'special'.

Naming oneself in medieval writing can also have primarily a petitionary purpose; authors name themselves to ask, especially, that their readers commemorate them in their prayers. At the end of his *Morte Darthur* Sir Thomas Malory asks his readers to pray for him both while he is alive and while he is dead: 'praye for me whyle I am on lyve that God sende me good delyveraunce. And when I am deed, I praye you all praye for my soule' (ed. Vinaver 1990: 1260). In the religious lyrics that he composed in the fourteenth century, John Audelay, Augustinian friar and priest of the chantry chapel belonging to Richard le Strange, Lord Strange of Knokin, Shropshire, repeatedly asks his readers to pray for him; in the final poem in the sole surviving manuscript of his works, Oxford, Bodleian Library, MS Douce 302, he represents this as a return for the service that he has done them:

> ȝef ȝe wil haue any copi,
>   Askus leeue and ȝe shul haue,
> To pray for hym specialy
>   That hyt made ȝour soules to saue,
>   Jon, þe blynde Awdelay.
> The furst prest to þe lord Strange he was,
> Of þys chauntre here in þis place,
> That made þis bok by Goddus grace,
>   Deeff, siek, blynd, as he lay,   sick
> *Cuius anime propicietur Deus.*   Whose soul may God comfort
>   (ed. Whiting 1931: no. 55, lines 44–53)

In the early Middle English debate poem *The Owl and the Nightingale*, a different petitionary function underlies what appears to be the author's inscription of his name within the text. Soon after the owl and the nightingale begin their debate over who is the better singer and the worthier citizen, the nightingale proposes that they should refer their disagreement to a third party, Master Nicholas of Guildford, because:

> 'He is wis an war of worde.
> He is of dome suþe gleu
> & him is loþ eurich unþeu.'

['He's wise and careful with his words; very discerning in judgment; and a man who hates every kind of vice.']
                              (ed. and trans. Cartlidge 2001: lines 192–4)

The reason for this praise is spelled out at the end of the poem, where a third bird, a wren, offers Nicholas an encomium:

'. . . he demeþ manie riȝte dom,
An diht & writ mani wisdom:
An þurh his muþe & þurh his honde
Hit is þe betere into Scotlonde.
To seche hine is lihtlich þing:
He naueþ bute one woning –
Þat his biscopen muchel schame,
An alle þan þat of his nome
Habbeþ ihert & of his dede.
Hwi nulleþ hi nimen heom to rede
Þat he were mid heom ilome,
For teche heom of his wisdome,
An ȝiue him rente a uale stude
Þat he miȝte heom ilome be mide?'

['He reaches many a correct decision, composing and writing much that is wise, so that by means of his words and deeds he makes things better as far as Scotland. It's not hard to find him, for he's only got one place to live, and that is a great shame to bishops and to all those who've heard of his words and deeds. Why won't they make it their policy to have him among them often, so that he can impart to them some of his wisdom?']

(lines 1756–67)

It is usually thought that Nicholas was the author of the poem, but his name is inserted in it not to advertise his authorship, but to benefit him in a tangible way – his naming constitutes an appeal to be granted multiple ecclesiastical benefices and advancement of other kinds.

If Nicholas was the author of the poem, he effaces himself within it behind a first-person narrator who represents himself as merely a reporter of the owl's and the nightingale's argument, which, he says, he overheard while he was in 'one sumere dale' ('a summer-valley') (line 1). This posture of self-effacement is one that is shared, of course, by authors of late fourteenth- and fifteenth-century English texts, particularly Chaucer, who in *The Canterbury Tales* conceals himself behind a narrator who claims that his role is to report accurately what others have said: 'Whoso shal telle a tale after a man', he says, 'moot reherce [must repeat] as ny [nearly] as evere he kan / Everich a word' that that man speaks (I.731–3) – as if the motley crew made up of his fellow pilgrims were worthy of the same respect as the *auctores* deferred to in Latin academic culture. But while the authors of late-medieval English literature explicitly minimize their own role in the production of their texts, their practice exposes how they contribute to them significantly.

Challenging Convention (1):
Chaucer's *House of Fame*

By Chaucer's day, a new 'cult of the author' had begun to emerge amongst the vernacular cultures of Europe, especially in Italy, where Dante, Boccaccio and – particularly – Petrarch were fêted; in 1341, and so around the presumed date of Chaucer's birth, Petrarch received a laurel crown from King Robert of Naples in an elaborate ceremony (see, for example, Lerer 1993: 26). Petrarch's laureation suggests how by the mid-fourteenth century people were celebrating the achievements of an author as an individual, rather than simply the writings that he had produced. The process might be helped along by authors themselves: in France, also in the fourteenth century, the courtly poet Guillaume de Machaut – like Dante, Petrarch, and, especially, Boccaccio a major influence on Chaucer – seems to have supervised the collection of his writings into organized, 'authorized' compendia that invited focus on his achievements as a writer by displaying the canon of his *œuvre* (compare Brownlee 1984).

In Chaucer's dream vision poem *The House of Fame* (*c.* 1379–80), it is especially the celebrity of authors who wrote in Latin rather than ones who used the vernacular languages that is contemplated explicitly: as he roams through the House of Fame, the narrator of the poem gazes at pillars on which such writers as Statius, Virgil and Ovid are standing. But implicitly the poem also contemplates what might happen if a vernacular author – somebody such as the narrator figure '"Geffrey"' himself – were unable to pose as merely a conduit of other people's words. At the beginning of his dream, the narrator finds himself in a temple that has walls adorned with images of the story of Æneas, and he sets out to recount what he sees there:

> . . . tho began the story anoon,   then
> As I shal telle yow echon.
>
> > (lines 149–50)

He has already paraphrased the opening lines of Virgil's *Æneid*; but much of the rest of his account of what he sees is drawn from Ovid's *Heroides*, which informs his report of Dido's experiences. The use of variant versions of the story draws attention to the fact that there is not one single, authoritative textual source of the story, as Helen Cooper's chapter discusses further below, and that the narrator must choose between different texts. He is further discomfited by the

realization that he is ignorant of the identity of the person who
crafted the images in the temple:

> 'A Lord,' thoughte I, 'that madest us,
> Yet sawgh I never such noblesse
> Of ymages, ne such richesse,
> As I saugh graven in this chirche;
> But not wot I whoo did hem wirche,   know
> Ne where I am, ne in what contree.'
>
> (lines 468–75)

Without identifiable sources for his material, the narrator must again
assume a considerable amount of responsibility for retelling the story
of Æneas; it is no surprise that he feels that he has lost all sense of
orientation, as the above quotation suggests. He exits abruptly from
the temple – a moment that might be interpreted as suggesting that
he is reluctant to assume the responsibility that he is called on to bear.
But outside the temple he finds only a barren desert – a dramatic image,
perhaps, of the mental landscape of a writer who finds himself without authoritative, or indeed any, sources.

Although the narrator is rescued from this state of paralysis by
the descent of a self-satisfied eagle who transports him to Fame's
palace, his problems only multiply. The eagle declares that his abduc-
tion of the narrator has a benign purpose, intended to provide him
with new '"tydynges / Of Loves folk"' (lines 644–5) that he can use
in his writing – a reward for his determination to write '"in reverence
/ Of Love and of hys servantes eke"' (lines 624–5). However, what
the narrator hears from the eagle about the House of Fame proves
far from reassuring. For one thing, the narrator has been accustomed to think of material that he might use in his writing as solid and
substantial: written words or painted pictures. The eagle's description of the House of Fame represents it as the receptacle, especially,
of every last word that is *spoken* in the world – '". . . every speche, or
noyse, or soun, / . . . / Mot nede come to Fames Hous"' (lines 783–6).
And the form in which what has been said enters the House is represented as distanced from the truth. Claiming that speech is sound
and that sound is nothing but '"eyr ybroken"' (line 765), the eagle
likens spoken words to stones dropped in a pool. Like stones in water,
words cause ripples to spread in air, and it is the outermost ripple –
the one furthest from its source – that reaches Fame's palace (lines
817–21).

means of exploring the philosophical questions raised by
us' *Consolation* concerning the relation between human and
love (Kaylor 1993). The substitution of 'If no love is' and 'And
is' for Petrarch's 'If it is not love' and 'if it is love' shape Troilus'
na as part of this wider question: where the poetic voice of
h's poem asks simply what it is that the speaker feels, Troilus
hether love exists at all. Chaucer's treatment of Petrarch's son-
en, shows him imposing his own 'sentence' on it, and suggests
e has the power to revise and shape its meaning.

tempting to read such instances of Chaucer's testing of the
that an author has only a minimal role in the creation of his
a form of 'irony' directed at the reader. The ending of *The House*
* has been read in this way too (Boitani 1984: 208). However,
iportant not to underestimate the extent to which Chaucer's
; in each case represents genuine experimentation, rather than
an elaborate parody of a demonstrably naïve notion. Since the
of Chaucer's conflation of multiple sources is likely to have been
ized by only a few of his contemporaries, it suggests that the
ially comic) discrepancy between conventional thinking and
e in *Troilus* is not primarily 'done for effect', but that – like the
lead ends of *The House of Fame* – it is a vital means of formu-
entirely new ideas about authorship. This is, perhaps, one
itly overlooked reason why Chaucer becomes so important to
:essors: by emphasizing the divergence between traditional ideas
iuthorship and the possible practice of an author, he provides
e of thinking about how authorship can operate. Yet for
r's successors, as for Chaucer himself, the new thinking never
ns the old ideas completely: rather, these ideas provide the means
iulating further new ideas about the role of an author.

Authorizing Strategies

ality towards the relationship between an author and his
predecessors that is apparent in Chaucer's writings is even more
uous in the works of John Lydgate. Lydgate discusses the role
uthor in the production of a text more directly than Chaucer
nd he is bolder in his attempts to assume control of his texts'
:e'; and yet his practice coexists with frequent gestures
s the theory of the deference due to previous authors (includ-
nacular ones, especially Chaucer). The beginning of *The Fall of*

If what the eagle says provides the narrator with reasons for wor-
rying about the reliability of the material that he is to find in the House
of Fame, what the narrator sees in the House itself is yet more troubl-
ing. As Fame's name suggests, she is responsible for broadcasting men's
reputations to the world. Yet when the narrator sees her in action,
summoning her trumpeter Eolus to spread her judgements to the
corners of the earth, he discovers that the reputations that she
accords people are based on nothing but whim. Some people who have
performed good works are given a bad reputation, some who have
performed bad works a good reputation, while those who ask
specifically to be granted anonymity have their fame trumpeted far
and wide. Only a very few receive the reputation merited by their
works (lines 1520–867). It is unsurprising, then, that the narrator
decides to pursue his search for '"tydynges"' elsewhere; what he has
discovered so far provides him with no reason for thinking that the
fame that people acquire represents the truth about them, and so he
is no further forward in his search for trustworthy grounds on which
to base his own writing.

The eagle willingly carries him to the House of Rumour. But this is
still worse. Where Fame's palace had at least the trappings of authority in its glorious walls of beryl and golden floors, the House of
Rumour is a whirling hut of twigs, filled with a great press of people
gabbling at the tops of their voices. Like Fame's own judgements, the
stories originating here compound falsehood and truth, as is strikingly
emblematized in the mingling of a 'lesyng and a sad soth sawe' ('lie
and a trustworthy true report') (line 2089) as they struggle to be the
first to escape through a window and broadcast their news to the world.
At this desperate point, the narrator gains some hope of resolution.
A man appears who 'semed for to be / A man of gret auctorite' (lines
2157–8), and the narrator (like all the other people present) hastens
to hear what he has to say. At this crucial moment, however, the narrative abruptly ends. One interpretation of the sudden conclusion of
the poem, with its refusal of any attempt to impose a meaning on the
material previously related, might be that the narrator is unable to deal
with new experience not mediated through the written sources to which
he is accustomed; at any rate, as has often been pointed out, his experiences in his dream up to this point have led him to question whether
anything that anybody says – in speech or in writing – genuinely does
possess 'gret auctorite', and whether, therefore, it is due his respect
as the person who might disseminate it further in his own writing.

Challenging Convention (2): Chaucer's *Troilus and Criseyde*

The urgency of questions concerning the role that an author might be required to assume brings the *House of Fame* to a grinding halt; but in *Troilus and Criseyde*, written just a few years later, Chaucer's ideas about authorship appear less raw. In *Troilus* Chaucer experiments more freely with the divergence between traditional ideas surrounding an author's contribution to his text and the actual practice of authorship. This divergence complements one of the most important themes of the poem: the issue of the extent of human free will. Troilus doubts that he has freedom to determine his fate in a world where divinity foresees all, and the narrator, likewise, suggests that his freedom to determine the contents of his text is limited, since he is dependent on a pre-existing narrative, ostensibly the work of the Latin-sounding (and probably fictitious) Lollius (compare, for example, Windeatt 1992: 259–67). However, the narrator's declarations of dependence are not supported by Chaucer's practice in writing *Troilus*.

It is not easy to represent the complexity and the slipperiness of Chaucer's thinking in the poem; but they may be exemplified through a consideration of the stanza in which Lollius is introduced. Lollius' name first occurs immediately before the song that Troilus sings in Book I as he commits himself to loving Criseyde; at this moment the narrator declares:

> . . . of his song naught only the sentence,   *meaning*
> As writ myn auctour called Lollius,   *wrote*
> But pleinly, save oure tonges difference,
> I dar wel seyn, in al, that Troilus
> Seyde in his song, loo, every word right thus
> As I shal seyn; and whoso list it here,   *desires to hear it*
> Loo, next this vers he may it fynden here.   *next to*
> (*Troilus*, I.393–9)

The stanza initially seems to manifest extreme deference towards the narrator's 'auctour', as the poet claims that he will follow 'naught only the sentence . . . but . . . every word' of his source. Alluding to the centuries-old debate concerning the choice a translator must make between being faithful to the letter of the text and being true to its spirit (see further Helen Cooper's essay below), the narrator not only effaces his own contribution to the text, but positions himself as

somebody who is peculiarly faithful to his letter and to the spirit of the original were mutually exclusive, yet by referring to 'na but every word' Chaucer's narrator appears be true to both.

However, the grammatical ambiguity of for a quite different interpretation. Althou the line 'As writ myn auctor called Lolliu and 'words', in fact it qualifies only 'senten the lines might be translated: 'I shall not song, as written by my "auctour" Lollius, bu that Troilus said in its entirety, word for wo the narrator is surpassing his source: that exactly what the narrator has decided that by the use of the phrases 'I dar wel seyn' a phrase may appear technically redundant, ically unaccountable, it can be read as mo direction, allowing the poet to assert a co he declares that what Troilus said was 'ev shal seyn' (my emphasis; compare Stillinge name of the ostensible source of *Troilus* l cally derived authority to the poem, Cha implication that his own authority is nece

This ambiguity is the more significant precise point in *Troilus* where Chaucer se of his actual sources, showing that he c ferent texts as he chooses. Chaucer's prin was Boccaccio's *Il Filostrato*, which he infu Boethius' *De consolatione philosophiae*; but th from neither of these texts. Rather, it is sonnets of Boccaccio's contemporary Petra lation. Chaucer not only transforms Petrar three seven-line stanzas of rhyme roya amplification, but also makes a pronoun of the first two lines. Where Petrarch asks is it that I feel? But if it is love, before Go Chaucer substitutes rather more general God, what fele I so? And if love is, wh (I.400–401; compare Thomson 1959). This type of changes that Chaucer consistently *Il Filostrato*, as he uses Boccaccio's relativel

as a
Boeth
divin
if lov
dilem
Petra
asks
net, t
how
It
theor
text a
of Fa
it is i
writir
mere
exten
recog
(pote
practi
many
lating
frequ
his su
about
a mo
Chau
aband
of for

Self-

The d
literar
conspi
of an
does,
'sente
towar
ing ve

Princes is one place in which the part that a new writer may play in conveying inherited material to his audience is subtly celebrated by Lydgate. The *Fall* is, in fact, a 'double' translation: a translation into English of the second French translation of Boccaccio's *De casibus virorum illustrium* ('On the Falls of Famous Men') that was made by the French humanist writer Laurent de Premierfait (in 1409). This mixed ancestry immediately raises questions about where the authority for Lydgate's version of the text is to be located; in an often-cited passage, the *Fall* emphasizes the part that somebody who inherits preformed material may play when he proceeds to work on it:

> Artificeres hauyng exercise   practice
> May chaunge and turne bi good discrecioun
> Shappis, formys, and newli hem deuyse,
> Make and vnmake in many sondry wyse,
> As potteres, which to that craft entende,   apply themselves
> Breke and renewe ther vesselis to a-mende.
>   (ed. Bergen 1924: I.9–14)

The lines indicate the insight and skill that a new 'artificere' may bring to his material, and raise the possibility that he may be able to improve on it – that he can 'a-mende' it (compare Strohm 2005: 93–4; Summit 2006: 218–21). The passage is based on what Laurent says in his text; but Lydgate subsequently adds to Laurent's material complementary assertions of his own, arguing that writers have licence to change things that were 'maad of auctours hem beforn' since they may make them 'more fressh and lusti to the eie' (lines 22–5). Elsewhere in the *Fall* he develops a new vocabulary to express the enhancements that an author may make to his raw material: he may 'overgild', 'enamel' and 'illuminate' it (Ebin 1988; Copeland 1992). And he enacts the process himself by using highly ornate or 'aureate' language to express the didactic moral 'sentence' inherent in his source material – at the same time as he refers that 'sentence' continually to the original source of the contents of his text, 'myn auctor Bochas'.

The marginalia that accompany Lydgate's works in many of the manuscripts in which they have been preserved similarly emphasize his own contribution to those works. The Latin marginalia that surround his poem *Reson and Sensuallyte* (*c.* 1407), an adaptation of part of the lengthy French allegorical work *Les Echecs amoureux* ('The Chess Game of Love'), include several that draw attention to the alterations that Lydgate has made to his source: they make such comments as 'Ista sunt verba translatoris' ('These are the words of the translator')

and 'Huc vsque verba translatoris' ('Thus far the words of the translator'). While the majority of the marginalia replicate the ones that
were also attached to the French text, providing a Latin summary of
the information that appears in the work, amongst these are examples that thus advertise the fact that *Reson and Sensuallyte* is a poem
that is not exclusively grounded in previous writing.

We might compare the function of the marginalia that are attached
to works by other late-medieval English authors (on these see also
Daniel Wakelin's essay later in this volume). The ones that accompany Thomas Hoccleve's 'advice to princes' poem *The Regement of Princes*
(1411–12) give the impression that the text is one that is entirely reliant
on previous writing, especially writing in the language of authority
and learning, Latin. The vast majority supply a passage of Latin that
is closely replicated in Hoccleve's English verse, together with a note
of the text from which it is drawn; they cite the Bible frequently, and
also the writings of Church Fathers such as St Augustine and the sixth-
century pope Gregory the Great; classical authorities such as the
rhetorician Quintilian; and Hoccleve's three principal sources for his
text, the pseudo-Aristotelian compendium of lore the *Secreta secretorum* ('Secret of Secrets'), the manual of princely instruction *De
regimine principum* ('On the Ruling of Princes') by the thirteenth-
century theologian Aegidius Romanus, and *De ludo scaccorum* ('On the
Game of Chess') by the fourteenth-century Italian Dominican writer
Jacobus de Cessolis, a work that relates the various orders of society
to pieces on a chessboard (see further Perkins 2001: 87–114). And yet,
while the marginalia thus present Hoccleve as merely the mediator of
multiple authoritative voices, they also might be said to surround his
own writing with an aura of authority. This was particularly important for Hoccleve because in writing the *Regement* he was faced with
a peculiar difficulty of self-legitimization. In his 'day-job' he was Clerk
to the Privy Seal, and so he served, and derived his income from, the
royal Lancastrian regime. The *Regement*, however, aims to counsel one
of the foremost representatives of that regime, Henry, Prince of Wales
– the future Henry V (Meyer-Lee 2007; compare Ferster 1996). The
allusions to previous writing in the marginalia to the text are thus a
means of bolstering Hoccleve's own authority just as much as they
are a way of effacing him, as they may at first appear.

The marginal Latin apparatus that accompanies copies of John Gower's
long English poem the *Confessio Amantis* provides commentary on the
contents of the text at certain points – material comparable in many

ways to the commentaries that, in Italy, Dante had created to accompany his exploration of the concept of love in *La Vita Nuova* ('The New Life') in the late thirteenth century or that Boccaccio, later, had supplied for his *Teseida*, the main source of Chaucer's *Knight's Tale*. This commentary, in part, invites readers to view a vernacular text as carrying the same authority as the Latin writing to which commentaries were traditionally attached. But in the case of the *Confessio*, the commentary sometimes serves to draw attention to the specific details and the meaning of Gower's writing. The commentary that accompanies Gower's tale of Florent – his version of the story told by Chaucer in *The Wife of Bath's Tale* – in Book I of the *Confessio* (I.1407–1882) identifies it as a tale 'contra amori inobedientes' ('against disobedient lovers'); but it might well be argued that the tale itself focuses less on disobedience in love than on the keeping of vows (Echard 1998: 33–4). The potential discrepancy between the commentary and the tale might be thought to undermine the authority of the former and to invite readers of the *Confessio* to transfer that authority instead to Gower's actual words in the body of the text (see further, for example, Yeager 1987).

Catherine Sanok, in her essay above, has suggested some of the ways in which female authors who wrote their texts – or had them written for them – well outside the spheres in which Chaucer and his contemporaries and successors moved imparted authority to their texts; but it is worth mentioning here that they also sometimes assert their importance as the *authors* of those texts even as, like their male counterparts, they too ostensibly efface themselves. As Nicholas Watson has pointed out, the task faced by Margery Kempe, like the other authors of visionary texts, was very different from that faced by the authors of other kinds of late-medieval writing: the subject matter of her *Book*, written *c*. 1436–8, was her own experience, not material that had previously been conveyed by other writers (Watson 1991). In her writing, then, she could not even claim to be deferring to the authority of those who had mediated her material before her. And yet her *Book* does defer to the language and conceits used by other mystical writers in their accounts of *their* experiences: famously, for example, the claim of the *Book* that Kempe was granted the feeling of a flame of fire in her breast in token of God's love strongly recalls the experience described by the fourteenth-century mystical writer Richard Rolle in his *Incendium amoris* ('The Fire of Love') (see further Windeatt, ed., 2000: 9–18). The *Book* also emphasizes Kempe's reliance on a scribe who could record her experiences as she could not. But it makes clear too the crucial role that Kempe played in its formation – her verification of the truth of its contents, for instance, and her clarification of any part of it that was unclear (ed. Windeatt 2000: 49). Just like other late Middle English literature, if in different ways, the *Book* emphasizes the contribution of its author at the same time as it denies it.

The tension between self-effacement and self-authorization that we can thus see in so much writing by late fourteenth- and fifteenth-century English authors may seem to have been left far behind by the end of the medieval period. In the humanist-influenced works written by the poet John Skelton (*c.* 1460–1529), who frequently referred to himself as laureated, explicit gestures towards earlier ideas about authorship seem to have disappeared. Skelton's florid celebration of himself as an author is one of the most prominent features of his writing: even in such an early work as the *Dolorus Dethe and Muche Lamentable Chaunce of the Mooste Honorable Erle of Northumberland*, written in 1489, when Henry Percy, the fourth earl of Northumberland was murdered, Skelton surrounded his text with a Latin paratext that proclaims his qualifications to eulogize the dead earl. The opening Latin verse is introduced by the line 'Poeta Skelton laureatus libellum suum metrice alloquitur' ('Skelton, the laureate poet, addresses his little book in verse'), which signals both Skelton's status and the respect due to the work that he has created. Skelton's roughly contemporaneous translation of the first-century BC *Bibliotheca historica* ('The Historical Library') by the Greek historian Diodorus Siculus emphasizes the way in which an author shapes his text. Based on a fifteenth-century Latin translation of the original Greek, Skelton's version interpolates into the prologue material that emphasizes how much work his translation has involved – his 'besy deligence', 'estudye laborious' and 'dilygent endeuoirment [endeavour]' (compare Griffiths 2006: 24–5; 38–55). Such self-celebration seems to project the same attitudes to authorship as are recognized in Pynson's edition of Lydgate's *Fall of Princes*. And yet such emphasis as Skelton places on his own role in the production of his texts can be interpreted as defensive, assertions that define themselves against the assumptions governing authorship that influenced so much medieval writing in the centuries before he wrote. There can be little doubt that Skelton's self-celebration would not have been such a prominent feature of his writing if the distinctively medieval ideas surrounding authorship had not existed.

References

Primary texts

Bergen, Henry, ed. (1924–7). *Lydgate's Fall of Princes*. EETS ES 121–4. London: Kegan Paul, Trench, Trübner & Co.

Brook, G.L., and Leslie, R.F., eds. (1963–78). *Laȝamon: Brut*. EETS OS 250, 277. London: Oxford University Press.

Cartlidge, Neil, ed. and trans. (2001). *The Owl and the Nightingale: Text and Translation*. Exeter: University of Exeter Press.

Furnivall, Frederick J., ed. (1897). *Thomas Hoccleve: The Regement of Princes*. EETS ES 72. London: Kegan Paul, Trench, Trübner & Co.

Macaulay, G.C. ed. (1900). *The English Works of John Gower*. EETS ES 81, 82. London: Oxford University Press.

Salter, F.M. and Edwards, H.L.R., eds. (1956–7). *John Skelton: The Bibliotheca Historica of Diodorus Siculus*. EETS OS 233, 239. London: Oxford University Press.

Scattergood, John, ed. (1983). *John Skelton: The Complete English Poems*. Harmondsworth: Penguin.

Schmidt, A.V.C., ed. (1987). *William Langland: The Vision of Piers Plowman – A Complete Edition of the B-Text*. 2nd edn. London: J.M. Dent.

Sieper, Ernst, ed. (1901–3). *John Lydgate: Reson and Sensuallyte*. EETS ES 84, 89. London: Kegan Paul, Trench, Trübner & Co.

Sullens, Idelle, ed. (1996). *Robert Mannyng of Brunne: The Chronicle*. Binghamton: Center for Medieval and Early Renaissance Studies.

Vinaver, Eugène (1990). *The Works of Sir Thomas Malory*. 3rd edn, revd P.J.C. Field. 3 vols. Oxford: Clarendon Press.

Whiting, Ella Keats, ed. (1931). *The Poems of John Audelay*. EETS OS 184. London: Oxford University Press.

Windeatt, Barry, ed. (2000). *The Book of Margery Kempe*. Harlow: Longman.

Secondary sources and suggestions for further reading

Boitani, Piero (1984). *Chaucer and the Imaginary World of Fame*. Chaucer Studies 10. Cambridge: D.S. Brewer.

Brown, Cynthia J. (1995). *Poets, Patrons, and Printers: Crisis of Authority in Late-Medieval France*. Ithaca: Cornell University Press.

Brownlee, Kevin (1984). *Poetic Identity in Guillaume de Machaut*. Madison: University of Wisconsin Press.

Copeland, Rita (1991). *Rhetoric, Hermeneutics, and Translation in the Middle Ages: Academic Traditions and Vernacular Texts*. Cambridge Studies in Medieval Literature 11. Cambridge: Cambridge University Press.

Copeland, Rita (1992). 'Lydgate, Hawes, and the Science of Rhetoric in the Late Middle Ages'. *Modern Language Quarterly*, 53, 57–82.

Ebin, Lois (1988). *Illuminator, Makar, Vates: Visions of Poetry in the Fifteenth Century.* Lincoln: University of Nebraska Press.

Echard, Siân (1998). 'With Carmen's Help: Latin Authorities in the *Confessio Amantis'*. *Studies in Philology*, 95, 1–40.

Ferster, Judith (1996). *Fictions of Advice: The Literature and Politics of Counsel in Late Medieval England.* Philadelphia: University of Pennsylvania Press.

Gillespie, Alexandra (2006). *Print Culture and the Medieval Author: Chaucer, Lydgate, and Their Books, 1473–1557.* Oxford: Oxford University Press.

Griffiths, Jane (2006). *John Skelton and Poetic Authority: Defining the Liberty to Speak.* Oxford: Clarendon Press.

Kaylor, Noel (1993). 'Boethian Resonance in Chaucer's "Canticus Troili"'. *Chaucer Review*, 27, 219–27.

Kerby-Fulton, Kathryn (1997). 'Langland and the Bibliographic Ego'. In Steven Justice and Kathryn Kerby-Fulton, eds., *Written Work: Langland, Labor, and Authorship* (pp. 67–143). Philadelphia: University of Pennsylvania Press.

Lerer, Seth (1993). *Chaucer & his Readers: Imagining the Author in Late-Medieval England.* Princeton: Princeton University Press.

De Looze, Lawrence (1991). 'Signing Off in the Middle Ages: Medieval Textuality and Strategies of Authorial Self-Naming'. In A.N. Doane and Carol Braun Pasternak, eds., *Vox intexta: Orality and Textuality in the Middle Ages* (pp. 62–82). Madison: University of Wisconsin Press.

Meyer-Lee, Robert J. (2007). *Poets and Power from Chaucer to Wyatt.* Cambridge Studies in Medieval Literature 61. Cambridge: Cambridge University Press.

Middleton, Anne (1990). 'William Langland's "Kynde Name": Authorial Signature and Social Identity in Late Fourteenth-Century England'. In Lee Patterson, ed., *Literary Practice and Social Change in Britain, 1380–1530* (pp. 15–82). Berkeley: University of California Press.

Minnis, A.J. (1988). *Medieval Theory of Authorship: Scholastic Literary Attitudes in the Later Middle Ages.* 2nd edn. Aldershot: Wildwood House.

Pearsall, Derek (1994). 'Hoccleve's *Regement of Princes*: The Poetics of Royal Self-Representation'. *Speculum*, 69, 386–410.

Perkins, Nicholas (2001). *Hoccleve's Regiment of Princes: Counsel and Constraint.* Cambridge: D.S. Brewer.

Spearing, A.C. (2005). *Textual Subjectivity: The Encoding of Subjectivity in Medieval Narratives and Lyrics.* Oxford: Oxford University Press.

Stillinger, Thomas C. (1992). *The Song of Troilus: Lyric Authority in the Medieval Book.* Philadelphia: University of Pennsylvania Press.

Strohm, Paul (2005). *Politique: Languages of Statecraft between Chaucer and Shakespeare.* Notre Dame: University of Notre Dame Press.

Summit, Jennifer (2006). '"Stable in Study": Lydgate's Fall of Princes and Duke Humfrey's Library'. In Larry Scanlon and James Simpson, eds., *John Lydgate: Poetry, Culture, and Lancastrian England* (pp. 207–31). Notre Dame: University of Notre Dame Press.

Thomson, Patricia (1959). 'The "Canticus Troilii": Chaucer and Petrarch'. *Comparative Literature*, 11, 313–28.

Watson, Nicholas (1991). *Richard Rolle and the Invention of Authority*. Cambridge Studies in Medieval Literature 13. Cambridge: Cambridge University Press.

Windeatt, Barry (1992). *Troilus and Criseyde*. Oxford Guides to Chaucer. Oxford: Clarendon Press.

Woolf, Rosemary (1968). *The English Religious Lyric in the Middle Ages*. Oxford: Clarendon Press.

Yeager, Robert F. (1987). 'English, Latin, and the Text as "Other": The Page as Sign in the Work of John Gower'. *Text*, 3, 251–67.

Part III
Writing in Middle English; Writing in England

Chapter 7

Language

Jeremy J. Smith

Defining Middle English

The term 'Middle English' generally refers to the period between the Norman Conquest of AD 1066 and the arrival of printing in England in 1476, as opposed to 'Old English' (before 1066) and 'New' or 'Modern English' (after 1476). It should of course be noted that the correspondence between language-state and date is approximate: people did not wake up on the morning after the Norman Conquest, or after the arrival of printing, speaking in a radically different way. However, the connection between the form of the language and these two historical events is, as we shall see, important.

The typology 'Old–Middle–Modern' with reference to English was established by scholars in the second half of the nineteenth century. The typology has limitations, but it does capture the differences between each stage. 'Prototypical' Middle English differs from Old English in all levels of language traditionally distinguished. Thus, in vocabulary, Middle English (unlike Old English) is the period when large numbers of words enter English from French; early loans were taken from Norman French, but after around 1250 a mass of Central French vocabulary starts to be recorded as part of English usage. In grammar, Middle English is traditionally seen as the period of 'reduced inflection'. In Old English there was a comparatively large number of inflectional markers – endings added to words – flagging categories such as case, number and gender. During the course of the Middle English period, these markers were significantly reduced, and other so-called 'discourse-tracking' mechanisms were introduced to compensate for the reduction, such as a more fixed word order, more use of prepositions, and a more distinctive system of pronouns (compare Present-Day English 'he', 'she', 'it' etc.). Developments in the sound-system (phonology) were reflected in the evolution of the writing-system; phonological variation was reflected in extreme written-system (graphological) variation between individual texts – hence Middle English has been called 'the age of written dialects'.

Similarly Middle English differs from Modern English in all levels of language. In the sixteenth century, there was an influx of Latin-derived vocabulary into English not only as a result of Renaissance 'humanism' but also as a result of the development of specialist vocabularies in the vernacular (such as scientific terms) that used Latin- and Greek-based formulations to express new concepts. This Latin material was later supplemented by new words taken from the languages with which English came into contact through imperial expansion. In grammar, inflectional distinctions that had survived from Old into Middle English were further reduced until the Present-Day English system emerged, with only a few markers left (for example of number and possession in the noun and pronoun: compare 'name' – 'names'; 'John' – 'John's'; 'she' – 'her'). In transmission, the standardization of the writing-system in the modern period made it hard to detect continuing change and variation in the corresponding sound-system. Major developments in phonology (such as the Great Vowel Shift of the fifteenth and sixteenth centuries, whereby the 'long vowels' of late Middle English were redistributed in a largely ordered way) undoubtedly took place. However, these changes can only be identified either by deduction – by noting which words are rhymed together, for example – or by the analysis of contemporary writings on pronunciation, such as those of the so-called orthoepists, spelling-reformers of the sixteenth century.

In this chapter, all the changes in the history of English outlined above will be exemplified in the light of wider changes in the status and use of the vernacular during the Middle English period. We shall note in particular the shifting relationships between English and the other languages that existed alongside it, especially French and Latin. It will be seen that form is constrained by function, and that the formal developments in the history of English are historically explicable only when they are seen from a functional perspective.

Latin, French and the Functions of English

To understand what the distinctive functions of Middle English were, some grasp of historical context is needed. William of Normandy's victory over the Anglo-Saxons in 1066 was followed relatively swiftly by the imposition of Norman political and cultural hegemony throughout the kingdom of England. By the time of William's death in 1087, the first two classes ('estates') of medieval society, clergy and nobility, were dominated by Normans.

This major change in England's social structure had a profound effect on the status of the English language, which had hitherto occupied a position unparalleled among the Western European vernaculars. English before the Norman Conquest was 'elaborated', that is, available for use in a range of linguistic registers and domains, from literature to science and theology, from poems such as *Beowulf* and *The Battle of Maldon* to the homilies of Ælfric and Wulfstan, the best-known prose writers of the late Old English period. When the Normans arrived, they thus encountered a sophisticated society that had developed a distinctive vernacular culture. Spoken Old English consisted of a range of different varieties, strongly affected – especially in the north and east of England – by the Norse dialects of Viking settlers. However, the impact of Norse was only rarely reflected in writing, since the Late West Saxon of south-west England had achieved the prestige associated with 'standard' languages, and was used for the composition and copying of manuscripts in various centres, largely monastic, outside its area of origin. This standardized form of English thus tended to exclude forms not found outside the south-west.

The Norman Conquest ended the prestige of Late West Saxon. For some time, and especially in places where Anglo-Saxon culture had strong institutional roots, such as at Worcester in the south-west Midlands, texts continued to be copied in standardized language after 1066, and some people tried to maintain cultural links with the Anglo-Saxon past. They included the so-called Worcester 'tremulous hand' scribe (discussed by Franzen 1991), who, at the beginning of the thirteenth century, glossed Old English texts available to him and also attempted to compose poems in Anglo-Saxon modes. Nevertheless, in general, dialectal variation and linguistic changes, hitherto not evidenced in written English, began to spread from the spoken to the written mode. These writings were clearly different from Old English: they are examples of Middle English.

But it is important to grasp that Britain between the Norman Conquest and the arrival of printing was a multilingual environment to an extent that is hard to comprehend from a twenty-first-century perspective. Middle English existed alongside many other languages. Some of these languages pre-dated the coming of the Anglo-Saxons: the Celtic languages of the north and west of Britain, which persist to a greater or lesser extent until the present day (as Scots Gaelic, Welsh and Cornish). And even Norse, the language of the Viking settlers who first came to Britain from the ninth century onwards, was still spoken in a comparatively 'pure' form in the far north of the British Isles, for example in Shetland and Orkney, where it endured (as 'Norn') until the eighteenth century.

The Norman Conquest meant that English in England existed alongside two further languages: Latin and French. Latin had already been in widespread use in Anglo-Saxon England, in documents and in works of theology, but its currency increased after 1066 because the Conquest coincided with a revival of Latin learning in Western Europe. The 'Channel State' of England and Normandy that resulted from William's victory aided the transmission of this culture to Britain. Latin – as in other Western European states – became the language of official record in England during the twelfth and early thirteenth centuries, used for, among other texts, the *Domesday Book* (1086) and *Magna Carta* (1215). Latin was also the literary language used by important twelfth-century writers working in England, such as Geoffrey de Vinsauf (author of the *Poetria nova*), Alexander Neckham (author of *De naturis rerum* – 'On the Natures of Things') and John of Salisbury (author of the *Policraticus*). And it was, of course, the spoken language of the liturgy, and the *lingua franca* of the learned.

Norman French, though the mother-tongue of the invading élite, could not at first compete with Latin in all its functions. However, as Michael Clanchy has pointed out, 'contact with England, with its long tradition of non-Latin writing, may have helped to develop French as a written language' (Clanchy 1993: 168). From the thirteenth century onwards, as Norman French developed in England into what modern scholars call 'Anglo-Norman' and evolved distinctive linguistic characteristics, it began to be used for both official and literary purposes. *Magna Carta*, for instance, was translated into Anglo-Norman late in the thirteenth century. Prototypical of Anglo-Norman literary writers is Wace, a Jersey man, whose two main works are the *Roman de Brut*, a verse history of Britain, and the *Roman de Rou*, a verse history of the dukes of Normandy (compare Andrew Galloway's essay above).

Throughout this period, English remained the primary spoken language of the majority of the population of England, which peaked at just over six million in the middle of the fourteenth century. There is some evidence that the Norman aristocracy themselves had begun to speak English by the beginning of the twelfth century; the change was encouraged by King John's loss of Normandy in 1204. However, French remained a necessary accomplishment for cultivated people – much as in nineteenth-century Russia – and the appearance of sourcebooks for the teaching of French, such as Walter of Bibbesworth's *Tretiz de langage*, during the thirteenth century correlates with this situation. The fairly common use of French for documentary purposes from the thirteenth century onwards may relate to the parallel switch from Latin to French in France.

English became increasingly widely used in the written mode as the Middle Ages progressed, as basic (or 'pragmatic') literacy became more widespread. Yet the primary functions of English were parochial – it was used for 'learning one's letters' before one progressed to learning Latin – and the language remained comparatively unelaborated (contrast the uses of Old English, described above). The national functions of written language, until the very end of the Middle English period, were carried out by Latin and French. There was therefore no need for a national form of English, and written English during the Middle English period manifested (as we shall see) a high degree of variation of the kind now more generally associated with speech.

Forms (1): The Lexicon

The extralinguistic context described in the previous section had an impact on the forms of Middle English at every level of language: lexicon, grammar, writing and speech. In the lexicon, as was indicated above, Middle English differs from Old English primarily in the appearance of a large number of loanwords from French (to be exemplified below), but other vocabulary also makes its first appearance in the language during this period.

Of these other elements, by far the most important is Norse. Norse, the language of the Vikings, was a language very similar in form, it seems, to certain Northern varieties of Old English; transfer of Norse vocabulary to Northern (or 'Anglian') English was comparatively straightforward. However, the existence of standardized West Saxon (see above) meant that Norse vocabulary was largely unrecorded in the written record until after the Norman Conquest, and those few words that do appear, such as *cnearr* ('ship'), relate to technological, military or cultural artefacts peculiar to Norse culture and for which West Saxon had no easy equivalent.

Norse loanwords only begin to appear more commonly in the written record of Middle English after the disappearance of the West Saxon standardized language. Many of the words borrowed from Norse express very common concepts, for example *bag, bull, egg, root, ugly, wing*. One slight difficulty in identifying Norse loanwords is that some words usually seen as Norse-derived, such as *call*, may in fact be derived from the Anglian dialect of Old English. Similarities between Anglian and Norse go back to the period before the Anglo-Saxon invasion of Britain, when Anglian was geographically the northernmost variety of West Germanic, closest geographically to the North Germanic varieties that developed into Norse. The greatest surviving Old English poem, *Beowulf*, is concerned with the deeds of North Germanic heroes living in what are modern Denmark and Sweden, and this connection between Anglo-Saxon and Norse cultures would seem to parallel the linguistic relationship.

The Norse impact on the lexicon is also seen in the new system of third person pronouns that replaced the Old English paradigm; thus Norse-derived *they, their, them* gradually came to be used in place of Old English-derived *hīe, hiera, him*. It is usual to see this development as driven by grammatical considerations; in the transition from Old to Middle English, it became desirable for more phonetically distinctive pronouns to be adopted from among the choices available, since pronouns were taking on a more significant role as inflectional distinctions were elsewhere being obscured (see below). But it is interesting that, in some dialects at least, *th*-type forms were not adopted throughout the paradigm at the same time. Whereas in Northern dialects of Middle English (including Older Scots), where the impact of Norse was strongest, *th*-types were indeed adopted throughout the paradigm, in Midland and Southern varieties *th*-forms appear first in the nominative (that is, subject) case and only later in other cases; thus the Chaucerian paradigm is *they* beside *here* ('their') and *hem* ('them'). The differential speed of the adoption of these forms probably arose because of the fact that the nominative form, as the subject form, and prototypically appearing at the beginning of clauses, is the primary reference-point back to an earlier noun phrase, and thus carries particular emphasis.

The appearance of the form *she* seems also to have been functionally conditioned, though its origins are controversial. Most scholars hold that it derives from Old English *hēo*; a stress-shifted variant, **hjo*, arose in areas where English was spoken with a Norse accent, and the rare cluster *hj-* was replaced by more common [ʃ], represented in Present-Day English writing by *sh-*. (A similar process may be seen in the replacement of initial *hj-* in the place-name *Hjaltland*, subsequently *Shetland*.) The fact that [ʃ]-types – generally – seem to appear earliest in Northern dialects again suggests that interaction with Norse is responsible for the rise of the form.

The status of Norse-derived vocabulary in Middle English does not seem to have differed from that of 'native' words derived from Old English. The other languages that had an impact on English during the Middle English period – Latin and French – had a rather higher social status, as was seen above, and this fact has implications for the kinds of words that were adopted.

Some Latin words were already present in Old English, either as adoptions made at that stage of the language (for example *gīgant* ('giant'), *pistol* ('letter, epistle')) or deriving from interaction between Latin and pre-Old English/Germanic during the time of the Roman Empire (for example *draca* ('dragon'), *strǣt* ('(paved) road')). These loans were somewhat restricted in number, and generally referred to specialist notions that were not to be found in native Germanic cultures.

During the Middle English period, a number of Latin words came directly into English, but these remained comparatively few until the fifteenth century, when large numbers of words were transferred from Latin to English as part of an attempt to dignify the vernacular. Forms such as *omnipotent* and *testament* were adopted, therefore, as part of the elaboration of the language that can be seen during the transition from Middle to Early Modern English. This process can be witnessed most obviously in fifteenth-century literary English, especially in the 'aureate' ('gilded') diction of poets such as John Lydgate – already mentioned in Jane Griffiths' essay – whereby terms from the Latin Church liturgy became part of a heightened linguistic register.

French was, as discussed above, the language of the post-Conquest élite, and the French element in English is directly related to the emergence of the new polity; only one pair of related words, *prūd* ('proud') and *prȳt(e)* ('pride'), seems to pre-date 1066 within the English written record.

French-derived vocabulary begins to appear in English texts in substantial numbers after the Conquest. Up until the middle of the thirteenth century, this vocabulary is largely taken from Anglo-Norman French, and is comparatively restricted in linguistic domain. Much of it relates to the relationship between governors and governed, for example *justice, obedience, mastery, prison, service*. The Anglo-Norman origin of many of these words is reflected in their spelling: compare the forms *war, wasp, carpenter, cauldron* with modern French *guerre, guêpe, charpentier, chaudron*, which are derived from the Central ('standard') dialect of the language. Although the spelling of some words in Present-Day English resembles the way they are spelled in Present-Day French, Norman French pronunciations have been retained, as in *quit* (with initial [kw]) and *fruit* (with an [u] vowel, from Norman French [y]); compare the [k] and [yi] in Present-Day French *quitter* and *fruit* respectively. Norman French endings in *-arie, -orie* are reflected in the Present-Day English forms *salary, victory*; compare Present-Day French *salaire, victoire*. The coexistence of Norman and Central French forms of certain personal names was exploited for literary effect in some Middle English texts. The author of *Sir Gawain and the Green Knight*, for instance, names his hero either *Gawa(y)n* (Central French) or *Wawan* (Norman French), depending on the exigencies of alliterative metre. Some Latin words were transferred into English not directly, but through the medium of French; indeed, sometimes it is hard to tell from which language these words were taken. Thus the form *castel* ('castle') may be a French word (compare its Present-Day French equivalent *château*), but it may equally well be derived directly from Latin *castellum* (a diminutive of *castrum* ('fort'), pl. *castra* ('fortified camp')).

From the middle of the thirteenth century to the end of the Middle English period French words entered the English lexicon in large numbers. The main source for this new vocabulary was Central French, reflecting the much more wide-ranging contact between English and French cultures during the later part of the Middle Ages. Some notion of the range of domains covered by this vocabulary is indicated by such words as *chancellor, homage, religion, chaplain, miracle, reverence, pardon, innocent, guard, defence, garment, chemise, sausage, salad*. The domains represented therefore include government, religion, the legal system, military matters, fashion and dress, and food.

A traditional illustration of the impact of French on the last of these domains is to show how the words *pork, beef* and *mutton* are foods that come from the *pig, cow* and *sheep* respectively. The first 'food' group of words derives from French *porc, bœuf* and *mouton*, terms that refer in French to both meat and animal; the second 'animal' group of words is derived from Old English. It has been usual to interpret this difference as arising from the social distinction between aristocratic (French-speaking) consumers and lowly (English-speaking) producers. Although this interpretation is doubtless crude, it does seem to derive from a real social distinction, though it may also reflect the traditional association of French with culinary culture. At the beginning of the twenty-first century French remains the international language of cuisine, even if English dominates the internet.

Words derived from French during the Middle English period are still habitually assigned to a different social or stylistic register in Present-Day English from English-derived ones occupying the same domains. For instance, the verbs *begin* and *commence* are evidently near-synonyms with their core meaning denoting inception; but the latter, French-derived word clearly has a 'higher', more formal meaning than the former. Such a distinction can be seen in many similar pairings, for example *hide – conceal, feed – nourish, make – oblige, look at – regard*, in which the French-derived word is the second in each pair.

This distinction in register, fairly obviously, would seem to have arisen during the Middle English period as a result of the initial social distinction between French- and English-users, which was sustained throughout most of the medieval period. The large-scale adoption of French words into English seems to correlate in date with the loss of Normandy, referred to above, and with the growing elaboration of English as a communicative medium; it seems that speakers of higher social classes, though now speaking English, continued to mark social difference by studding their English with French vocabulary – a habit that persisted through subsequent generations. Such a phenomenon is commonly noted in what are often referred to as 'language death' situations; as French died as a major language in England, it threw off numerous items of vocabulary into the language that took over its functions, that is, English.

Forms (2): Grammar

'Grammar' may be considered to have two components: word-form (morphology) and the functional roles of words (syntax); the two are of course intimately connected. Just as the Middle English lexicon shows the impact of contact with other languages, so does Middle English grammar.

The impact of French on Middle English grammar was comparatively slight, and restricted to two areas: lexical morphology (word-formation)

153

and some elements of phrasing. This impact may thus be swiftly exemplified. Old English vocabulary was characteristically extended in the same way as Present-Day German, through compounding; hence Old English *brecan* ('(to) break') could be made more intensive in meaning by the adoption of the prefix *for-*, in *forbrecan* ('(to) destroy') (the Present-Day English word 'destroy' derives from French). Such compounds tend to be replaced by borrowed forms, as in this case. French, moreover, supplied suffixes such as *-able* which could be applied to native stems, as in *knowable, unspeakable*. In phrasing, certain usages seem to be based on French models, for instance *in vain, without fail, to do justice, to hold one's peace*. Many of these phrases contain French-derived vocabulary (such as *justice, peace*), but they are also calques on French expressions (compare, for example, Present-Day French *en vain, sans faille*). Some phrases containing only Old English-derived words seem to be modelled on French usage, for example *at first hand* (compare Present-Day French *de première main*).

The impact of Norse on the grammar of English was, it seems, stronger; before discussing Norse 'influence' on grammar, however, a general characterization of Middle English grammar has to be attempted. As was indicated at the beginning of this chapter, the major difference between Old and Middle English grammar relates to inflectional morphology, and to the effects that this had on syntax. Old English was (comparatively) highly inflected; element order was consequently (comparatively) flexible. Thus, to take a simple example, in Old English the clause 'The man binds the servant' could be expressed in three ways:

(1) *Se wer þone cnapan bindeþ* (subject – object – verb, literally 'The man (subject) the servant (object) binds').
(2) *Se wer bindeþ þone cnapan* (subject – verb – object, literally 'The man (subject) binds the servant (object)').
(3) *Þone cnapan bindeþ se wer* (object – verb – subject, literally 'The servant (object) binds the man (subject)')

In each case the different form of the 'the'-word (*se, þone*) and the inflectional ending (*-an* in *cnapan*) flags the role of the Noun Phrase in question. By contrast, in Present-Day English, 'The man binds the servant', fairly obviously, does not denote the same as 'The servant binds the man'.

In short, Old English Noun Phrases sustained formal distinctions of case, traditionally marked as nominative, accusative, genitive and dative, prototypically used for marking subject, object, possessive and adverbial functions respectively. There were also inflectional distinctions reflecting gender-assignation, since Old English distinguished 'grammatical gender': thus *se stān* ('the stone') (masculine), *sēo giefu* ('the gift') (feminine), *þæt wīf* ('the woman') (neuter). There were also distinct sets of markers for number (singular, plural), for example *stān* ('stone'), *stānas* ('stones').

These distinctions broke down during the transition from Old to Middle English. The masculine/feminine/neuter 'grammatical' gender system disappeared; although inflectional distinctions remained in the personal pronouns of Middle English, these were assigned according to 'natural' gender. This pattern was already becoming established in late Old English, where (for example) *wīf* ('woman'), a neuter noun, was occasionally referred to by the pronoun *hēo* ('she') beside 'grammatical' *hit* ('it'). The distinctive case-forms largely disappeared, leaving only inflectional markers of plurality and possession. Modifiers generally ceased to be marked for agreement with their nouns, so that, for instance, *the* appeared in place of the many forms available in Old English. However, a distinction between *this/that – these/those* was sustained, albeit with a wide range of variation in the forms used for these words.

In Old English there were two distinct adjectival paradigms depending on whether or not the adjective was preceded by, in particular, the equivalent of 'the', 'these, 'those' – thus *se gōda wer, þone gōdan wer* ('the good man') (where the adjective is 'weak' because it comes after forms for the word for 'the'); but *gōde weras* (where the adjective is not preceded by a form for 'the' and is therefore 'strong'). Some dialects of Middle English retained vestiges of this old adjectival weak/strong distinction, but indicated it exclusively by the absence or presence of the ending *-e*; compare the Chaucerian distinction in the singular adjective between *the olde man* (weak) and *the man is old* (strong).

Old English, like Present-Day English, distinguished strong, weak and irregular paradigms of the verb, each group characterized by distinct methods of forming its past tense, for example *sing/sang* (strong verb), *love/loved* (weak verb), *is/was* (irregular verb); compare Old English *singan/sang, sungon* or *sungen* (past tense 'indicative' singular, indicative plural and 'subjunctive' plural respectively: see further below), *lufian/lufode, lufodon* or *lufoden*, and *beon/wæs, wǣron* or *wǣren*. During the transition from Old to Middle English, however, the range of different verb inflections was much reduced; the operation of analogy also meant various reassignments and removal of forms perceived as irregular.

Complex Verb Phrases arose in place of some Old English simple verbal forms, often to express distinctions that had been lost through the obscuration of inflectional endings. Thus Old English distinguished between (for example) *bundon* ('(we/you/they) bound') (past plural indicative), and *bunden* ('(we/you/they) may have bound') (past plural subjunctive); the obscuration of the inflectional distinction between *-on* and *-en* led to the replacement of the subjunctive verbal ending by complex verb phrases with *may* and *might* (which come from Old English *mæg, mihte* ('can, could')). *Shall* and *will* were increasingly used as auxiliary verbs indicating future time rather than as lexical verbs signalling obligation and volition respectively (as was the case in Old English). Other characteristic Middle English innovations in the Verb Phrase included the development of phrasal verbs such as *put up* and *stand by*; such verbs are still common in Present-Day English, especially in informal usage.

Phrasal verbs were also a characteristic feature of Old Norse, and it is usual to see their appearance in Middle English as related to Norse usage. Morphological innovation seems to have been most advanced in Northern varieties of English, and may first be detected in Old English texts in Northern dialects (for instance the tenth-century Lindisfarne Gospels Gloss); this would suggest that Norse had a role in the development. It seems likely that Norse encouraged inflectional obscuration that was already under way in Old English.

Inflectional obscuration and loss had implications for what is the major development in English grammar during the transition from Old to Middle English: the appearance of comparatively fixed word order, as in present-day usage. To compensate for the loss of case distinctions, the Subject–Verb ordering of Old English, which was prototypical for main clauses, was extended to all clauses (in subordinate clauses in Old English it was usual for the main verb to be left until the end of the clause). At the same time prepositional use was extended, and – as we have already seen – there emerged pronominal paradigms with more distinctive forms than were found in Old English, as pronouns became more grammatically important. The process seems to have been complementary, that is, inflectional obscuration and a more fixed element order encouraged each other. This change, traditionally referred to as the 'synthetic-analytic' shift, is a good demonstration of the way in which language change works across a system, with interconnectedness between its constituent parts; as was commonly asserted by the structuralist linguists of the early twentieth century, 'tout se tient' ('everything is connected to everything else').

Forms (3): Writing- and Sound-Systems

Classical and medieval grammarians were well aware of problems to do with relating speech to writing, and developed theoretical frameworks to describe them. Thus in the early centuries of the Christian era the ancient 'doctrine of *littera*' was developed to correlate speech with alphabetic writing-systems of the kind used for Greek or Latin. Writers such as Donatus (in his *Ars grammatica*, of the fourth century AD) and Priscian (in his *Institutiones grammaticae, c.* AD 500) distinguished the following categories: *nomen* ('the name (of the letter)'), *potestas* ('sound-value'), and *figura* ('written symbol'), with the term *littera* ('letter') denoting any unit of speech.

However, although there is a connection between them, writing and speech are also distinct modes of transmission, and it is now a commonplace of linguistic enquiry that writing and speech deserve studying in their own right. In discussing these modes, modern linguists generally distinguish the following categories:

phoneme: defined either as the smallest speech-unit that distinguishes one word from another in terms of meaning, or as the prototypical sound being aimed at by speakers within a speech community. Replacement of one phoneme by another changes the meaning of the word in which it occurs. It is conventional to place phonemes in slash brackets, thus: /../. Linguists also make use of the term *allophone*: the realization of the phoneme in speech. Replacement of one allophone with another realization of the same phoneme does not change the meaning of the word in which it occurs. It is conventional to place allophones in square brackets, thus [..].

grapheme: the written language equivalent of the phoneme, that is, the alphabetic unit being aimed at by the scribe. Replacement of one grapheme by another changes the meaning of the word in which it occurs. It is conventional to place graphemes in angle brackets, thus: <..>. Linguists also use the term *allograph*: the realization of the grapheme in writing. Replacement of one allograph by another realization of the same grapheme does not change the meaning of the word.

The terms *phoneme* and *grapheme* will be adopted in the rest of this chapter.

The period from the Norman Conquest to the arrival of printing in Britain is particularly interesting for students of the speech–writing relationship. Since – unlike Latin or French – written English for much of the medieval period served only local purposes, there was no need for a spelling-system that was common to different areas. Spelling-systems that offered a fairly close grapheme–phoneme mapping arose; these eased the teaching of reading and writing by the 'phonic' method, which seems to have been usual in medieval times, as witnessed by the 'abecedaries' or primers that were in use by the fourteenth century.

As a response to this functional situation, spelling-systems evolved that reflected the wide range of phonological systems that existed in England during the medieval period. Some systems seem to modern eyes baroquely exotic, but they made sense in their own terms. Perhaps the best-known of such systems is that developed by Orm in the late twelfth century for his collection of metrical homilies, the *Ormulum*:

> Þiss boc iss nemmnedd Orrmulum
> forrþi þatt Orrm itt wrohhte.

[This book is named Ormulum / because Orm created it.]

Doubled consonants are used here to indicate which vowels should be pronounced 'short'. The evidence is that Orm is simply an egregious example amongst many less ambitious contemporary modifiers of writing systems inherited from Old English and subsequently modified in the Middle English period to reflect Latin or French orthographic practice: a point returned to below.

The outcome of this process was that the most important survey of Middle English linguistic usage that has yet been published, the *Linguistic Atlas of Late Mediaeval English* (1986), records no fewer than 500 ways of spelling – for example – the word 'through' during the period 1350–1450. These include *throgh, thorw, þorow, thurhgh, yruȝ, dorwgh, yora, trowffe, ȝurch, trghug*.

Written Middle English reflected linguistic variation in the spoken language; it also reflected linguistic change. In Present-Day English there is a temporal lag between changes in the spoken mode and developments in the writing-system, and there are many features of Present-Day English spelling (for example <ea>–<ee> distinctions, or the retention of 'silent' <gh>) that are fossil representations of spoken distinctions that disappeared in most varieties of English several centuries ago. But in Middle English, writing-systems were modified to reflect change in speech: thus in texts from south of the River Humber, Old English <ā> appears as <o> or <oo>, reflecting the raising and rounding of the vowel in pronunciation (compare, for instance, Old English *hām* with Middle English *hom* or *hoom*). The fact that for most of the period Middle English was not a language of record may also have contributed to the readiness with which it reflected change in the spoken medium. Since it was not used to communicate material that might be consulted in the future, its orthography was not required to become fixed, in a way that would make it as accessible to readers to come as it was to those living in the present.

Dialect Issues

In Barbara Strang's phrase, Middle English is *'par excellence*, the dialectal phase of English, in the sense that while dialects have been spoken at all periods, it was in [Middle English] that divergent local usage was normally indicated in writing' (Strang 1970: 224). In other words, dialect differences in all levels of language are manifested in Middle English texts. To illustrate these differences, two versions of a single text, the anonymous *Cursor Mundi* ('Cursor of the World'), composed in the early fourteenth century, will be examined.

Cursor Mundi survives in nine fourteenth-century versions, some being full copies of the text while others are fragments. The poem seems to have circulated widely during the later medieval period, and texts were modified freely to accommodate their language to their copyists' dialects. Passages from two versions are presented here:

(1) London, British Library, MS Cotton Vespasian A.iii (= C), written in a Northern English dialect (the West Riding of Yorkshire) in the early fourteenth century;
(2) Cambridge, Trinity College, MS R.3.8 (= T), written in a Midland English dialect (Staffordshire) in the late fourteenth century.

> C: *The Cursor o the world*
> Man yhernes rimes for to here,
> And romans red on maneres sere,
> Of Alisaunder þe conquerour;
> Of Iuly Cesar þe emparour;
> O grece and troy the strang strijf,   5
> Þere many thosand lesis þer lijf;
> O brut þat bern bald of hand,

Þe first conquerour of Ingland;
O kyng arthour þat was so rike,
Quam non in hys tim was like,   10
O ferlys þat hys knythes fell,
Þat aunters sere I here of tell,
Als wawan, cai and oþer stable,
For to were þe ronde tabell;
How charles kyng and rauland faght,   15
Wit sarazins wald þai na saght;
[Of] tristrem and hys leif ysote,
How he for here becom a sote,
Of Ioneck and of ysambrase,
O ydoine and of amadase   20
Storis als o [s]erekin thinges
O princes, prelates and o kynges;
Sanges sere of selcuth rime,
Inglis, frankys, and latine,
To rede and here ilkon is prest,   25
Þe thynges þat þam likes best.

[One likes to hear rhymes and romances read in various ways – of Alexander the conqueror, of Julius Caesar the emperor; the fierce war of Greece and Troy, where many thousands lose [*sic*] their lives; of Brutus, that warrior bold of hand, the first conqueror of England; of King Arthur who was so powerful, whom none in his time was like, of marvels that happened to his knights, whose many adventures to defend the Round Table I hear tell of, such as Gawain, Kay and other sturdy knights; how King Charles and Roland fought – they wanted no peace with the Saracens; of Tristram and his beloved Isolde, how he became a fool because of her; of Yonec and of Ysumbras, of Ydoine and of Amadas; stories also of various things – of princes, prelates and of kings; various songs of different rhyme, English, French and Latin. Each one is eager to read and hear the things that best please them [*sic*].]

T: *Here bigynneþ þe boke of storyes þat men callen cursor mundi*
Men ȝernen iestes for to here
And romaunce rede in dyuerse manere
Of Alisaundre þe conqueroure
Of Iulius cesar þe emperoure
Of greke & troye þe longe strif   5
Þere mony mon lost his lif
Of bruyt þat baron bolde of honde
Furste conqueroure of engelonde
Of kyng Arthour þat was so riche
Was noon in his tyme him liche   10
Of wondris þat his knyȝtes felle

And auntres duden men herde telle
As wawayn kay & oþere ful abul
For to kepe þe rounde tabul
How kyng charles & rouland fauȝt   15
Wiþ Sarazines nole þei [neuer be] sauȝt   they will never be
                                     reconciled

Of tristram & of Isoude þe swete
How þei with loue firste gan mete
Of kyng Ion and of Isombras
Of Idoyne and of amadas   20
Storyes of dyuerse þinges
Of princes prelatis & of kynges
Mony songes of dyuerse ryme
As englisshe frensshe & latyne
To rede & here mony are prest   25
Of þinges þat hem likeþ best.
              (ed. Morris 1874–93: 1–2, with modifications)

MS C has a number of features that characterize it as Northern. Late Old English *ā* appears as <a> in *strang* ('strong') (line 5), *bald* ('bold') (7); the weak adjective ending *-e*, which was lost early in Northern English, has disappeared in *the strang strijf* ('the fierce war') (5), even though the stress-pattern of the verse indicates that it probably appeared in the authorial original; the present plural inflection of the verb is *-is* in *lesis* ('lose') (6); the pronouns *þer, þam* ('their', 'them') appear in 6, 26; and *sere* ('various') (12, 23) is a Norse loanword that seems to have had only a Northern currency.

By contrast, MS T displays features typical of a Midland dialect. Old English *ā* appears as <o> or <oo> in, for example, *longe* (5), *bolde* (7), *noon* ('none') (10). There is some evidence of the retention of the weak adjective ending, as in *þe longe strif* (5); the present plural inflection of the verb is the Midland *-en* in *callen* ('call') (in the rubric), *ȝernen* ('desire') (1). In line 26, *hem* appears for 'them', and *mony* appears in place of C's *sere*. Many other differences could be adduced. Such dialectal differences are commonly attested in Middle English texts, and were drawn upon for the *Linguistic Atlas of Late Mediaeval English*.

Literary authors of the Middle English period were well aware of dialectal differences. The best-known demonstration of this awareness is probably in Chaucer's *Reeve's Tale*, where a subtle interplay is offered between the Northernism of the young students, the Norfolk usage of the narrator and the London usage in which the bulk of the text was written (for a useful discussion, see Machan 2003: 116–30).

Other writers could exploit the local resources of their language for literary effect, and a good demonstration may be found in a Cheshire text of the late fourteenth century, the poem *Pearl*, which survives alongside other texts in London, British Library, MS Cotton Nero A.x. *Pearl* is a religious dream vision in which, as Catherine Sanok's essay has described, a grieving dreamer receives spiritual comfort through interaction with the Pearl-maiden, who seems to be his dead daughter transmuted into one of the Blessed Virgins of the biblical Book of Revelation. Her role is to adore the Lamb of God, whom the dreamer is allowed to glimpse towards the end of the poem.

At one point in the poem, the following lines appear:

> Of sunne ne mone had þay no need;
> Þe self God watʒ her lombe-lyʒt,
> Þe Lombe her lantyrne, wythouten drede.
> (ed. Andrew and Waldron 2002: lines 1045–7)

[They had no need of sun or moon; God himself was their lamp-light, the Lamb their lantern, without fear.]

Many editors of the text have modified *lombe-lyʒt* ('lamp-light') to *lompe-lyʒt*, which is obviously more recognizable for a modern reader, but in dialectal terms this emendation is unnecessary. The <b> in *lombe-* seems to be a 'reverse' spelling, sometimes used in this dialect for the pronunciation [p] as well as [b] (see Gordon, ed., 1953: 93). The context indicates that the author – whose interest in word-play is attested in numerous places throughout his text – is fully aware of the ambiguities of the word. The form *lombe-lyʒt*, fairly obviously, links with the metaphor in the following line, *þe Lombe her lantyrne*, and thus the modification of the form by editors ignores a subtlety whereby the author was exploiting dialectal resources for literary effect.

Function and Form within the Middle English Period

During the latter half of the late-medieval period, the functions of English changed. A harbinger was the appearance of an exceptional thirteenth-century example of a document in English, a version of Henry III's famous 1258 *Proclamation* to his rebellious barons; this, however, seems to have been a special production for special circumstances. As

Tim Machan has pointed out, 'the original document was quite clearly composed in French, the language typically used for note-taking, political resolutions, and drafts of public documents' (Machan 2003: 58), and the appearance of an English version is usually interpreted as a response to a rebel demand for the 'ethnic cleansing' of anyone who – like the king – could not speak English. English was first used in speech in Parliament in 1362, and only began to be used fairly regularly in public documents from the end of the fourteenth century, as in, for example, the *Appeal* of Chaucer's contemporary Thomas Usk (in which Usk accuses the former mayor of London John of Northampton of various illicit dealings) and *The Petition of the Folk of Mercerye* (which expresses the grievances of the London Mercers' guild at the mayoralty of Nicholas Exton). From the second decade of the fifteenth century English starts to be employed regularly in government documents.

The development of a documentary function for English was accompanied by the appearance of major literary texts in English. Substantial works such as the *Cursor Mundi* were followed by the emergence of major literary writers in English in the later 1300s: Chaucer, Gower, Langland, the *Gawain*-poet. It is no coincidence that scribes were active in producing both public documents and literary manuscripts, as Alexandra Gillespie's essay has explored: the recent discovery that the scribe of the Hengwrt and Ellesmere manuscripts of Chaucer's *Canterbury Tales* – now identified by Linne Mooney as Adam Pinkhurst, the Adam of Chaucer's 'Wordes unto Adam, His Owne Scriveyn' – also wrote out *The Petition of the Folk of Mercerye* is highly significant.

These changes in the functions of English link with developments in its form. Towards the end of the medieval period, when English came to be used in writing that was addressed to a wider readership than it had addressed previously, the written variation of the earlier Middle English period became inconvenient, and a communicatively driven process of dialectal muting began to reduce the range of written variation that had existed hitherto. Written Standard Modern English emerged slowly and uncertainly, based on many of the usages current in late-medieval and Tudor London, as printed versions of (in particular) the Bible gave educated people models for their own usage. The spoken language sustained its diversity, but the reflection of this diversity in a more permanent form had to wait for the dialect surveys of the nineteenth and twentieth centuries, and the rise of electronic recording techniques.

Jeremy J. Smith

References

Primary texts

Andrew, Malcolm and Waldron, Ronald, eds. (2002). *The Poems of the Pearl Manuscript: Pearl, Cleanness, Patience, Sir Gawain and the Green Knight.* 4th edn. Exeter: University of Exeter Press.

Burrow, J.A., and Turville-Petre, Thorlac, eds. (2005). *A Book of Middle English.* 3rd edn. Oxford: Blackwell.

Chambers, R.W., and Daunt, Marjorie, eds. (1931). *A Book of London English 1384–1425.* Oxford: Clarendon Press.

Gordon, E.V., ed. (1953). *Pearl.* Oxford: Clarendon Press.

Morris, Richard, ed. (1874–93). *Cursor Mundi.* EETS OS 57, 59, 62, 66, 68, 99, 101. London: N. Trübner & Co.

Secondary sources and suggestions for further reading

Barber, C.L. (1993). *The English Language: A Historical Introduction.* Cambridge: Cambridge University Press.

Baugh, A.C. and Cable, T. (2002). *A History of the English Language.* 5th edn. London: Routledge.

Benskin, M. (2004). 'Chancery Standard'. In Christian J. Kay, Simon Horobin and Jeremy J. Smith, eds., *New Perspectives on English Historical Linguistics II: Lexis and Transmission* (pp. 1–40). Amsterdam: Benjamins.

Blake, Norman, ed. (1992). *The Cambridge History of the English Language Volume 2 (1066–1476).* Cambridge: Cambridge University Press.

Brünner, Karl (1970). *An Outline of Middle English Grammar* (Grahame Johnston, trans.). Oxford: Blackwell.

Burnley, J.D. (1983). *A Guide to Chaucer's Language.* Basingstoke: Macmillan.

Clanchy, M.T. (1993). *From Memory to Written Record: England 1066–1307.* 2nd edn. Oxford: Blackwell.

Franzen, Christine (1991). *The Tremulous Hand of Worcester.* Oxford: Clarendon Press.

Horobin, Simon and Smith, J.J. (2002). *An Introduction to Middle English.* Edinburgh: Edinburgh University Press.

Jones, Charles (1972). *An Introduction to Middle English.* New York: Holt, Rinehart and Winston.

Laing, Margaret, ed. (1989). *Middle English Dialectology: Essays on Some Principles and Problems.* Aberdeen: Aberdeen University Press.

Machan, Tim William (2003). *English in the Middle Ages.* Oxford: Oxford University Press.

McIntosh, A., Samuels, M.L. and Benskin, M., with M. Laing and K. Williamson (1986). *A Linguistic Atlas of Late Mediaeval English.* Aberdeen: Aberdeen University Press.

Mooney, Linne R. (2006). 'Chaucer's Scribe'. *Speculum*, 81, 97–138.

Mugglestone, Lynda (2006). *The Oxford History of English*. Oxford: Oxford University Press.

Samuels, M.L. (1963). 'Some Applications of Middle English Dialectology'. *English Studies*, 44, 81–94. (Reprd in Laing 1989).

Smith, J.J. (2005). *Essentials of Early English*. 2nd edn. London: Routledge.

Strang, B.M.H. (1970). *A History of English*. London: Methuen.

Wright, J. and Wright, E.M. (1928). *An Elementary Middle English Grammar*. London: Oxford University Press.

Chapter 8

Translation and Adaptation

Helen Cooper

During the Middle Ages, literature was routinely translated and adapted from one language into another, and the surviving corpus of Middle English texts reflects that process particularly clearly. As the previous chapter has discussed, after the Norman Conquest, English was relegated to the lowest status of the three languages of England, with French replacing it as the language of high culture, the aristocracy and government, and Latin extending its dominance both within the Church and as a language of record. The tradition of poetic composition in Old English, which had produced works of the stature of the secular epic *Beowulf* and the religious *Dream of the Rood*, was almost completely disrupted by the Norman colonization, and English literary writing had effectively to be reinvented. The most significant literature produced in post-Conquest England was at first composed in Anglo-Norman, the insular variant of continental French that diverged from its parent language ever further over the ensuing centuries. For much of the twelfth century Anglo-Norman texts were in the very forefront of vernacular composition in Western Europe, and constituted some of the earliest and the most famous works of 'French' literature. Anglo-Norman, however, increasingly became a language that had to be learned at every social level below the royal court; and the understanding of Latin remained almost entirely confined to male clerics, that small segment of the population who had a formal education. Translation was therefore an everyday practice in post-Conquest England, but its process was almost always 'downwards' through the linguistic hierarchy, from the most authoritative language (Latin itself) into the courtly vernacular of Anglo-Norman, and from both of those into the various dialects of English, the language unmarked by education or hierarchy – the language of the marketplace, the provincial manor-house and the tavern. As this chapter will explore, the differences in culture and status between the three languages meant in turn that the processes of translation encouraged a degree of adaptation to match the interests and capacities of the various target audiences.

The ubiquity of literary translation in medieval England was further encouraged by the belief that there was no particular virtue in originality (compare Jane Griffiths' essay above). Many of the great narratives that feature in Middle English literature were already in existence: stories of biblical history and of the fall of Troy, of King Arthur and Charlemagne, not to mention saints' lives, local legends and folktales. The skill lay in recasting classical material to cater for contemporary interests, in upgrading popular material for audiences of high cultural sophistication (often including women), or in adapting French texts for a broader appeal among English-speaking audiences. Secular stories allowed an author the greatest degree of freedom, but religious material was generously capacious too: a saint could have his or her life written in twenty lines or several thousand, gaps in the biblical narrative (such as the childhood of Christ) could be filled in, and the major events of biblical history could be given dramatic form, as happened in the great Corpus Christi cycles of the later Middle Ages. 'Translation', by derivation, means 'carrying across'; and the carrying was done not only between different languages, but between different social levels and different genres. 'Interpretation', a word derived by Isidore of Seville from *inter partes*, between two parties, conveys the more active role that the translator often had, in explaining matters that words alone might leave obscure. The concept reflects the more generous recasting of a story or a text that was frequently undertaken (Copeland 1991: 89–90). Direct translation of the word-for-word variety (*verbum pro verbo* in the Latin phrase) was unusual unless the translation was intended as a crib, to provide access to an original, for instance in interlinear glossing (the insertion of meanings in the vernacular between the lines of a Latin text). The translation of discursive material more often aimed to offer an equivalence of sense (*sensus pro sensu*), which allowed for differences in idioms and expressions. Strict fidelity to the source text, however, was comparatively rare, and, outside the special case of the Bible (see below), comparatively little sought after. Since classical times, accurate translation had indeed been regarded as a process inferior to the art of creative adaptation (Copeland 1991; Kelly 1979; Morse 1991: 179–230). Middle English literature was largely grounded on the superior form of the art.

Medieval translation accordingly comes in a wide range of forms, from the most basic linguistic explanation to what is effectively a new text. A radically rewritten text may overtly recall its model (as Milton was later to base *Paradise Lost* on the Book of Genesis), or may leave it as no more than a level of allusion (a modern example would be the American makeover of Jane Austen's *Emma* in *Clueless*), though much of the point of such works lies in their recognizable relationship to their source texts. There is a point midway between such re-creations and literal translations where it becomes both impossible and pointless to try to distinguish translation from adaptation: the fourteenth-century English romance *Ywain and Gawain*, for instance, faithfully follows its source text, Chrétien de Troyes' *Yvain*, in terms of event and occasionally wording, but it also cuts back on some of the elaboration of the original in ways that emphasize what happens in the narrative rather than emotional analysis. In the Middle Ages, furthermore, adaptation could fulfil the function served by literary criticism in a more recent age, where, rather than the critic spelling out what he or she perceives to be a correct or interesting interpretation of a work, the adaptor rewrites the original so as to bring out such an interpretation, or indeed to substitute an alternative meaning (*sententia* in Latin, *sens* in French, *sentence* in Middle English) perceptible within the same narrative. This process can sometimes largely run in tandem with a sense-for-sense translation at the verbal level, but it depends on a generous alertness to how words carry meanings, and it can also serve to open up larger areas of meaning that the original text left obscure or even denied.

The Problems of Translation

Translation was never a straightforward business, for a whole array of reasons ranging from the practical and textual to the cultural and ideological, and the prefaces attached to a number of translations show that many of these problems were well recognized (Wogan-Browne et al. 1999). At the most basic level of the individual word, there were no bilingual dictionaries and few wordlists, so the meaning of a rare or unfamiliar word might have to be guessed; if an earlier commentator had supplied a definition or a discussion, that might well be incorporated into the translated text. In the early Middle Ages in particular, before the vocabulary of English had been enriched by the abundance of French borrowings that poured into it later, there might even be no equivalent native term for a word that a translator found in his source. As late as the 1380s, Chaucer felt obliged to gloss the new borrowing *autumpne* in his translation of Boethius' *De consolatione philosophiae* with 'that is to seie, in the laste ende of somer' (*Boece*, I. Metrum 5, lines 25–6). A source text, moreover, in a manuscript culture, was likely to have gone through a good many copyings and recopyings since it was first composed, with the possibility for error being introduced at every stage. Comparing a modern edited text of an original work with a medieval translation may thus give an underestimate of the translator's ability: he may have been doing a good job with a bad text rather than a bad job with a text of edited quality. For all kinds of reasons, therefore, it is rash to assume that a 'wrong' translation is necessarily the result of a writer's incompetence in the source language.

What looks like mistranslation may also in fact be intentional creativity in getting around a problem. Robert Mannyng, for instance, found himself faced with the term 'manuel' in the title of the Anglo-Norman *Manuel des péchés* that he was translating at a date (1303) before the borrowing of 'manual' into English had taken place or 'handbook' had entered the language as a general term. He therefore makes a virtue of necessity in announcing and justifying his own title, *Handlyng Synne*:

> Men clepyn þe boke handlynge synne.   call
> Yn frenshe þer a clerk hyt sees,
> He clepyþ it manuel de pecchees.
> Manuel ys handlyng wyþ honde,
> Pecchees ys synne to vndyrstonde . . .
> And weyl ys clepyd for þys skyle . . .   reason
> We handyl synne euery day
> Yn wrde & dede al þat we may.   word
>   (ed. Sullens 1983: lines 80–4, 87, 89–90)

And he proceeds to develop the idea for a further fifty-five lines, with the same ingenuity that he shows in choosing the title in the first place. The incompatibility of languages provides Mannyng with a useful opportunity to insert a little moral homily that encapsulates the subject matter of the whole treatise.

The business of translation was affected by further constraints and considerations beyond the linguistic. The process of 'carrying across' from the capacities of one set of readers (who might be Latin-literate, francophone, educated) to another (lay, English-speaking only, perhaps female), for example, required a degree of interpretation as well as verbal translation. Early patronage of translation in England generally stemmed from the wealthiest individuals, the aristocracy, who wanted Latin texts in their own Anglo-Norman. This is the case with the first known post-Conquest translation into one of the vernaculars of England, *The Voyage of Saint Brendan* composed by one Benedeit around 1120 for the first or second wife of Henry I (according to which manuscript one believes). The work is based on the Latin prose *Navigatio Sancti Brendani*, but the translation is into octosyllabics, a form increasingly associated with narrative of the more fictional varieties, and Benedeit nudges the pious tenor of the original into something a bit more like science fiction. Brendan's voyage from Ireland to see God's wonders in the deep (which was probably historical in origin, and which may have taken him to North America) has the potential to emphasize either God or the wonders more, and the clerical Latin and lay Anglo-Norman texts make opposite choices (see O'Donoghue 1994). Translation into Middle English got under way only at the end of the twelfth century, and was more frequently motivated by piety than the possibility of reward. One of the very earliest such works was the *Ormulum*, so called after its author, who names himself as Orm: this blockbuster paraphrase of the readings from the Gospels that accompanied the Mass over the year, written so that English 'folc' can follow the readings in thought, word and deed, incorporates a good deal of commentary so that its audience's understanding is guided in ways not allowed for in the original biblical text (ed. Holt and White 1878: see especially lines 13–34).

The Bible and Devotional Translation

Biblical translation presented particular problems, though those were more often doctrinal than linguistic. Paraphrases of biblical material were common in both Anglo-Norman and Middle English, as they had been in Old English; a work such as the *Cursor Mundi* (early fourteenth century: compare Jeremy Smith's chapter above) consists of a massive compendium of biblical history with a good deal of interspersed apocryphal material, such as the legends surrounding the provenance of the Cross. The text of the Latin Bible itself, however, was taken as the Word of God; translation therefore demanded accuracy as an act of faith, and in addition, the Church tried to maintain a tight monopoly on how the text should be interpreted. Although a French version of the Bible was widely known and not regarded as threatening, opening access to the text to lay people by translating it into English was potentially more dangerous, and translations were therefore typically accompanied by commentaries to ensure correct interpretation. The Psalter was on several occasions the basis of a translation, since its recitation was a central part of the liturgical cycle; in the 1340s the Yorkshire hermit and mystical writer Richard Rolle produced a word-for-word translation, 'swa that thai that knawes noght Latyn by the Ynglis may com til mony Latyn wordis' (Wogan-Browne et al. 1999: 246, lines 63–4). To accompany it, Rolle also wrote an expanded paraphrase that incorporates the commentary of the twelfth-century theologian Peter Lombard. The fifteenth-century gentlewoman Dame Eleanor Hull likewise incorporated a commentary into her translation, derived from a French intermediary, of the Penitential Psalms (ed. Barratt 1995).

The whole issue became especially contentious when the first attempt to make a complete English translation of the Bible was undertaken in the 1380s by the followers of the Oxford theologian John Wyclif as part of a religious reform movement fiercely suppressed by the orthodox Church as heretical. The aim of the Wycliffite translators was to produce a text equivalent to the Latin Vulgate for those who understood only English. The first attempt showed its anxiety to preserve the Word of God by an extreme literalism, not least in word order; a revision had to be undertaken very soon afterwards to make it more comprehensible. The Latin 'Num quem diligit anima mea, vidistis?' for instance, from the Song of Songs 3:3, was altered from the baffling 'Whether whom looueth my soule, ʒe seʒen?' to 'Whether ʒe sien hym, whom my soule loueth?' (ed. Forshall and Madden 1850: Vol. III, 76; the seventeenth-century Authorized Version of the Bible offers 'Saw ye him whom my soul loveth?'). The later version was given a preface in which the reviser justifies the anglicization of the Latin syntax and word order (ed. Forshall and Madden 1850: Vol. III, 57; Hudson 1978: 67–72). The overt eroticism and dialogue form of the Song of Songs presented additional problems that the two translators attempted to solve in very different ways, and in this case the reviser was the less idiomatic. The earlier translator added indications as to who was speaking – 'The vois of the Chirche' or 'of Crist' – but those amounted to an interpolation in the text of the kind that the whole Wycliffite programme opposed. The reviser tried to incorporate equivalent information into his translation by adding the French feminine ending *-esse* to his ungendered English vocabulary in an attempt to reproduce the gender indicators of the Latin, with results that can make his version much stranger than the earlier one. The Latin *amica*, '(female) friend' – 'beloved' in the Authorized Version – is rendered in the first version of the Wycliffite Bible into the close synonym *leef*, 'dear', but in the revised translation into something scarcely English at all:

> Surge, propera, amica mea, columba mea, formosa mea, et veni. Iam enim hiems transiit, imber abiit et recessit.
>
> (Song of Songs 2:10–11)

> (first Wycliffite translation) Ris, go thou, my leef, my culuer [dove], my shapli, and cum; now forsothe winter passede, weder ʒide fro, and is gon awei.

> (revised translation) My frendesse, my culuer, my faire spousesse, rise thou, haaste thou, and come thou; for wyntir is passid now, reyn is goon, and is departyd awei.
>
> (ed. Forshall and Madden 1850: Vol. III, 75)

And here, for comparison, is Chaucer's rendering of the passage:

> Rys up, my wyf, my love, my lady free!
> my dowve sweete,
> The wynter is goon with alle his reynes weete.
> (*The Canterbury Tales*, IV.2138–40)

There is a strong case for arguing that this is the best 'translation'; but its context decisively removes it from any fidelity to the original text, since the lines form part of the elderly January's seduction speech to his young and unimpressed wife May in *The Merchant's Tale*. The allusion is heavily ironic, but as with all irony, it relies on the reader picking up what the text leaves unspoken. It relies, in fact, on the Song of Songs being recognized in English even when its first full translation from Latin was scarcely completed.

The fierce suppression of the Wycliffite movement brought almost any English devotional writing under suspicion in the fifteenth century (Watson 1995), but works setting out the basics of orthodox faith, saints' lives (which were disapproved of by the Wycliffites) and continental works of recognized orthodoxy continued to be translated. The fifteenth century has some claim to be the golden age for English saints' lives of all lengths, in both prose and verse; the life of St Katherine by the Augustinian friar John Capgrave, for instance, runs to over 8,000 lines. Lay devotion was also encouraged through a carefully managed selection and presentation of orthodox texts. One work that managed to obtain approval from the heretic-hunting Archbishop of Canterbury Thomas Arundel, and consequent wide dissemination – it survives in some seventy manuscripts and early prints – was Nicholas Love's *Mirror of the Blessed Life of Jesus Christ* (ed. Sargent 2004), a translation of the *Meditationes vitae Christi* ascribed, wrongly, to St Bonaventure. Perhaps because of that anxiety over heresy, perhaps because of the status of his source, Love is much more meticulous than most translators about marking those points where he elaborates on his original, indicating the beginning of his own interpolations with an 'N', and inserting a 'B' where he reverts to (Pseudo-)Bonaventure's text. It was certainly anxiety that impelled a similar pattern of initialled interventions in another devotional translation, *The Mirror of Simple Souls*, from the French of Marguerite Porete, a mystic who had been burned for heresy around 1310. Here the interventions are made not humbly, to avoid confusion with an authoritative source, but with authority, to keep the reader's comprehension within safe bounds of orthodoxy. A second translation of the work was made into Latin: an unusual move, but it had the desired effect of putting the text out of reach of the uneducated altogether. The fervid adoration of the Godhead expressed in the text was never, however, likely to achieve the popularity of Love's treatise; and even that was easily surpassed in the ownership stakes by the Wycliffite translations of the Bible, which, as Alexandra Gillespie's chapter has pointed out, survive in whole or in part in some 250 manuscripts despite all the official attempts to suppress them.

Secular Adaptation

The Bible in Latin was an esoteric text, sealed from the common people; the same text in English was dangerous because accessible. A comparable phenomenon of a text shifting in significance as it shifted language operates in secular literature too, though without the element of danger. Works tended to become less abstruse as they moved down the hierarchy of languages, or at least to encode a different kind of appeal. Nowhere is this clearer than in the Middle English translations of French and Anglo-Norman romances, which began to appear in the late thirteenth century. Several translators noted that whilst the nobility or gentry might be able to speak French, everyone in England could speak English; and one result of this democratization was that, although almost all the French and Anglo-Norman romances in circulation in England are courtly in ideology and often in origin too, the term can be applied to very few romances in English. Even those English romances that are close adaptations of French originals tend to be more down to earth, more action based, removed from the more self-indulgent or fantasy elements of the courtly ethos: they are 'popular' not merely because of their choice of the language that was accessible to most. Adaptations such as *Ywain and Gawain* and *Sir Tristrem*, the latter taken from the Anglo-Norman of Thomas, are both shorter and sparer than their originals, and imply rather than spell out their emotional interest. It is something of a paradox that the Middle English romance that we would perhaps be most likely to describe as courtly, *Sir Gawain and the Green Knight*, has no direct French source at all; it is, furthermore, written in the distinctly uncourtly form of alliterative verse, and in a provincial dialect that would have been difficult for contemporaries from London and the south to comprehend. It operates within the broader context of its writer's, and presumably its audience's, familiarity with French romance (Putter 1995), and succeeds brilliantly at translating, 'carrying across', that culture into English modes; but in this most courtly of Middle English romances, linguistic translation is not involved.

Secular romance rarely felt under any obligation to cite its authority, to name its source, and its adaptors took much greater liberties with their source texts than translators of devotional works. Across all languages, however, some authors of fiction muddy the waters by claiming to have a written source when they are in fact inventing, and especially so if, like Geoffrey of Monmouth in his Latin *Historia regum Britanniae* ('History of the Kings of Britain'), completed *c.* 1138, they claim to be writing history rather than fiction. Geoffrey's work not only presents itself as recounting historical facts, but declares that those facts came from a book given to him by Archdeacon Walter of Oxford – a book for which there is no independent evidence and little plausibility. Both Wace, who produced a French version of Geoffrey's work for the Angevin court around 1155, and Laȝamon, who in turn adapted Wace into Middle English some fifty years later (both works carrying the title *Brut*, after Brutus, legendary founder of Britain: see also Andrew Galloway's essay in this volume), emphasize their use of written originals to add authority to their versions of the past, but Wace is, of course, no more reliable than Geoffrey, or Laȝamon than either. Writers whose work makes no such claim to fact sometimes still assert that their stories come from written sources. Chrétien de Troyes claimed to have such a source for his story of the Grail, as did the Anglo-Norman Hue de Rotelande for his *Ipomedon* (*c.* 1190), but there is not the slightest evidence that they did, and in Hue's case precious little evidence that he expected anyone to believe him. The fourteenth-century Middle English redactor of *Sir Percyvell of Galles* (a version of the Grail story without the Grail, and indeed so freely adapted as effectively to be an original work) and Hue's various Middle English translators all ignored such statements. Of all the English romances drawn from French, only instances of the Breton *lai*, a kind of mini-romance, consistently acknowledge the existence of source material, and that is as much a generic ploy as a recognition of linguistic origins, since the whole genre is characterized by its consistent self-definition: a Breton *lai* is a poem that tells us it is a Breton *lai* (Laskaya and Salisbury, eds., 1995). The insistence of these texts on their derivation from traditional Breton material serves to assert the value of, and expectations arising from, those traditions: traditions that were probably oral in origin, as the poems assert, even though in practice most of the English *lais* are silently adapted from written French intermediaries.

Of all the secular romance adaptations, Sir Thomas Malory's *Morte Darthur*, completed in 1469 or 1470, is the greatest, and its relationship to its originals is much the most complex. It is often described as a translation of various thirteenth-century French Arthurian prose romances, notably parts of the *Lancelot-Grail* cycle and the *Tristan* (Dover 2003); and in one respect in particular, Malory's decision to write in prose rather than the verse that had been the norm for earlier English versions of *Lancelot-Grail* material, the *Morte* is one of the closest renderings of this material that we have. Although Malory will often translate, however, he also abbreviates, adapts, invents, goes in for some radical restructuring, and incorporates into his prose two late fourteenth-century English poems, *The Alliterative Morte Arthure* and *The Stanzaic Morte Arthur*. The work looks as if it is generous in acknowledging its origins, but in practice there is a subtle kind of falsification taking place. Malory's references to what 'the Freynshe booke sayth' are most often made for strategic reasons, not because they necessarily correspond with what is really in the French; and his English borrowings, which are just as close as the ones from the French, are made silently, presumably because such romances did not carry the cachet or the cultural weight of the more courtly language. Although he often follows his sources word for word so closely that there are places where it is possible to correct the surviving text by reference to them, the end result of the work is very different from its models. Much of the *Lancelot-Grail* is unashamed fantasy, though it reads the downfall of the Round Table as divine retribution for sexual sin: Arthur's incestuous begetting of Mordred, Lancelot and Guinevere's adultery. Malory models his own version much more on factual chronicle, with its locations being given a 'translation' into real place-names: Camelot itself, for example, is identified as Winchester. He further nudges his text, switches between sources, and occasionally feeds in invention of his own to produce a version where Arthur's death is a 'day of Desteny', and where Guinevere 'was a trew lover, and therefor she had a good ende' (ed. Vinaver 1990: 1237, 1120). His translation may thus look as if it should be categorized at the literal end of the spectrum of translation, yet he produces something radically different in its larger meaning.

The *Morte Darthur* itself marks the transition between high French Arthurian romance and the new age of prose fiction. William Caxton printed Malory's text as one among a substantial number of prose romances, most of which he translated himself from the corpus of such works that were all the fashion at the time at the Burgundian court in the Low Countries, and which he translated with a concern for faithfulness unusual in secular fiction. This accuracy may in part be a reflection of the fact that the texts were being 'carried across' at the same social level on each side of the Channel, as the rise of the wealthy and upwardly mobile urban classes and the increasing importance of money over land reduced the gap between royal and aristocratic society and the lower echelons: there was no longer any need for cultural interpretation between a courtly francophone readership and a potentially more popular English one.

English as a language was coming up in the world by the end of the Middle Ages. That rise in status was measured not only by the extension of the use of English into all aspects of political and governmental life, but by the increasing frequency with which works of Latin antiquity were translated directly into English. The 'romances of antiquity' of the twelfth century had been adapted from Latin into French for cultured audiences on both sides of the English Channel; now, the cultured audiences in England spoke English. Although there was no sustained effort of translation of the Latin classics until the sixteenth century, Chaucer and Gower both produced versions of stories from Ovid and other of the major classical authors, and Chaucer's career is indeed marked by a continuous engagement with both Ovid and Virgil. Throughout the fifteenth century, however, English readers who thought they were reading translations of the classics might well in practice be reading versions of free French adaptations. Caxton's *Eneydos* (1490) was based on a creative French adaptation of Virgil, and drew down on itself the scorn of the Scottish poet Gavin Douglas when he made the first full translation of Virgil's own text into any form of English early in the sixteenth century. Similarly, Caxton's *Recuyell of the Historyes of Troye* (1473–4), which became the standard popular account of the Troy story for the next two hundred years, was a translation of a recent French prose work by the Burgundian Raoul le Fèvre, whose own sources were likewise medieval rather than classical. The classical authors most likely to be translated before the sixteenth century were from the late end of the classical period, from either side of AD 400. The first, both in importance and in the date when he was translated, was Boethius, whose *De consolatione philosophiae* had the rare honour of being turned into both Old and Middle English, by King Alfred, Chaucer, and the early fifteenth-century writer John Walton; a later royal translator was Elizabeth I. *Apollonius of Tyre*, a Latin romance of obscure (but possibly Greek) origin, also appeared in both Old and Middle English; its many adaptors included Gower in the fourteenth century (within the *Confessio Amantis*) and Shakespeare in the early seventeenth (in *Pericles*). The structure of meticulous argument in Boethius' *Consolation* elicited a corresponding carefulness from its translators; the anonymous *Apollonius* tended to be treated more like a fairy-story, with a faithful replication of the plot rather than the words (those words included the *gymnasium* where Apollonius exercises; the word baffled later writers, who substituted ball games, sword-and-buckler fights, and, in Shakespeare's case, a tournament: see Archibald 1991). Other translations were more immediately practical: the treatise on the art of war by the Latin writer Vegetius was translated for Thomas, Lord Berkeley, in 1408 (an earlier Anglo-Norman translation had been made for the young Edward I or II), and Palladius' Latin treatise on agriculture was translated for Humphrey, Duke of Gloucester, before 1447 (Hanna 1989). A further late-classical work, Claudian's eulogy on a Roman consul, was repackaged as a tribute to Richard, Duke of York, in 1445 (Edwards 2001). This last text is especially interesting, in that the translation appears to be the first attempt to write an English equivalent of Latin hexameters, and the sole manuscript lays out the original and the translation as parallel texts, on facing pages – a format that represents a move towards translation practices that are familiar to us. By the end of the fifteenth century, translation was taking the first steps towards a recognizable English humanism.

The 'Great Translator' Geoffrey Chaucer

All the examples cited so far are picked out from the hundreds of translated and adapted texts that make up a high proportion of Middle English literature. In an attempt to bring the topic and its complexities into a single focus, the rest of this chapter will concentrate on a single author: Geoffrey Chaucer, famously described by the contemporary French poet Eustache Deschamps as 'grant translateur' (ed. Brewer 1978: 39–41). Chaucer's works illustrate almost every point on the spectrum of varieties of translation and adaptation. The works he promotes as most authoritative are translated closely from named originals and designed to offer an accessible version of those for people who cannot understand the source language; at the other extreme, the very un-authoritative *fabliaux*, the comic tales for which analogous stories are often known in French, Flemish and Italian, present themselves as effectively sourceless, and indeed often have such a loose connection to their possible originals that it may well not be certain what those were. His exceptional self-awareness about the processes of translation, expressed in all modes from commentary on his source texts to parody, makes all the issues involved in the process unusually visible.

These issues emerge even in Chaucer's translations that look most literal. Fragment A of *The Romaunt of the Rose*, which is probably his earliest work to survive, both declares its title ('It is the Romance of the Rose': line 39) and follows its original closely; he presumably made the translation because the French *Roman de la rose* itself was such a cult work that there was a demand to have it in English. What is surprising, indeed, is not that the translation was made, but that it did not gain wider currency – it survives in a single manuscript that was itself the source for an early print. The *Romaunt*'s tetrameter couplets generally reproduce the octosyllabics of the thirteenth-century French source as faithfully as the constraints of form and language will allow. Such constraints are significant, however: it may be possible to translate prose more or less faithfully, word for word or sense for sense, but the demands of rhyme and metre make verse altogether more difficult. As early as the *Ormulum*, Orm was noting anxiously that in order to keep his metrical units, his 'rime', he would have to adapt the Gospel original; and, in the *envoy* to his poem *The Complaint of Venus*, Chaucer becomes one of many poets who lament the shortage of rhyme words in English compared with the Romance languages. Those constraints still allow the translator plenty of room for manœuvre, however, and some of the choices made in the *Romaunt* translation show a process of poetic 'carrying across' in more than just the narrow sense of language. In particular, the phrasing sometimes moves away from the French to recall the alliterative formulae of Middle English lyric and romance: 'byrde in bour', 'rose in rys' (lines 1014–15).

Chaucer's translation of Boethius' *De consolatione philosophiae* demonstrates its concern for a vernacular readership in a different way, through its careful explanation of its source text by the incorporation of a number of glosses drawn partly from the Latin of one of Boethius' fourteenth-century explicators, Nicholas Trevet, and partly from the French translation made a century earlier by one of the authors of *Le Roman de la rose*, Jean de Meun, which Chaucer was using as a crib. Chaucer's concern with explication over formal equivalence is also evident from his decision to translate the alternating passages of prose and verse in Boethius' original entirely as prose. For equivalents of Boethius' poetry in Chaucer's œuvre, one has to look to his short poems *Gentilesse* and *The Former Age*, and to the passages incorporated into *Troilus and Criseyde*, in particular Troilus' great hymn to love that he sings when his relationship with Criseyde is at its height. In Chaucer's prose translation, part of this passage runs:

> That the see, gredy to flowen, constreyneth with a certein eende his floodes, so that it is nat leveful [permitted] to strecche his brode termes or bowndes uppon the erthes (*that is to seyn, to coveren al the erthe*) – al this accordaunce of thynges is bounde with love, that governeth erthe and see, and hath also comandement to the hevene. And yif this love slakede the bridelis, alle thynges that now loven hem togidres wolden make batayle contynuely, and stryven to fordo the fassoun [fabric] of this world, the which they now leden in accordable [harmonious] feith by fayre moevynges.
>
> (*Boece*, II.Metrum 8, lines 8–21)

The equivalent in *Troilus*, now transformed from a speech by Philosophy into the hymn of a joyful lover, adds the music of rhyme royal (it is one of Troilus' great arias that punctuate the narrative) even while Chaucer's tough engagement with the Englishing of the original still shows through:

> 'That, that the se, that gredy is to flowen,
> Constreyneth to a certeyn ende so
> His flodes that so fiersly they ne growen
> To drenchen erthe and al for evere mo;   drown
> And if that Love aught lete his bridel go,
> Al that now loveth asondre sholde lepe,
> And lost were al that Love halt now to-hepe.'   now holds together
>
> (*Troilus*, III.1758–64)

The stanza is still a faithful translation of the sense, and many in Chaucer's immediate original audience must have recognized it either from the Latin or from his own translation, even though the narrative requires that the source remain unidentified, that the verse should appear as a spontaneous outpouring. The new context, however, shifts the larger meaning away from natural philosophy towards emotional rapture. Readers divide as to whether they read the speech ironically, as a measure of how much Troilus is misunderstanding, or sympathetically, as a measure of how much the new experience of fulfilled love enables him to participate in Philosophy's own comprehension of the love that binds the universe.

The passage raises an unusual, and perhaps typically Chaucerian, problem. Even a translation that closely renders sense for sense can still change the meaning of the original, can offer the same verbal *sensus* but a different large *sententia*: a faithful translation of a whole work, or even of a few words (as happens in the case of the appearance of the Song of Songs in the middle of *The Merchant's Tale*, quoted above), can become radically unstable in its meaning as it shifts between contexts. The problem becomes acute in the case of the *Melibee*, the prose tale that Chaucer gives himself as pilgrim-narrator in *The Canterbury Tales* after his first effort, *Sir Thopas*, is cut short on the grounds of poetic incompetence. This is accurately Englished, without even the 'contamination' of commentary, from the fourteenth-century *Livre de Melibée et de Dame Prudence* of Renaud de Louens, itself a translation of a thirteenth-century Latin text by the jurist Albertanus of Brescia. The original is never identified, even though, like the *Roman de la rose*, though for rather different reasons, it had become something of a pan-European hit. It is tempting to assume that Chaucer is joking in giving himself such a heavily derivative tale to tell, given how creatively he adapts the sources of all the other pilgrims' tales, and given its twinning with *Sir Thopas*; but it is hard to justify not taking seriously a treatise on peace that was known and admired across Europe. One's interpretation may well vary, moreover, depending on how the work is encountered. The weighty ethics of its message suggest that Chaucer might initially have made the translation as a contribution to the contemporary political debate on the desirability of peace with France (see further Helen Barr's chapter); if so, its first audience would have understood it very differently from those who first encountered it in the context of the *Tales*. There, Chaucer precedes the work with a discussion of the problem of variant texts, but even that obscures more than it clarifies. He claims that the tale has been told 'in sondry wyse / Of sondry folk' (which is not for any practical purposes true), and compares the case of the Gospels, which record Christ's actions and words differently from each other and yet all truthfully, with a single 'sentence' (*CT*, VII.941–52). It is a defence that is beside the point as far as the tale that follows is concerned; yet it makes an accurate and theologically significant observation about the 'translation' of Christ's life into written form, an issue of no small import in the era of the Wycliffite controversy, and therefore potentially carrying a cultural weight much larger than the immediate context.

Homage and Challenge

The work where Chaucer's attitude to translation is at its most extended and most playful is his *Troilus and Criseyde*. He seems to have done his homework carefully on this, as the work shows signs of his reading in French and medieval Latin versions of the story, but the poem is in both outline and detail an adaptation of the *Filostrato* of his older Italian contemporary Boccaccio (edited in parallel with *Troilus* in Windeatt 1984). There is no firm evidence that Chaucer actually knew who had written this work, though Boccaccio was still alive when he made the diplomatic visits to Italy during which he presumably acquired his Italian manuscript, and it seems unlikely that he would have borrowed so much from the Italian poet without encountering his name (he also brought back a copy of Boccaccio's *Teseida*, the source of *The Knight's Tale*, and at least saw, if he did not himself own, *The Decameron*). Boccaccio, however, is never mentioned anywhere in Chaucer's works. Instead, Chaucer twice names an entirely fictional source for *Troilus*, 'Lollius', and makes frequent further references to him as his 'auctour', his authority for the story. It is conceivable that he thought that a classical author named Lollius had really existed, but he most certainly knew that his actual source was contemporary Italian. Throughout the poem, moreover, he is most likely to appeal to his source text when he is making things up: as with Malory's *Morte Darthur*, a source citation in this poem is a rhetorical strategy, not a footnote reference. When he does translate or make a close adaptation from any of his sources for the poem, which also include Boethius' *Consolation* and Dante's *Divine Comedy*, he does so silently. As Jane Griffiths has discussed in her essay, *Troilus* even contains the first translation of a Petrarch sonnet into English (the 'Canticus Troili' at I.400–20); but far from flagging the fact – it would, after all, be another century and a half before this would have served the purposes of advertisement, when Petrarch's poems to Laura had achieved iconic status – he ascribes that too to 'myn auctour called Lollius' (I.394).

The contrast between what Chaucer makes of the story of Troilus and what Boccaccio did with it has fuelled much of the criticism on the poem, but it is not an approach that was open to his original audience: none of his early readers is likely to have known the *Filostrato*, and so the shift of meaning between Chaucer's text and his original source was not visible to them. The issue of his treatment of his sources becomes especially pressing when the source in question carries significant authoritative weight. Chaucer could safely expect a high proportion of his readers to recognize biblical material, however he treats it; the most learned among them would also recognize his borrowings from Boethius, and he always treats those seriously. Even when Troilus gets Philosophy's arguments about free will wrong, they remain serious arguments, as their length indicates: see *Troilus* IV.960–1078. On the other hand, Dante elicited much more complex reactions from him, which were probably invisible to all his readers: he may well have been the only Englishman of the period to have read *The Divine Comedy*. Dante was sufficiently authoritative to be one of the authors Chaucer names (as a source in *The Monk's Tale*; in *The Wife of Bath's Tale* as an authority on the nobility of virtue; and in *The Friar's Tale* as worthy of a professorial chair in hell studies), but he treats him with a unique mixture of admiration and scepticism, imitation and resistance. So lines from St Bernard's prayer to the Virgin in the *Paradiso* (33.1–51) appear (ascribed to the saint) in the Invocation to the Virgin Mary in the Prologue to *The Second Nun's Tale* (*CT*, VIII.36–56), but also, unascribed, in Troilus' eulogy of love spoken over the naked body of his beloved on their first night together (III.1262–7; compare *Paradiso* 33.14–18). The lines here have an evident potential for irony, for marking how inadequate is Troilus' worldly idea of love as sexual desire compared with divine Christian love, and it has been given an influential reading in those terms (Robertson 1962: 474–502); but they also give secular love a weight unprecedented in earlier Middle English poetry that is difficult to dismiss lightly. Chaucer's most extended borrowing from Dante is the story of Hugelyn, Dante's Ugolino, in *The Monk's Tale*, but that is an adaptation rather than a translation, and he radically changes the *sentence* of the story: rather than telling of just punishment for treachery, the tale describes the grim deaths of a man and his innocent children on the basis of what may be no more than rumour (*CT*, VII.2407–62).

Not all of Chaucer's borrowing from Dante invites such questioning. The Second Nun's Prologue contains both some of Chaucer's own most powerful religious poetry and some of the most magnificent versions of Dante in all the long history of the translation of his writings into English:

> Thow Mayde and Mooder, doghter of thy Sone,
> Thow welle of mercy, synful soules cure,
> In whom that God for bountee chees to wone,   chose; dwell
> Thow humble, and heigh over every creature,
> Thow nobledest so ferforth our nature,   ennobled; to such an
>   extent
> That no desdeyn the Makere hadde of kynde   humankind
> His Sone in blood and flessh to clothe and wynde.
>
> (*CT*, VIII.36–42)

Equally powerful is the final stanza of *Troilus*, where Chaucer commits his work to the unwritten author of all things:

> Thow oon, and two, and thre, eterne on lyve,   eternally living
> That regnest ay in thre, and two, and oon,
> Uncircumscript, and al maist circumscrive . . .
>   (V.1863–5: cf. *Paradiso* 14.28–30)

Chaucer recognized in Dante, in fact, a poet who could endow his own style with sublimity.

According to the poet John Lydgate, Chaucer's translations from Dante went beyond such short extracts to encompass what he calls 'Dante in Inglissh' (ed. Brewer 1978: 53). Of Chaucer's surviving poetry, this can apply only to *The House of Fame*; but apart from a handful of lines in the proems to each book of the poem, *The House of Fame* is most certainly not a translation of *The Divine Comedy*. It is, rather, a 'carrying across' in the most extreme sense, to produce a work that counter-models its ideas on Dante's and challenges him at every step, starting by recasting Virgil not as the poet's leader but as his misleader (Boitani 1984 and Cooper 1999 give differing accounts). The goddess of Chaucer's poem, Fame herself, is likewise cast as the opposite of Dante's idea of *fama* as true report. Dante tells the stories of those who have died as if he had, as the poem claims, direct knowledge of the judgements of God; Chaucer insists that the truth of anyone's life, let alone their fate after death, is unknowable, and the nature of their reputation, or fame, bears a purely arbitrary relationship to what they actually deserve. Virgil also comes under attack for claiming to know an authoritative version of the past, after Chaucer opens one major section of the poem with the opening of the *Æneid* itself, lines that would have been widely familiar to anyone with more than the most minimal Latin schooling:

> I wol now synge, yif I kan,
> The armes and also the man
> That first cam, thurgh his destinee,
> Fugityf of Troy contree,
> In Itayle, with ful moche pyne
> Unto the strondes of Lavyne.   i.e. Italy
> *(The House of Fame*, lines 143–8)

This is as accurate a translation of the opening two-and-a-bit lines of the *Æneid* as the poetic form will allow (at the rate of a couplet per hexameter; the interpolated 'yif I kan', at one level a typical Chaucerian disclaimer, also provides the necessary rhyme for 'man'). But having so firmly established his Virgilian credentials, Chaucer goes on to offer a summary of the story of Æneas and Dido that directly contradicts the meanings that Virgil would have it carry. Virgil's Æneas is a model of *pietas*, the fulfilling of his duties towards the gods and all those to whom he owes obligations; Chaucer's comment on him is the acid

> Ther may be under godlyhed   righteousness/ piety
> Kevered many a shrewed vice.   covered
> (lines 274–5)

The faithfulness of the opening quotation is in fact belied by the radical redirection that Chaucer gives to the meaning that his retelling of the story exemplifies. This reinterpretation (the act of a middleman, *inter partes*) stems in large measure from the fact that Chaucer also acts as middleman between two different source texts: Ovid, through the mouth of Dido in his *Heroides*, had already invited a much more sceptical reading of the Trojan hero, and Chaucer explicitly reminds his audience that he as well as Virgil can serve as an authority for the story. As with the Gospels, the translation of history into text can result in more than one version, but here there is no possibility of any underlying consensual truth. From offering an exemplary image of 'godlyhed', the *Æneid* therefore shifts to offer an exemplary image for the unreliability and unverifiability of texts that relate history, and it is this idea that is to govern the rest of the poem and that is expounded iconographically in the House of Fame itself. Translation from one language into another might in itself be expected to be a value-neutral process; but when it is a matter of translating the Latin classics, with their weight of authority and the cultural capital invested in them, the procedure invites treatment as an act of homage, which Chaucer refuses to make.

In a number of respects, Chaucer's work as *grant translateur* moves the whole programme of English translation into new areas. Devotional translation occupies only a small part of his output (the short poem *An ABC*, or the adaptation of the legend of St Cecilia that became *The Second Nun's Tale*), and after the *Romaunt* he is more likely to borrow than to translate from French, creating genuinely original works. His closest translations from Latin are much more intellectual than was usual in Middle English: the philosophy of Boethius, the political thought of Albertanus, the pastoral theology assembled from various sources for *The Parson's Tale*. His borrowings from the classics most often consist of adaptations or retellings rather than direct translation (most extensively, in the series of stories borrowed from Ovid's *Heroides* in *The Legend of Good Women*), but his interest in classical authors nonetheless aligns him more with his continental contemporaries or with the English Renaissance than with his immediate Middle English context. And his cosmopolitanism, his readiness to appropriate the new Italian literature as well as the customary French, also renders him unique in the late fourteenth century. That does not mean, however, that he was a Renaissance man out of his time. His openness to non-anglophone literatures and his alertness to the theoretical possibilities within translation are both characteristic of Middle English; but in his exploitation of what translation and adaptation could do, he has scarcely been matched by any writer in any age.

References

Primary texts

Barratt, Alexandra, ed. (1995). *The Seven Psalms: A Commentary on the Penitential Psalms Translated from French into English by Dame Eleanor Hull*. EETS OS 307. Oxford: Oxford University Press.

Brewer, Derek, ed. (1978). *Chaucer: The Critical Heritage*. London: Routledge & Kegan Paul.

Doiron, Marilyn, ed. (1968). 'Marguerite Porete: *The Mirror of Simple Souls*'. *Archivio Italiano per la Storia della Pietà*, 5, 243–382.

Forshall, Rev. Josiah and Madden, Sir Frederic, eds. (1850). *The Holy Bible . . . Made by Wycliffe and his Followers*. 4 vols. Oxford: Oxford University Press.

Holt, Robert and White, R.M., eds. (1878). *The Ormulum*. 2 vols. Oxford: Clarendon Press.

Hudson, Anne, ed. (1978). *Selections from English Wycliffite Writings*. Cambridge: Cambridge University Press.

Laskaya, Anne and Salisbury, Eve, eds. (1995). *The Middle English Breton Lays*. Kalamazoo: Medieval Institute Publications.

O'Donoghue, Denis, ed. (1994). *Lives and Legends of Saint Brendan the Voyager*. Reprd edn. Felinfach: Llanerch Press.

Sargent, Michael G., ed. (2004). *Nicholas Love: The Mirror of the Blessed Life of Jesus Christ*. Exeter: University of Exeter Press.

Singleton, Charles S., ed. and trans. (1977). *Dante Alighieri: The Divine Comedy*. Bollingen Series 80. Princeton: Princeton University Press.

Sullens, Idelle, ed. (1983). *Robert Mannyng of Brunne: Handlyng Synne*. Binghamton: Center for Medieval and Early Renaissance Studies.

Vinaver, Eugène, ed. (1990). *The Works of Sir Thomas Malory*. 3rd edn, revd P.J.C. Field. 3 vols. Oxford: Clarendon Press.

Windeatt, B.A., ed. (1984). *Geoffrey Chaucer: Troilus and Criseyde*. London: Longman.

Wogan-Browne, Jocelyn, Watson, Nicholas, Taylor, Andrew and Evans, Ruth, eds. (1999). *The Idea of the Vernacular: An Anthology of Middle English Literary Theory 1280–1520*. Exeter: University of Exeter Press.

Secondary sources and suggestions for further reading

Archibald, Elizabeth (1991). *Apollonius of Tyre: Medieval and Renaissance Themes and Variations*. Cambridge: D.S. Brewer.

Boitani, Piero (1984). *Chaucer and the Imaginary World of Fame*. Chaucer Studies 10. Cambridge: D.S. Brewer.

Cooper, Helen (1999). 'The Four Last Things in Dante and Chaucer: Ugolino in the House of Rumour'. *New Medieval Literatures*, 3, 39–66.

Copeland, Rita (1991). *Rhetoric, Hermeneutics, and Translation in the Middle Ages: Academic Traditions and Vernacular Texts*. Cambridge Studies in Medieval Literature 11. Cambridge: Cambridge University Press.

Dover, Carol, ed. (2003). *A Companion to the Lancelot-Grail Cycle*. Cambridge: D.S. Brewer.

Edwards, A.S.G. (2001). 'The Middle English Translation of Claudian's *De consulatu Stilichonis*'. In A.J. Minnis, ed., *Middle English Poetry: Texts and Traditions* (pp. 267–78). Woodbridge: York Medieval Press.

Hanna, Ralph, III (1989). 'Sir Thomas Berkeley and his Patronage'. *Speculum*, 64, 878–916.

Kelly, Louis (1979). *The True Interpreter: A History of Translation Theory and Practice in the West*. Oxford: Blackwell.

Machan, Tim William (1985). *Techniques of Translation: Chaucer's "Boece"*. Norman, OK: Pilgrim Books.

Morse, Ruth (1991). *Truth and Convention in the Middle Ages: Rhetoric, Representation, and Reality*. Cambridge: Cambridge University Press.

Putter, Ad (1995). *Sir Gawain and the Green Knight and French Arthurian Romance*. Oxford: Clarendon Press.

Robertson, D.W., Jr. (1962). *A Preface to Chaucer: Studies in Medieval Perspectives*. Princeton: Princeton University Press.

Watson, Nicholas (1995). 'Censorship and Cultural Change in Late-Medieval England: Vernacular Theology, the Oxford Translation Debate, and Arundel's Constitutions of 1409'. *Speculum*, 70, 822–64.

Chapter 9

Contemporary Events

Helen Barr

Event as Text

If, as the previous two chapters have suggested, the particular linguistic circumstances of English authors in the medieval period inform the literature that they produced, so too do the distinctive historical circumstances. Medieval English authors wrote through riots, wars, the dethronement of kings, rebellions by heretics, and large-scale changes to the very structure of society. To argue that this period of English history was more turbulent or more fractured than any other would be untenable, but there is no doubt that the writers of English literary texts in the Middle Ages lived through some very unsettling events, and in some cases took part in them. What this chapter will attempt to chart is the inseparability of events from Middle English texts, and something of the variety of textual strategies that 'produce' events in medieval England: events that now often go by names that would have been unrecognizable to those who actually lived through them. Textual events in medieval England were produced both through sponsored commentary (what we would now call 'spin'), and through attempts to reinsert marginalized voices within the mainstream of contemporary discourse. Works also survive in which the pressure of the contemporary moment erupts through the text, scarcely, perhaps, under the author's control, and others where the very instability of textual continuity and coherence can be seen to reproduce the chaotic contemporary climate of the work's composition.

First, however, it is important to sound a word of caution about the relationship between text and events. Even in our contemporary world, with its immediate proliferation of media of all kinds, transparent, unmediated access to 'what happened' is unavailable. Text weaves an event into being. In the Middle Ages, there are specific factors that render a 'naked event' even more unknowable. The first of these factors is the nature of medieval literacy. If we turn to documents (legal, chronicle or parliamentary) to tell us 'what happened', it is important to bear in mind that those that survive were written chiefly in Latin and/or French and produced usually by clergy, lawyers or men of noble rank, as the last two chapters have explained. Accounts of contemporary happenings found in such records are inevitably shaped by the institutional perspectives of those who produced them, and the projected audience to which they were addressed. Sermons, drama and poetry, even if written in English, were written by a minority elite. The sites of production shape how events are discussed and also, silently, have the potential to efface the perspectives that might have been offered from those who were unable to record their views in non-perishable material forms. The vast majority of those whose lives were touched (or transformed) by wars, epidemics, social revolt, trials for heresy, or political upheavals could not write. Yet although their stories, their perspectives, remain largely untold to us, it is clear that they were told to each other. Information about public events could travel very fast indeed across both regional and social boundaries (Richmond 1998). Proclamations were made in market squares and other public places that made the news of London the gossip of the counties and the coasts. 'What was happening' was the subject of tales and rumours exchanged in churches, law courts and taverns (Hanna 1996: 267–82). Of most of this news, however – news that was oral, non-institutionalized and ephemeral – only faint traces remain.

There is a second issue that underlies the above: what is the relationship between event and *any* text? I can think of no better articulation of this question than a conversation that occurs in Chaucer's *House of Fame*. In Book II, the narrator (a portly civil servant called Geoffrey) is carried up to the heavens by an irrepressibly chatty eagle who is improbably well versed in the laws of physics. The eagle explains to Geoffrey how sound works. Cast a pebble on the water, he says, and what you will see is an endless series of concentric rings. The pebble is the sound uttered but it sinks below the surface. The originary utterance is lost; the circles are all the traces that are left (lines 789–822; compare Jane Griffiths' essay above). The significance of this analogy can be extended. We might want to think of an event as a thing, something graspable, palpable – like a pebble in fact. But as Chaucer's eagle explains, we never get to see the pebble, let alone hold it. Pebble as event vanishes. Its wake is left, the circles and the spaces between them brimming always away.

Rhetoric and Power

Chaucer's analogy shows us that our knowledge of an event is inseparable from the language that shapes it. Put another way, our apprehension of events is through rhetoric. This has important consequences for Middle English texts, especially in instances where participants in events, or those who become caught up in them, are not themselves able to narrate their stories in a way that is legible to posterity. In such cases, it is easy to mistake access to literacy and powerful textual models for 'what actually happened', and in so doing, to collude with the writings of the powerful in effacing the testimonies of those perhaps most affected by the events in question.

This situation is especially pertinent to the series of civil uprisings in 1381 that posterity has named 'The Peasants' Revolt'. Following the imposition of a seriously punitive poll tax, protestors marched on London, broke into aristocratic houses and destroyed countless documents that were felt to be associated with fiscal tyranny or that, more generally, withheld their rights. The force of the disturbances can be gauged by the fact that during their course, the Archbishop of Canterbury, Simon Sudbury, was dragged from his altar and murdered, and the boy-king Richard II forced to parley with an angry crowd of rebels in a field at Mile End, just outside the city walls of London. Contemporary accounts of the uprisings, chiefly written in Latin or French, insistently depict the insurgents as violent, senseless rustics, whence derives the name of 'Peasants' Revolt'. Those who took part in the revolts, however, were not simply peasants. From legal records, it is clear that participants included members of the gentry, clerics in minor orders and, overwhelmingly, artisans such as bakers and thatchers. To compare the chronicle accounts with the legal records lays bare the demonizing rhetoric of the contemporary chroniclers and their anxiety to subsume the identities of all protestors into an animalistic, filthy mob. These events were written about by those and for those who had most to fear from them, and were inevitably shaped by their perspectives. This chapter starts with this scenario because it provides a very clear example of the cost of rhetoric to the disempowered, but also because responses to 1381 show us how very self-conscious writers could be about the language they deploy.

Both Chaucer and his contemporary John Gower write about 1381. Gower's response to the rebels is very much in keeping with the dominant demonizing perspective of writers. In the first book of his Latin work *Vox Clamantis* ('The Voice of One Crying'), events in London are recounted in a frenzy of lavish and extravagant rhetoric drawn from scriptural and classical sources. London itself is cast as the city of Troy. Gower is not alone in forging this connection. Troy exerted a powerful influence over the social imagination of later medieval London. Chaucer, the anonymous authors of the alliterative poems *St Erkenwald* and *Wynnere and Wastoure* (ed. Turville-Petre 1989), and, in the fifteenth century, John Lydgate – amongst others – draw on the renaming of London as Troy Novant, or New Troy. The re-christening granted epic and mythic status to the city and was explicitly exploited in civic pageants and processions such as the grand spectacle in 1392 when the city staged an elaborate reconciliation with its offended king, Richard II (ed. Carlson, trans. Rigg 2003).

In Gower's *Vox*, Troy is attacked by successive plagues of animals, including asses, swine, flies and frogs, all escaped from their natural places of confinement. There is widespread inversion of social hierarchy, and an insistence on demonic noise. The marauding mob, given names such as Bet, Gib, Hick and Col, are descendants of Cain, who enter Troy where there is no Hector to defend it. The narrator laments that 'Prelia Thebarum, Cartaginis, illaque Rome / Non fuerant istis plena furore magis' ('The battles of Thebes, Carthage and Rome were not more filled with madness than these': lines 983–4). Sudbury's murder becomes the death of Helenus, the high priest of Troy's Palladium. The work is crammed with elevated, stylized comparisons, from England as the Garden of Eden to the rebels' march on London as the Day of Judgement. Gower mobilizes the elevated discourses of Scripture and classical myth to condemn the protestors to a rhetorical space that is outside civilization: animal, senseless, noise. His powerful rhetoric disables the political voice of the dissidents and silences their credible political aims.

It is well known that Chaucer's *Nun's Priest's Tale* contains his only unambiguous reference to 1381. The tale is not, however, a narrative account of events couched in rhetoric apparently beyond the reach of the dissidents, but a response to the rhetoric of the events itself.

191

Chaucer's poem exposes the rhetorical plot on which Gower's 1381 narrative is constructed, mischievously tweaking Gower's orgiastic account of events, especially his white-hot rhetoric. The end of *The Nun's Priest's Tale* relates a fox chase. Made aware that her cockerel, Chauntecleer, has been seized, a widow, her whole household and the farm animals (including 'Colle oure dogge' (line 3383) – a name the creature shares with one of Gower's prototypical peasants) join pursuit. The description focuses on demonic noise, beasts tearing free from where they ought to be confined, and social inversion. The narrator comments that the cacophony exceeded even that of Jack Straw and his men, and it seemed that the very heavens would fall (lines 3375–401). Jack Straw was one of the leaders of the revolt, and this is the place of Chaucer's unambiguous reference. While it might seem that Chaucer's fox chase reproduces the demonizing rhetoric with which his contemporaries described the peasant rebels of 1381, what is actually going on is a mordantly funny satire on Gower's contemporary earnest. When the fox first seizes the cockerel, the narrator explicitly draws attention to the need to find sufficiently lofty rhetoric to narrate the tragedy, in particular the grief suffered by Chauntecleer's 'wife', Pertelote, and the other hens. The narrator laments his impoverished skills, comparing his feeble talent to that of Geoffrey of Vinsauf, who wrote a handbook on rhetorical ornamentation:

> O Gaufred, deere maister soverayn,
> That whan thy worthy kyng Richard was slayn
> With shot, compleynedest his deeth so soore,   by the shot of an
>   arrow
> Why ne hadde I now thy sentence and thy lore
> The Friday for to chide, as diden ye?
> For on a Friday, soothly, slayn was he.   truly
> Thanne wolde I shewe yow how that I koude pleyne   complain
> For Chauntecleres drede and for his peyne.
>   Certes, swich cry ne lamentacion
> Was nevere of ladyes maad whan Ylion   Troy
> Was wonne, and Pirrus with his streite swerd,
> Whan he hadde hent kyng Priam by the berd,   seized
> And slayn hym, as seith us *Eneydos*,   *The Æneid*
> As maden all the hennes in the clos.
>
>   (*CT*, VII.3347–60)

Commentators have usually seen this passage as a tilt at Vinsauf's rhetoric. But it might be argued that Gower, not Vinsauf, is the target. The passage, in miniature, recalls Gower's effort to marshal every rhetorical trick in the book. It must have delighted Chaucer to rhyme a reference to Virgil's *Æneid* with the yard of some cackling hens (*Eneydos / clos*). And the ludicrous comparisons continue beyond the passage quoted: Pertelote's grief is likened to that of Hasdrubal's wife at the burning of Carthage, the distress of the other hens to the trauma of the senators' wives in Nero's blazing Rome. These are exactly the similes that Gower uses in *Vox Clamantis*, but while Gower's Troy is a civil uprising in London, Chaucer's Trojan lamentation describes a barnyard débâcle in which a fox runs off with a chicken – and the chicken escapes.

As a whole, *The Nun's Priest's Tale* is one of the funniest and zestiest of Chaucer's works, but, as in all comedic works of value, serious matters are raised. The tale explicitly engages with issues of causality, morality, and seriousness and play. The treatment of rhetoric is part of this examination. Chaucer's exposure of the over-elaborate, hysterical response of his fellow poet to 1381 can be seen to comment on the moral responsibility of writers when they narrate events. The happenings of 1381 clearly did horrify contemporary observers and some of the consequences were deadly, but demonizing writers, Gower included, omit from their accounts any concession to the undoubtedly careful planning of the rebels and their explicitly political targets, such as the destruction of the records of the hated poll tax. Scholars have shown how careful sifting of the evidence, and a refusal to buy into the rhetoric of the powerful, demonstrate that the unrest was not just a mindless and brutal opportunity for bloodshed and looting (Hilton and Aston, eds., 1984). Gower does buy into the rhetoric of the powerful. Chaucer exposes it. 'Taketh the moralite, goode men', says the narrator cheerily at the end of *The Nun's Priest's Tale* (line 3440). Inscribed in the bonhomie, however, is a matter of grave importance. To take the morality, to make moral sense of events, means to take care in the exercise of rhetoric. Text is the only event we can grasp. As Chaucer's tale shows us, how that event is written matters very much indeed.

Writing for the Powerful

The rhetorical basis of events is seen not only in Middle English texts that deploy formal schemes and tropes. Some Middle English writers were commissioned to comment on contemporary events and the textual shapes into which these events then became forged were prompted by the desire or the pressure of writing for a powerful patron (compare Alexandra Gillespie's essay in this volume). Some of the clearest examples of how pressure from the powerful affected the textual stance of the writer can be seen in responses to the Hundred Years War. The phrase 'Hundred Years War', invented by nineteenth-century French historians, concretizes a complex period of political upheavals between around 1337 and 1453. Although the term is used to describe hostilities between England and France, within these 'hundred' years there were long stretches of peace and truce, and to pitch the battle-lines solely between England and France deletes significant roles played by other nations, especially Scotland. The surviving literary works that engage with these events are clearly not concerned with reporting 'facts' from the front line. Rather, reflection on the events creates a textual occasion – an occasion that may serve the mutual interests of patron and writer.

Little is known about the figure of Laurence Minot, who wrote a series of short poems about the first twenty years of hostilities against France. Most critics are of the view that his accounts are of little historical value (see James and Simons, eds., 1989: 15), an observation that, perhaps, misses the point. The early years of the wars gave Minot an opportunity not to send dispatch reports, but to glorify Edward III (who reigned from 1337 to 1377). Whether Minot's efforts were the result of direct patronage from the court or an attempt to gain a courtly patron remains unclear. What emerges unambiguously, however, is a portrait of Edward III as a romance hero. Minot contrasts Edward's illustrious exploits against the craven disasters of both the French and Scottish armies. Military crassness and cowardice by the Scottish and French kings serve as a foil to Edward III's military triumphs. Minot creates a romance framework in which true, brave Edward is pitted individually against Philip of Valois, the French king who had denied Edward his claim to the French crown. While Philip is consistently characterized as a coward, 'a caitif', and as incompetent, Edward is 'oure cumly king', whom God will help to achieve his 'reght [right] in France' (ed. James and Simons 1989: nos 4, 6). Edward's vanquished adversaries are timorous unfortunates whose inevitable demise is narrated without a shred of pity: '. . . sum ligges [lies] yit in that mire / All hevidless [headless], withouwten hire'. The movement from history to romance is gilded by Minot's formally wrought verse, which furnishes his heroes with a burnished frame. Pomp and circumstance, however, are rarely separable from xenophobia: French beards get pulled, foreign pratfalls applauded, and enemies mocked:

'thare lerid [taught] Inglis men tham a new daunce'. For Minot, the occasion of the French wars allows him to adopt the poetic voice of a minstrel to *perform* the English chivalry of Edward III.

A more complex instance of a poet using the French wars as an occasion for performance can be seen in the works of Thomas Hoccleve. Hoccleve, Clerk of the governmental office of the Privy Seal as well as an admirer of Chaucer's poetry, wrote a long 'advice to princes' poem called *The Regement of Princes* for the future Henry V, as Jane Griffiths has already discussed. The poem treats the standard values and ethics that a king should cultivate. The final part is an unambiguous call for peace in the hostilities between England and France:

Allas! What peple haþ your were slayn!	war
What cornes wast, and doune trode and schent!	wasted; destroyed
How many a wif and maide haþ be by layn!	raped
Castels doun belte & tymbred houses brent,	pulled down; burnt
And drawen doune and al to-torne and rent!	torn to shreds
The harm may nat rekened be, ne told:	
This were wexiþ al to hoor and old.	grows; grey

(ed. Furnivall 1897: lines 533–41)

The Hoccleve persona paints a plaintive picture of the cost of the war by constructing a rhetorical series of *exclamationes*. He then calls on the kings of both France and England – 'o worthi princes two' (line 5363) – to make peace at once. Writing in 1411 (although the poem probably was not completed and presented to Prince Henry until late in 1411 or 1412), 'Hoccleve' argues that the war has grown too old and grey. In 1413, however, with Henry now king, the situation had changed. Hoccleve wrote *A Poem to Sir John Oldcastle*. Oldcastle was a heretical knight who had reputedly organized a recent rebellion. The poem is an appeal to Oldcastle to renounce heresy, but simultaneously it casts the knight as a foil against which Henry V's military prowess is blazoned. It appears that the poem was written as Henry set sail to renew war against France. Oldcastle is enjoined to resume his rightful status as a soldier:

Conquere meryt and honour, let see,
Looke how our cristen Prince, our lige lord
With many a lord & knyght beyond the See,
Laboure in armes; thow hydest thee!
And darst not come shewe thy visage!
(ed. Furnivall and Gollancz 1892: lines 498–502)

The narrative strategy is reminiscent of Minot's polarization of Edward and Philip. It depends on the rhetorical construction of Henry as manly Christian champion and Oldcastle as feminized heretical coward. Hoccleve's change of heart from peace to war is plainly motivated by the need for patronage and accompanied by a remarkably nimble-footed change of rhetorical colours. Hoccleve's verses on the French wars illustrate how texts can produce events from diametrically opposed perspectives if patronage is at stake. The verses are governed less by a concern to speak about the wars than by a desire to construct a rhetorical portrait of his patron. Rather as Chaucer's *Book of the Duchess* can be seen to be less a poem about the lady Blanche than a poem 'between men' – that is, the woman serves as a go-between to establish a bond between poet and patron – so too, the French wars can be seen as an occasion for Hoccleve: an occasion to establish a relationship between himself and Henry V.

For both Hoccleve and Minot, responses to the Hundred Years War are literally shaped by the need and/or desire to write for the powerful. While the particular tropes used in each case are different, both writers construct English kings as manly champions engaged in individual warfare, in a rhetorical production of contemporary events that might be compared with the modern-day fetish with 'personality politics'. The opportunism of sponsored rhetoric, with the ostensible subject of the verse more a means than an end, is seen most readily in Hoccleve's transparent change of position.

Writing for a Cause

The construction of kingliness and kingship in Middle English texts is crucially dependent on the cause espoused by the work. As the example of Hoccleve shows, even 'advice to princes' texts are not neutral guides for kingly ethics in the abstract but are inflected towards the demands or the concerns of the contemporary moment. The fashioning of kingship takes on a more cutting political edge in texts that respond to the deposition of Richard II in 1399. Richard acceded to the English throne as a boy-king after Edward III's death in 1377. Twenty-two years later, Richard was dead, deposed by Henry Bolingbroke and his supporters. Quite what happened in 1399 is probably lost to us (surviving chronicles contain conflicting accounts), but a broad outline is clear. While Richard was absent on a military expedition to Ireland, Henry, the banished son of John of Gaunt, returned. Landing on the

Yorkshire coast, he led his army through England, arriving eventually at London, and claimed the throne in September. Richard had come back but was captured at Flint Castle, where he either surrendered or was forced to give up the throne. He died at some point between September and January 1400, probably murdered. Right from the start of his reign, with power devolved to the barons during his minority, Richard's rule was plagued by civic factionalism. His part as king was played out against a wider backdrop of baronial jealousies and aristocratic competitiveness.

Yet it is exactly this important stage that is deleted from surviving literary accounts of Richard's downfall. Time and again in literary texts, for instance in Gower's *Cronica Tripertita* ('Tripartite Chronicle'), what we get is not coverage of the events of 1399 with all the actors playing their respective parts, but an intense focus on the central figure himself, not as victim, but in stage villain role. Writers such as Gower, and the anonymous poet of the early fifteenth-century alliterative poem *Richard the Redeless*, produce a particular type of monarch: the king as tyrant. In the case of *Richard the Redeless*, the role of the king is conditional upon the cause that the poem espouses. The deposition of an anointed monarch was as dangerous and politically volatile an act as could be committed, whatever justifications might be sought. The new Lancastrian regime was haunted by the spectre of usurpation and sought strenuously to promulgate documents and poetry in order to legitimize its existence (Strohm 1998). One of the measures taken was to disseminate throughout the realm doctored copies of the rolls of parliament, which gave a thoroughly Lancastrian account of the events of the 1399 parliament that deposed Richard. These rolls contained thirty-three accusations of wilful misgovernment against the former king (ed. and trans. Given-Wilson 1993: 168–89). *Richard the Redeless* (composed shortly after January 1400) is part of this thoroughgoing Lancastrian production of 'correct' text, both as a whole and in details: some of the key thirty-three articles are rehearsed in alliterative verse (ed. Barr 1993: I.96–142).

This Lancastrian positioning clearly shapes the production of Richard as villain in the work. While it purports to be written as an advice to princes poem to Henry IV, its target is the capricious rule of Richard. Personally, it seems, Richard cultivated bands of retainers who rampaged through the country, murdered innocent bystanders (II.2–66; 101–39) and intimidated parliament (III.317–42). Supposedly, Richard was responsible for the murder of his uncle Thomas Woodstock, a brother of John of Gaunt, and of Richard Fitzalan, Earl of Arundel.

Figure 9.1 The Westminster Abbey portrait of Richard II (1390s).
Reproduced by permission of the Dean and Chapter of Westminster.

He was responsible also, according to the text, for the life-imprisonment of Thomas Beauchamp, Earl of Warwick (III.26–31). More concerned with fashion and festivity than rightful government (III.175–206; 209–39 and 264–8), Richard so despoiled his country that only Henry, his divinely appointed successor, could come to the rescue (II.141–92; III.351–70). This is a thoroughly Lancastrian portrait. The intensely personal focus on the character of Richard himself creates a polarization of the decadent king and the righteous saviour Henry. This strategy is clearly tendentious, but its political value is much more insidious than the polarization of characters seen in Minot and Hoccleve. With baronial factionalism edited out, it is much harder to read Henry's accession as an act of usurpation. The vile business of deposition is obscured. The focus on Richard and his crimes rather than the wider picture of baronial ambition and jockeying for position reproduces the Lancastrian rhetoric that the new regime wished to be taken for parliamentary fact.

There is a cruel paradox here. It is well known that Richard promulgated glorious images of himself and his state regalia to display and assert his power. In the portrait of the king in Westminster Abbey (see the illustration opposite), the space is filled with a close-up of the face of the king in frontal pose that adopts the iconographic representation of Christ in majesty. And yet, when the writer of *Richard the Redeless* comes to justify Lancastrian rule, it is exactly this placing of Richard centre stage, but a Richard stripped of his majestic colours, that allows the poet to leech the ugliness of deposition out of the picture.

Writing by the Disempowered

Richard the Redeless is a very clear example of the interdependence of political positioning and the way that human subjects and agency are produced in texts. But the powerful did not have everything their own way. Particularly intriguing examples of how the supposedly disempowered could create text in which their voices speak loud and clear can be seen in works that stem from the context of Wycliffism, or Lollardy, the movement that used the radical ideas of the Oxford philosopher and theologian John Wyclif (who died in 1384) to challenge the institutionalized Church in England. Wyclif's views were disseminated first by the preaching of fellow academics, but, as Alexandra Gillespie has described above, percolated through to members of the nobility, clerics within the traditional Church hierarchy, and men and women as various as teachers, carpenters, fishmongers and tinkers. Wyclif's call for the Bible, then in Latin, to be translated into English so that all could understand it threatened to break the monopoly on scriptural interpretation enjoyed by the male clerical establishment. In 1401, on the passing of the statute *De heretico comburendo* ('Of the Burning of Heretics'), crucial aspects of Wyclif's teaching were defined as heretical, and provision was made for the execution of those who refused to recant Lollard views. In 1409, the publication of the Constitutions of Thomas Arundel, the Archbishop of Canterbury, supplemented these measures. Arundel decreed a severe clampdown on the writing and reading of books in English, preaching, and the meeting of groups who might discuss and disseminate heretical ideas. Although the measures failed to stifle religious discussion, many individuals found themselves on trial for suspected Lollard sympathies.

Hundreds of sermons and miscellaneous works survive that were written by Wycliffite sympathizers. One of these explicitly addresses the interrogation of heretical suspects. *The Testimony of William Thorpe* is a quasi-autobiographical account of the examination of a Lollard preacher by Archbishop Arundel in August 1407. Although Thorpe states that he was being held in Saltwood Castle prison, in the diocese of Canterbury, no formal record of further action or prosecution against him remains; the 'factual' status of the encounter between Arundel and Thorpe, therefore, is uncertain. What *is* clear is how Thorpe uses the occasion of what is meant to be a trial to give full coverage to many key aspects of Lollard thinking, including challenges to orthodox teaching regarding the sacraments of the Church. Thorpe's is a text that proclaims its religious allegiances boldly and eloquently. Not only does it take on a figure of ecclesiastical authority: it also ambushes a key discourse of ecclesiastical authority, the trial of the heretic, and makes it yield up meanings opposite to those that Church officials would have wished to wring from their unwilling suspects. As a Lollard, Thorpe ought to be on the disempowered end of an ecclesiastical trial. Not so in this text: it is the archbishop who is made to answer for his views.

A classic instance in the text where Thorpe fashions himself not as suspect but interrogator occurs in a discussion of the practice of confession, a vital part of Christian practice since 1215, when oral confession to a priest at least once a year was made mandatory for all, as Marilyn Corrie's chapter has already noted. The truly penitent were offered absolution, but a penance was imposed so that the repentant sinner made amends for his or her wrongdoing. Wyclif and his followers argued that confessing out loud to a parish priest was unnecessary. Internal contrition alone was sufficient to wipe out sin. Only God could know if a sinner was truly repentant. Such views bypassed the role of parish priests.

When Arundel accuses Thorpe of having advised a man that he should not make confession to any human being, only to God, Thorpe sidesteps the indictment. He gives a carefully eloquent reply that arrogates ecclesiastical discourse to his own ends. Drawing on scriptural text and the teaching of St Augustine, Thorpe argues that the advice and counsel of priests can be very helpful for a person who is 'distroublid' with sin (ed. Hudson 1993: 83) and is unsure of how to purge himself. Thorpe restricts the role of the clergy to that of counsel only. He argues that God is more ready to forgive sin than the devil is eager to stir it up. For anyone who is wholeheartedly ashamed of his or her transgressions and acknowledges them faithfully to God, purposing to make amends, the grace of God is sufficient to allow the individual to come to God's mercy. Arundel retorts hotly (rather in the manner of a suspect under the spotlight) that Holy Church does not approve of this teaching. Thorpe responds coolly that Holy Church *must* approve it because the people need to be taught to keep God's commandments, hate sin, believe in God, trust to his mercy, and be brought into perfect charity. Thorpe's strategy is very simple: if there is a problem, it lies with the Church, not with him. He confounds the margins from which he is meant to be writing. While Arundel had wanted all expression of Wycliffism eradicated, Thorpe puts Lollard teaching centre stage by rewriting the Archbishop's script.

Thorpe's *Testimony* is a text that imaginatively creates an event of great moment. When so much writing was determined by the kinds of powerful institutions mentioned above, it is significant that a writer using the English vernacular could mount such a challenge. Thorpe's self-styling creates a discursive space to promulgate teaching that the Church would not sanction. A Wycliffite hero is created who is intelligent, learned, quick-witted and unencumbered by all the stolid paraphernalia of the established Church. Thorpe creates a dramatic event that dismantles the control that institutionalized texts attempted to impose on their subjects. The significance of this textual event lies as much in the assertion of contemporary subjectivity as it does in voicing key tenets of Wycliffite thought.

Writing as Social Practice: The Pressure of the Contemporary Moment

All the works discussed so far can be seen to shape events assertively, especially, perhaps, the *Testimony*, where Thorpe seizes the occasion to produce his own event from whatever happened in his meeting with the Archbishop. But to focus on the cause espoused by the writing risks effacing a fundamental relationship between text and event that is pertinent not just to medieval culture, but to any culture. How far is the writing of any text in and of itself *necessarily* a contemporary event; that is, to what extent does the very practice of writing create a text that is inevitably the social product of its times? Malory's *Morte Darthur* provides some intriguing answers to these questions.

It is tricky to calibrate the *Morte's* engagement with contemporary events. It might be thought that Malory's adaptation of the French romances on which his text is largely based (compare Helen Cooper's chapter above) re-creates a past Arthurian world of chivalry, loyalty, knightly courtesy and adventure, a world divorced from Malory's own involvement in the political turmoil of his own times. But the *Morte* is more complex than this. On the one hand, there are its overt gestures towards contemporary events. Malory says that he finished writing his Arthurian epic in 'the ninth yere of the reygne of Kyng Edward the Fourth' (ed. Vinaver 1990: 1260), that is, in 1469 or 1470 (the ninth regnal year of Edward IV fell between 4 March 1469 and 3 March 1470). The inscription locates the writing of the *Morte* at a particularly turbulent time of civil strife, a time that the influence of Shakespeare's *Henry VI* plays has led to be called 'The Wars of the Roses'. The seeds of this unrest can be traced back to Henry IV's accession in 1399. The Lancastrian dynasty never entirely shook off claims that it was illegitimate. While Henry V's military exploits in France brought him popularity, his reign was brief (1413–22). His son, Henry VI, acceded to the throne as an infant. During his reign the English lost all their territorial advantages in France. The king suffered periods of insanity, and political weakness in the face of strong baronial opposition led eventually to the series of civil wars fought between 1453 and 1485. On the one side was the House of Lancaster, whose badge was a red rose, and on the other the House of York, whose badge was a white rose. Edward, the son of Richard, Duke of York, seized the throne from Henry VI in 1461. One of his most powerful supporters was Richard Neville, Earl of Warwick, known to posterity as 'Warwick the

Kingmaker'. In 1469, Warwick turned against Edward IV and ruled briefly in his name before Edward reasserted his power. In 1470, Warwick and other powerful nobles turned sides and restored Henry VI to the throne, forcing Edward to flee the country. Henry's tenure of the crown for a second time was short-lived. Edward returned to England and, with Warwick killed at the battle of Barnet in 1471, reclaimed the kingship and ruled until his death in 1483.

Although it was standard practice to express dates in terms of the regnal year of the monarch, that Malory should have dated his work with reference to 'Kyng Edward' at a moment when the contest for his crown was so acute might be taken as an indication that what was happening outside the prison cell in which he was writing was not far from his mind. And there are other signs in the *Morte* that for Malory the boundaries between the writing of legend and writing about contemporary England were permeable. In his famous authorial interpolation not long before the final battle in the *Morte*, Malory is prompted to moralize upon the times by the desertion of Arthur's subjects to the side of his nephew, and illegitimate son, Mordred:

> Lo ye all Englysshemen, se ye nat what a myschyff here was? For he that was the moste kynge and nobelyst knyght of the worlde, and moste loved the felyshyp of noble knyghtes, and by hym they all were upholdyn, and yet myght nat thes Englyshemen holde them contente with hym. Lo thus was the olde custom and usayges of thys londe, and men say that we of thys londe have nat yet loste that custom. Alas! thys ys a greate defaughte [fault] of us Englysshemen, for there may no thynge us please no terme.
>
> (ed. Vinaver 1990: 1229)

The narration of the battle on Salisbury Plain slips into a present perspective with the use of the collective first person pronouns 'we' and 'us'. It also slides into syntactical incoherence. In the second sentence, Malory introduces Arthur as if he were to be the grammatical subject, but the unnamed king becomes an indirect object ('by hym') and then shifts unsteadily out of narrative focus. Arthur is superseded by the deixis of 'thes Englysshemen', and then by the reference to their counterparts in Malory's own day: 'us Englysshemen'. The interpolation bursts into the narrative and disrupts the time logic of the syntax. The intervention is deliberate on Malory's part; the rupture of the syntax of his story is perhaps less conscious. The final destructive moments of the Round Table become inexorably entwined with the civil strife of Malory's own contemporary moment.

More difficult to gauge are the less overt gestures to fifteenth-century England and the extent to which the *Morte* as a whole becomes symbolically resonant of the late-medieval factionalism in which, prior to his imprisonment, Malory himself took part (Field 1993; Hardyment 2005). While I have previously discussed how relationships between poet and patron, or propaganda, have been the cause of writing, here I want to reflect on how the very *practice* of writing collates text and event (Pocock 1987). Writing is inevitably socially contingent because it is a material form of social practice. Texts must necessarily be written in language, and since the use of language is both a social product and an act of social behaviour (as the institutional conditions of medieval literacy force us to remember), texts are not separable from the culture that produces them. Their subjects (in both senses of the word: the subjects who produce them and their subject matter), their narrative modes and diction are all part of what has been called 'the ensemble of social practices' (Balibar and Macherey 1981).

A writer's choice of tropes or diction to narrate what is happening within the time-logic of the text under construction describes simultaneously what is happening in the time-logic of the present tense of the writing. The very choice of diction tears down the boundaries between the world of the text and the world of the writing. Consciously or not, the pressures of the contemporary moment can be seen to influence the linguistic choices of the writer so that even if the ostensible subject of the writing takes place in a narrative world that is not mimetic of the social formations or subjects of contemporary society, the linguistic choices that construct and maintain that world are inevitably drawn from contemporary resources. Throughout the *Morte*, Malory's diction clusters around the lexis of wholeness and rupture. One of the insistent ways in which this discourse is constructed is through focus on bodies that are wounded and torn. Time and again the bodies of the knights display wounds that must be searched to make them 'hole'. The episode of 'The Healing of Sir Urry' that concludes Malory's penultimate tale, 'The Book of Sir Launcelot and Queen Guinevere' (ed. Vinaver 1990: 1145–54), is based entirely on this notion. Urry has been enchanted by a sorceress 'so that he shulde never be hole untyll the beste knyght of the worlde had serched hys woundis. And thus she made her avaunte [boast], wherethorow hit was knowyn that this sir Urry sholde never be hole' (1145). Starting with King Arthur (who fails), Malory rolls out a gargantuan list of knights (some of whom have died in earlier books), who search Urry's wounds in vain. Only Lancelot is able to heal the knight: 'he ransaked the three woundis, that they bled a lytyll and forthwithall the woundis fayre heled and semed as they had bene hole a seven yere' (1152). In a corporate ritual that has the purpose of staging the sight of a body made whole, only Lancelot succeeds, but he succeeds against a backdrop of failure, a failure in which King Arthur takes first place. Lancelot's feat takes up a small narrative space at the end of a roll-call of endeavour that fails to close Urry's wounds. The miracle of Lancelot's accomplishment cannot efface the liturgy of unwholeness that has gone before. Still less can this brief fantasy of wholeness stave off the slander and strife with which the next book opens, and the inevitability of the destruction of the Round Table. Lancelot's healing of Urry stages a brief moment of desire fulfilled, a desire very promptly overtaken by the rupture of what comes next.

Whether Malory was conscious of it or not, this diction of wholeness and rupture, of plenitude and fracture, inscribes the fragility of the fellowship itself. Nowhere is this seen more plangently than at Arthur's feast at Pentecost that precipitates the quest for the Holy Grail in Malory's 'Tale of the Sankgreal', the narrative that immediately precedes 'The Book of Sir Launcelot and Queen Guinevere'. Arthur clearly knows that from this point the fellowship is destroyed forever. Right at the point of the Round Table's plenitude, its last place filled by Sir Galahad, who has just arrived at Arthur's court, Malory gives Arthur a speech that diverges from the diction of his French source:

'Now', seyde the kynge, 'I am sure at this quest of the Sankegreall shall all ye of the Rownde Table departe, and nevyr shall I se you agayne *holé togydirs*, therefore ones shall I se you *togydir* in the medow, *all holé togydirs*! Therefore I wol se you all *holé togydir* in the medow of Camelot, to juste and to turney, that aftir youre dethe men may speke of hit that such good knyghtes were here, such a day, *holé togydirs*.'
(ed. Vinaver 1990: 864 (italics inserted))

The repeated phrase 'holé togydir(s)' is Malory's addition. It sounds a threnody. Just at the point of wholeness comes dispersal, testimony to the fracture that lies at the heart of the *Morte Darthur* (compare Mann 1991). Unachievable unity haunts Malory's work. Right from the start, the legitimacy of Arthur's conception is contentious, and Malory goes on to forge Arthur into an English king who is unable to build unity from the valorous deeds of his most noble knights, unable to hold in fellowship factions and feuds, and unable, finally, to prevent his own death by the illegitimate fruit of his own loins. Whatever Malory thought he was doing, the diction of torn wholeness that he deploys to narrate his story imports vocabulary resonant of contemporary fracture and discord into his Arthurian sources. The lexis of plenitude and rupture mediates between the record of divisions and tensions already present in Malory's source material and the civil strife of the present times in which he was writing. Malory's practice of writing 'words' his Arthurian materials into a tale of contemporary disintegration on an epic scale.

In exploring the relationships between Middle English literary texts and contemporary events, this chapter has been keen to stress the 'textuality' of history. The chapter has avoided words such as 'context' and 'background' because they imply separation between a literary text and the cultural milieu of which the text is part. Some works can clearly be seen to have been commissioned to produce versions of events that pander to those who commissioned them; others are the result of a desire for recognition – whether their authors aspire to patronage, or give voice to censored views. But if we widen the scope of thinking about events as texts, and think of writing as a 'social practice', then it is evident that all literary texts must be nourished in some shape or form by the present tense of their writing.

It is not only in the Middle Ages that rhetoric represents what might be legitimate protest as the riot of an animalistic mob. Nor is it an exclusively medieval practice to edit out the ugly details of a political situation by intense focus on the polarized personalities of the leaders involved. Thorpe was not the first marginalized dissident to attempt to wrest discourse back from powerful institutions, nor will he be the last. And it probably goes without saying that *Le Morte Darthur* hardly stands alone as a work in which a writer's linguistic choices weave contemporary resonance into a textual world non-mimetic of contemporary social formations. Although the happenings, and the participants in them, that have been discussed in this chapter are bound to a specific moment in time, many of the issues that they reveal are less time-bound.

Yet the particular factors that affected the writing of medieval texts mean that those texts must be read especially closely for the histories they reveal. For all its joky ducking of morals, *The Nun's Priest's Tale* surely teaches us that. While we might not be able to reach a 'naked event' – the pebble below the water – the rings that brim need to be watched with keen scrutiny. What is at stake is power: not just political power, nor simply power over the interpretation of 'what happened'. What is also at stake, as I have demonstrated, is power over identity and selfhood, both collective and individual.

References

Primary texts

Barr, Helen, ed. (1993). *The Piers Plowman Tradition: A Critical Edition of Pierce the Ploughman's Crede, Richard the Redeless, Mum and the Sothsegger and The Crowned King*. London: J.M. Dent.

Carlson, David R., ed., and Rigg, A.G., trans. (2003). *Richard Maidstone: Concordia facta inter regem et cives Londonie*. Kalamazoo: Medieval Institute Publications.

Dobson, R.B., ed. (1983). *The Peasants' Revolt of 1381*. 2nd edn. London: Macmillan.

Furnivall, Frederick J., ed. (1897). *Thomas Hoccleve: The Regement of Princes*. EETS ES 72. London: Kegan Paul, Trench, Trübner & Co.

Furnivall, Frederick J. and Gollancz, Israel, eds. (1892). *Thomas Hoccleve: The Minor Poems*. EETS ES 67, 73. London: Kegan Paul, Trench, Trübner & Co.

Given-Wilson, Chris, ed. and trans. (1993). *Chronicles of the Revolution 1397–1400: The Reign of Richard II*. Manchester: Manchester University Press.

Hudson, Anne, ed. (1993). *Two Wycliffite Texts*. EETS OS 301. Oxford: Oxford University Press.

James, Thomas Beaumont and Simons, John, eds. (1989). *The Poems of Laurence Minot 1333–1352*. Exeter: University of Exeter Press.

Macaulay, G.C., ed. (1902). *The Complete Works of John Gower Volume 4: The Latin Works*. Oxford: Clarendon Press.

Stockton, Eric W., trans. (1961). *The Major Latin Works of John Gower*. Seattle: University of Washington Press.

Turville-Petre, Thorlac, ed. (1989). *Alliterative Poetry of the Later Middle Ages*. London: Routledge.

Vinaver, Eugène, ed. (1990). *The Works of Sir Thomas Malory*. 3rd edn, revd P.J.C. Field. 3 vols. Oxford: Clarendon Press.

Secondary sources and suggestions for further reading

Aers, David (1999). '*Vox populi* and the Literature of 1381'. In David Wallace, ed., *The Cambridge History of Medieval English Literature* (pp. 432–53). Cambridge: Cambridge University Press.

Balibar, Etienne and Macherey, Pierre (1981). 'On Literature as an Ideological Form'. In Robert Young, ed., *Untying the Text: A Post-Structuralist Reader* (pp. 79–99). London: Routledge & Kegan Paul.

Barnie, John (1974). *War in Medieval Society: Social Values and the Hundred Years War, 1337–99*. London: Weidenfeld & Nicolson.

Coleman, Janet (1981). *English Literature in History 1350–1400: Medieval Readers and Writers*. London: Hutchinson.

Dalrymple, Roger, ed. (2004). 'Literature and History'. In *Middle English Literature: A Guide to Criticism* (pp. 139–63). Oxford: Blackwell.

Field, P.J.C. (1993). *The Life and Times of Sir Thomas Malory*. Cambridge: D.S. Brewer.

Gordon, Dillian, Monnas, Lisa and Elam, Caroline (1997). *The Regal Image of Richard II and the Wilton Diptych*. London: Harvey Miller.

Hanawalt, Barbara, ed. (1992). *Chaucer's England: Literature in Historical Context*. Minneapolis: University of Minnesota Press.

Hanawalt, Barbara and Wallace, David, eds. (1996). *Bodies and Disciplines: Intersections of Literature and History in Fifteenth-Century England*. Medieval Cultures 9. Minneapolis: University of Minnesota Press.

Hanna, Ralph, III (1996). *Pursuing History: Middle English Manuscripts and their Texts*. Stanford: Stanford University Press.

Hardyment, Christina (2005). *Malory: The Life and Times of King Arthur's Chronicler*. London: HarperCollins.

Harriss, Gerald (2005). *Shaping the Nation: England 1360–1461*. Oxford: Clarendon Press.

Hilton R.H. and Aston, T.H., eds. (1984). *The English Rising of 1381*. Cambridge: Cambridge University Press.

Hudson, Anne (1988). *The Premature Reformation*. Oxford: Clarendon Press.

Justice, Steven (1994). *Writing and Rebellion: England in 1381*. Berkeley: University of California Press.

Mann, Jill (1991). *The Narrative of Distance, the Distance of Narrative in Malory's Morte Darthur*. The William Matthews Lectures 1991. London: Birkbeck College.

Patterson, Lee (1991). *Chaucer and the Subject of History*. Madison: University of Wisconsin Press.

Pocock, J.G.A. (1987). 'Texts as Events: Reflections on the History of Political Thought'. In Kevin Sharpe and Steven N. Zwicker, eds., *Politics of Discourse: The Literature and History of Seventeenth-Century England* (pp. 21–34). Berkeley: University of California Press.

Richmond, Colin (1998). 'Hand and Mouth: Information Gathering and Use in the Later Middle Ages'. *Journal of Historical Sociology*, 1, 233–52.

Strohm, Paul (1989). *Social Chaucer*. Cambridge, MA: Harvard University Press.

Strohm, Paul (1998). *England's Empty Throne: Usurpation and the Language of Legitimation, 1399–1422*. New Haven: Yale University Press.

Swanson, R.N. (1993). *Church and Society in Late Medieval England*. 2nd edn. Oxford: Blackwell.

Part IV

Middle English Literature in the Post-Medieval World

Chapter 10

Manuscripts and Modern Editions

Daniel Wakelin

Before 1473–4, when William Caxton printed the first book in English, all Middle English literature circulated in manuscripts: in copies written by hand. But few people now read this literature from the original manuscripts, for the manuscripts are rare and precious, preserved in just a few libraries, and far fewer people are trained to read the handwriting than are able to read the language. Instead, people now read Middle English literature in printed editions that 'give out' the text (the first meaning of Latin *edere*, the root of the word *edition*) or publish it in a form more accessible in cost and appearance than a manuscript would be. But such editing involves not only reproducing a text from a manuscript but changing it in some way. After all, the act of copying or reproducing implies change in who, where, how or why one needs a text; so when an edition reproduces a Middle English work in order to serve that changing situation it changes what was in the manuscript. We must be aware of these changes if we wish to know how Middle English literature appeared to its earliest readers and how our editions might influence our interpretation of this literature. However, many of the changes in editions respond to the changes found among manuscripts themselves; in the light of such changes, modern editions seem like just one more method of not only reproducing Middle English literature but repackaging it for new readers.

No reproduction preserves an original perfectly. Even the excellent photographic facsimiles available as books (listed in Beadle 1998:

323–31), CD-ROMs or websites, such as the Parker-Library-on-the-Web Project (the site of the Parker Library in Corpus Christi College, Cambridge), lose the expensive and emotive charge of the real object. Moreover, as well as *losing* something, most facsimiles *add* something to the Middle English manuscript. The most useful facsimiles also contain, within the same book or website, interpretative commentary or 'metadata'. And the mere decision to reproduce a manuscript in facsimile expresses interpretative assumptions. Why edit this one? After all, only a few dozen of several thousand Middle English manuscripts are available in this way. The choice of what to 'edit' as a facsimile might reflect a fetish for fine illustrations or for Chaucer or Langland above other poets, as most facsimiles of Middle English literature include illustrations or the poetry of these men. Or what might have been a rough and plain manuscript, such as a miscellany used by some scholar is, when reproduced in such an excellent facsimile as *The Winchester Anthology* (a reproduction of London, British Library, MS Additional 60577: ed. Wilson 1981), imbued with new value and – although the manuscript was put together over time and lost sections over time – new solidity. The manuscript is changed, then, by dint of being edited even in a facsimile.

Furthermore, to read a facsimile of Middle English handwriting is difficult; and photographic facsimiles are also expensive. Therefore, most people have read Middle English literature in the typeset or printed forms of editions. Some editions offer very precise transcriptions from the manuscripts, preserving every point of spelling, punctuation and sometimes even the page-layout. But these precise transcriptions, known as 'diplomatic' editions, are more commonly used for letters, documents and political works, and few editors publish literary works in this way. J.R.R. Tolkien published such a transcription of one important manuscript of the beautiful religious treatise *Ancrene Wisse*; he even preserved the exact division of the prose into separate lines in the manuscript, the odd medieval punctuation marks and some of the symbols that abbreviated words (ed. Tolkien 1962: vi). Yet, although this seems, on the surface, a close reproduction, the deeper intentions, effects and reasons for recording the text have changed. Tolkien's diplomatic transcription emphasizes the philological curiosity of thirteenth-century English, and the need to attend to it, as a historian of the language, word by word; such reading differs from the devout meditation that *Ancrene Wisse* invites from its implied readers – although, interestingly, both readings should be ruminative and slow. Finally, the decision to preserve the unfamiliar Middle English of the manuscript in every detail creates difficulties that were probably seldom felt by the earliest readers. It is in order to obviate this difficulty that most editors therefore not only transcribe the texts that they find in manuscripts: they also deliberately change them somehow.

Changes by Editors

The first change is, like one of the changes made in facsimiles, the selection of texts. Most editors do not reproduce a whole manuscript but only elements of it. For manuscripts were shaped by circumstances that have changed: the expense of materials and the methods for circulating exemplars (traced by Alexandra Gillespie in this volume) often led people to produce miscellaneous manuscripts that collected up whatever texts came to hand and that they wanted to preserve wherever they could. Modern editors, less constrained by shortages of parchment or the difficulty of finding exemplars, tend to reproduce only parts of any miscellaneous manuscript. For example, one famous miscellany (London, British Library, MS Cotton Caligula A.ix) collects together two such different poems as the bird debate *The Owl and the Nightingale* and Laʒamon's *Brut,* alongside another debate-poem and a chronicle in French and some French saints' lives; but these works are printed separately now (Cartlidge, ed., 2001: xxvii). Some editions are still collections, but what they collect has changed, under the influence of changing constraints: marketability and the underpinning assumptions about the themes, authors, genres and languages worth editing. For example, the famous manuscript Harley 2253 in the British Library gathers more than half of the secular short poems recorded before 1400 as well as a mixture of works in Latin and French. Yet Brook's edition of *The Harley Lyrics* (1948) includes only the short, English lyrics, and not the manuscript's longer works such as the romance *King Horn* (fols 83r–92v) or the debate-poem 'In a þestri stude y stod a lutel strif to here' ('I stood in a dark place to hear a little dispute') (fols 57r–58v), despite the brevity of the debate-poem and the use of debate in lyrics that are included in the edition, such as 'My deþ ich loue my lyf ich hate' (ed. Brook 1948: no. 24). Nor does the edition print the manuscript's Latin and French religious instruction and its saucy fabliaux (although Brook does print one lyric in a mixture of English, French and Latin (poem no. 19)). Even when a manuscript only includes lyrics, editors are selective: for example, one editor prints just fifty-seven of the seventy-four poems in the famous collection Sloane 2593 in the British Library, because these items might be defined, on formal grounds, as carols (ed. Greene 1977: 306); another editor chooses just six and disperses them throughout his anthology grouped by themes such as 'The Blessed Virgin' or 'Sex'. One of these poems, 'I haue a gentil cook', is punningly *not* about sex, but the editor adds the subheading 'Sex' and so the double entendre becomes explicit – and he changes the scribe's spelling 'cook' to 'cok' to help further (ed. Hirsh 2005: no. 39; see also nos 9, 13, 16, 33 and pp. 125–6). Reproducing these poems in their new settings changes the value and meaning of the text reproduced.

The new setting also loses things that the whole manuscript can tell us. The Harley manuscript tells us something about trilingualism or attitudes to the mix of secular and pious writing in the early fourteenth century. Another manuscript, the Findern manuscript (now Cambridge, Cambridge University Library, MS Ff.1.6), has canonical poems such as Chaucer's *Parliament of Fowls* among short poems of love-longing, which might have been composed by women at leisure in a provincial household (ed. Hirsh 2005: nos 18, C1–C3); thus it might tell us more about women's literacy and taste for Chaucer, say, than might a paperback edition of Chaucer's dream visions. One of the most characteristic losses is the loss of illustrations, which accompanied a number of late fourteenth- and fifteenth-century works (many described in Scott 1996). Some humble illustrations clarified the text's reference and devotional function: for example, in the manuscript of one Carthusian monk (London, British Library, MS Additional 37049), alongside the poem 'O man unkynde' is a drawing of Christ, who speaks the poem, gesturing to the wounds that he wants us to 'Beholde *and* see' (reproduced in ed. Hirsh 2005: fig. 5; see further Brantley 2007). Grander were the sixty-odd gorgeous pictures in one copy of Lydgate's *Troy Book*, pictures that likely turned this poem into a luxurious status symbol, and that convey the bustle and grandeur of Lydgate's vision of antiquity (Scott 1996: figs 363–66, no. 93). Modern editions tend to include few of the illustrations found in early manuscripts, or to shunt them to the cover, cutting the connection of text and image. Similarly, there are constraints from typesetting and conventions for the layout of books today that prompt editors to change other visual elements such as the page-layout (explored at the end of this chapter). Overall, changing conventions about what is worth reproducing and the setting in which it is reproduced mean that, even if reproduced identically letter by letter, the text in manuscript looks different from the text in a modern edition.

Finally, and most importantly, most editors do not reproduce a text letter by letter as it is found in any one manuscript: they change details of the text itself. One lyric in the aforementioned manuscript Sloane 2593 illustrates some of these changes. Here is a 'diplomatic' transcription of it (from a photograph):

> ¶   I syng A of a mydē . þᵗ is makeles
> a
> kyng of all kyng~ . to here sone che ches
>
> ¶   he cā also stylle . þ~ his mod~ was
> As dew in aprylle . þᵗ fallyt on þe gras
> (ed. Hirsh 2005: fig. 2)

Here is its appearance in one of many modern editions:

> I syng of a mayden
> That is makeles.   a triple pun: without equal, lover, or stain
> Kyng of alle Kynges,
> To here sone she ches.   she chose for her son
>
> He cam also stylle,   as silently
> Ther his moder was,
> As dewe in Aprylle
> That fallyt on the gras.
> (ed. Hirsh 2005: no. 13)

The scribe uses some abbreviations, such as the macrons over and the squiggles after some letters; the editor silently expands these abbreviations. The scribe uses the letters thorn and yogh (þ and ȝ) but the editor replaces them with modern equivalents. The scribe spells the word *she* oddly as 'che' here, and again on the facing page in the lyric 'I haue a ȝong suster'; but the editor regularizes the spelling to modern *she* – although he does not do so in his edition of 'I haue a ȝong suster' (ed. Hirsh: no. 33). Many editors likewise modernize spelling, most often of the letters *u*, *v*, *i* and *j*, which were used differently in Middle English from now; some editors of popular student editions, such as Beadle and King's *The York Plays: A Selection in Modern Spelling* (1984) or Lester's *Three Late Medieval Morality Plays* (1981), update the spelling even more. We might think that these changes are acceptable – especially in drama that still offers itself for performance – but we must be aware of them. Most editors also remove scribal errors from the text, a sensible attempt to remove the inadvertent changes made by the scribes: for example, in the lyric above the scribe left out the *a* in 'mayde*n*', and squeezed it below, and added a superfluous *A* earlier in the line; the editor helpfully changes these errors in the manuscript in order to avoid enshrining a mistaken change by the scribe. Other Middle English poems to the Virgin, however, including others in the same manuscript, begin with the singable exclamations 'A a a a' (ed. Greene 1977: nos 188, 232.A), and that might be echoed in the *A* here.

These changes are helpful, but they make the poem look more polished, more artistic perhaps, as does the new layout. In the manuscript the poem is ten lines in rhyming couplets without any space between them, but in the editions the lines have been halved and arranged into five separate quatrains, the first and last rhyming *abcb* and the middle ones rhyming *abab*. Which is right? The lines might be considered to form quatrains, because the second stanza does have the cross-rhyme of 'stylle' and 'Aprylle' and, in the manuscript, a *punctus*, a single dot, divides each long line in half. Moreover, before 1400 scribes often copied English stanzas in long lines, following convention or saving parchment; they do so in the Harley lyrics, for example (Solopova 2000: 379–81, 389). Most editors change this poem into quatrains – more like those of William Blake or Emily Dickinson, say. And there is one further element of the manuscript not reproduced in print: to the right of each couplet is a square 'bracket' joining the rhymes. This feature, common in English poetic manuscripts (Tschann 1985: 6), highlights the sound of the poem, whereas editors, spacing out the stanzas without brackets, highlight the organizing silences. Such small changes to spelling and layout might not seem important: they were for a long time dismissed in editorial theory as changes to the 'accidentals' of the text, to the merely visual elements of it rather than the essence of the text (the 'substantives'). However, some recent critics have contended that such changes remove information that might affect how we interpret each poem (McGann 1991: 13–15; McKenzie 1999: 18–23), or whether it looks fit to be interpreted at all. That seems true here.

Reproducing Variation among Manuscripts

However, the biggest changes in modern editions affect the 'substantive' texts themselves. A lot of Middle English works survive in more than one manuscript, but most editions (with exceptions noted below) have the space to reproduce just one. Deciding which to reproduce is difficult because the manuscripts often vary from each other a good deal. This variation is frequent in small differences – like a difference between the word 'Iusticer' in one manuscript of a Middle English translation of the French writer Alain Chartier's *Traité de l'Espérance* ('Treatise of Hope') but the more familiar 'iuge' in another (ed. Blayney 1974: 67, line 14) – and common on a larger scale too. For some critics, this variation or change from one manuscript to another is the essence of 'medieval' literary culture (Zumthor 1992: 45–9). Some such critics have objected to the need in modern editions to reproduce just one of the variant forms of any text and have suggested new forms of edition to represent the variation (Cerquiglini 1999). Hitherto, though, editors have most often had three broad options.

Firstly, some have simply printed more than one manuscript in a 'parallel text'. For example, Laʒamon's early thirteenth-century verse *Brut* has been printed thus, for one manuscript uses a consistently more archaic style than the other (ed. Brook and Leslie 1963–78). It has been argued too that a parallel text edition is the only sensible arrangement for many romances (Fellows 1998: 19–23), as their manuscripts often show frequent variation, like that seen here in *Sir Degrevant*:

Sir Degreuant þan hir mete		Syr Degriuaunt withouten lett
In an alay with-owtyn let;	hindrance	In an aley he hyr mete,
Ferly faire he hir gret.	Extraordinarily	And godlyche he hyr gret.
		(ed. Casson 1949: lines 689–91)

But to read an edition in parallel is difficult – especially when the editor modernizes as little as here. And some texts do not show, as this one does, clear parallels between the variant versions. At one extreme, the two earliest manuscripts of *The Canterbury Tales*, despite being copied by the same scribe, who may even have known Chaucer (Mooney 2006), differ from each other quite a lot, both in the 'accidentals' of particular lines and in the range of tales included and their order. The differences (seen in the facsimile ed. Ruggiers 1979, which prints the Hengwrt manuscript with the variants in the Ellesmere manuscript in parallel) are fiddly to understand; and the further fifty-odd manuscripts of this work introduce yet more variants. How could one present them readably?

The second option, then, is an edition based on one manuscript. Such an edition might be a 'best-text' edition, which reproduces just one manuscript for its seeming excellence, although perhaps incorporating a few points from another manuscript. An example is an edition of *The Canterbury Tales* that boldly prints just the Hengwrt manuscript (which omits *The Canon's Yeoman's Tale* as well as numerous smaller details found in other manuscripts), in order 'to remind us of what is actually in the best manuscript' (Blake, ed., 1980: 12). Similar is a 'scribal' edition, which also reproduces only one manuscript closely, but with less interest in claiming that the manuscript is the 'best' (Moffat with McCarren 1998: 31–6). For example, one editor of the fourteenth-century mystical work *The Scale of Perfection* calls his edition 'scribal', because it reflects just one scribe's effort to reproduce the author Walter Hilton's work – including some Christocentric expansions in the first section of the text that are likely not by Hilton (Bestul, ed., 2000: 8–9). (Yet the edition does not reproduce copies of Hilton's other works found in the same volume (Bestul, ed., 2000: 7–8).)

The third and final common option for handling variant manuscripts has a long pedigree in editions of classical Latin and Greek works. The manuscripts of those works tend to have been made centuries after the text was composed and tend to differ among themselves a lot as a result. In response, scholars have devised elaborate procedures, including mapping textual lines of descent in 'recensions', or *stemmae*, to explain the variation between copies, in order not to reproduce any one *manuscript* but to reconstruct anew the authorial or at least earliest knowable form of the *text* (Moffat with McCarren 1998: 27–31). This 'textual criticism' has produced many excellent editions and its procedures have been adopted and adapted for Middle English literature. So, to return to the variants of *The Canterbury Tales*, most modern editions, such as *The Riverside Chaucer*, conflate the Hengwrt and Ellesmere manuscripts somehow, and incorporate sections found in neither manuscript, such as the Epilogue to *The Man of Law's Tale* (Benson, ed., 1987: 1126). Sometimes such editions make informed reconstructions of the author's own words, even if these words are not recorded in any manuscript. For example, the greatest edition of *Piers Plowman* frequently gives lines recorded nowhere but which the editors feel instinctively would be Langland's (Kane and Donaldson, eds., 1988: 130), such as these lines of devious quibbling (spoken by the figure of Mercy) about God's deception of the arch-deceiver Satan:

'And riȝt as [þe gilour] þoruȝ gile [bigiled man formest]   first
So shal *grace* that bigan [al] make a good [ende
And bigile þe gilour, and þat is good] sleighte.'   stratagem
(ed. Kane and Donaldson 1988: XVIII.160–2)

The lines are offered as Langland's B-text of his poem, but the square
brackets – included in any good edition and vital to attend to – warn
us that no manuscript of the B-text includes them; it was the editors
who added the dizzying *traductio* on *guile* and the charming contrast
of God *beginning* all (the universe) and putting an *end* to all the world's
sorrow. Langland did have this idea at one point: he revised the B-
text some years later into the so-called C-text, and the manuscripts
of the C-text do include these lines (ed. Russell and Kane 1997:
XX.163–5). However, the editors have assumed what no manuscript
proves: that Langland devised these lines for his earlier B-text too. They
have removed one possible change between Langland's B-text and C-
text, and in doing so have changed the manuscripts of the B-text that
they reproduce.

Such reconstructions can be considered either an imaginative triumph or a great deception (Moffat with McCarren 1998: 36–40). People
often have strong feelings about the editorial procedures of conflating
and emending, or not, as well as anthologizing, selecting, moderniz-
ing, punctuating and glossing. All these procedures change the
manuscripts purportedly being reproduced. Yet the above emendation
to *Piers Plowman*, like the changes made by editors of other works, seems
prompted by the ways in which poets or scribes *themselves* changed
the works that they produced and reproduced. Therefore, we cannot
divide manuscripts neatly from editions, just as we cannot always divide
'medieval' and 'modern'. The people who made and used manuscripts reworked texts for new occasions, and altered the language and
accompanying paratexts – in ways similar, if not identical, to those
of editors.

Variation in Manuscripts

The tendency to change the work begins with the author himself,
challenging the distinction between author and editor. Some authors
rewrote or re-edited their works for circulation in different versions.
Sometimes the prompt was political upheaval, as in some fifteenth-
century works that shifted in policy or patron, following the fluctuating

allegiances of the Wars of the Roses. For example, William Worcester seems to have drafted parts of his treatise *The Boke of Noblesse* for Henry VI in the 1450s, but he then revised it for Edward IV in 1475 (and his revisions are still visible, in his handwriting, on the only manuscript); then, after Worcester's death, his son repackaged it for Richard III (Wakelin 2007: 95). But the prompt was not always political: the author of *Ancrene Wisse* composed his treatise firstly for a close-knit group of three anchorites but adapted it for a wider audience less well known to him (Millett, ed., 2005: xxxvii–viii). Moreover, at least one poet was unembarrassed about changing dedicatees for his poem, for he left the change visible within one manuscript: Thomas Hoccleve says that he wrote his *Dialogue with a Friend* for the Duke of Gloucester ('For him it is / þat I this book shal make') but in an autograph copy of the text he added a stanza in which he sends the book as a gift to the Duchess of Westmorland, presumably fishing for a new patron (ed. Burrow and Doyle 2002: Durham fols 19v, 95r). Many Middle English poets mention the purpose for which they are writing; but here Hoccleve reveals the changing purpose behind reproducing his *Dialogue* in another copy.

Writers also edited their works for more curious, creative purposes. The most important example is Langland's rewriting of *Piers Plowman*, which was so complex that most editors and critics identify three different versions of it, the A-text, B-text and C-text, in supposed order of composition (as noted above). However, in fact the multiple manuscripts of each single version in turn differ from each other so much that one editor has plausibly suggested that some might be further revisions, with the poem 'in a continuous state of composition', as Langland endlessly composed and recomposed it (Pearsall 1985: 99–100; see also Pearsall 1992: 40–6). A more self-contained but intriguing example is offered by the variant versions of Chaucer's Prologue to *The Legend of Good Women*: what is now thought to be the earliest version, the F-Prologue, seems to allude to Queen Anne and the other version, G, may date from after her death, for allusions to her are absent from it (Benson, ed., 1987: 1060). However, besides this change in patron, there are also artistic changes: for example, the delicate lyric 'Hyd, Absalon, thy gilte tresses clere' is sung in the F-Prologue by the narrator 'in preysyng' of the beautiful Queen Alceste – perhaps in parallel praise of Queen Anne – and in the G-Prologue by a troupe of ladies in honour of a daisy. Apart from the refrain, the lyric is reproduced almost identically; yet it changes in its function – from praise to an expression of joy – by being edited into a new context (F.241–77, G.194–227). There may be similar changes in *The Canterbury Tales*: after Chaucer's death, people tried, with difficulty, to arrange the unfinished poem into an acceptable order, but some changes to the text look like authorial reorganizations. In the earliest, Hengwrt manuscript *The Merchant's Tale* did not follow *The Clerk's Tale* and lacked the Merchant's Prologue, as we now know it, in which the Merchant laments his dreadful marriage. The Merchant's Prologue instead was what in the Ellesmere manuscript and most modern editions becomes the Franklin's response to *The Squire's Tale*, in which he praises the Squire for his gentility and eloquence; the only difference in the earlier manuscript is the phrase 'Quod the Marchant' instead of 'Quod the Frankeleyn' (ed. Ruggiers 1979: xxv, fol. 137v; ed. Benson 1987: V.673–708). The substitution of a prologue that suggests links between the Merchant's dreadful marriage and his sexist tale (Benson, ed., 1987: 13) might reflect Chaucer's later editing of his work, as might the juxtaposition of *The Merchant's Tale* with *The Clerk's Tale*. The poetic creation of *The Canterbury Tales* as a whole was in part a work of editing, for Chaucer compiled some of the poem from tales written earlier, such as *The Knight's Tale* and *The Second Nun's Tale* (Benson, ed., 1987: 3). In Middle English literature, then, there was sometimes a blurred division between a writer and an editor.

Yet commoner still was for works to be changed by scribes and readers. Firstly, as Jeremy Smith describes above, scribes changed the orthography and morphology of the texts that they copied according to their local variety of English, and they sometimes updated archaisms. Secondly, scribes of course made some inadvertent changes to texts, by oversights, the omission of stanzas, slips of the pen and so on. Finally, they changed texts for new readerships or new audiences: for example, later scribes further abridged and expanded *Ancrene Wisse* for devout lay readers rather than anchorites (Millett, ed., 2005: xxi–ii). Some clear adaptations are found in the texts of carols; other religious lyrics were also adapted for different purposes. For example, Lydgate's poem in the voice of Jesus, 'Vppon the cross nailid I was for the', circulated in several fifteenth-century manuscripts but in one early sixteenth-century songbook acquired a long burden – like a repeated 'chorus' – making it suitable for singing in the traditional form of a carol, to music by Sheryngham (ed. Greene 1977: no. 263.a). This was a longstanding trend: other religious poems appear in some manuscripts without a 'burden' and in others with one, turned into a carol, fit to sing and dance to. Very occasionally the burden has been added in a visibly different ink and handwriting (Wakelin 2006: 36–7), a clear instance of editorial rewriting for a new convivial occasion.

Some editing does not seem merely to respond to changes in use, or to the mobility of oral transmission. It has long been recognized that scribes were likely to emend the text to simplify any more difficult word or section (the *difficilior lectio* in classical editing) with a simpler one. It is well known that some scribes of Chaucer's and Langland's poetry did this (Windeatt 1979; Kane and Donaldson, eds., 1988: 130–1), like one scribe of *Piers Plowman* who replaced the archaic alliterative words *gome* and *wye* – familiar to readers of alliterative verse – once with the more common *man*, and once, wrongly, with the adjective *wyle* ('wily') (San Marino, CA, Huntington Library, MS HM 114, fols 113v, 15v). Rather than condemn such changes, recent editors and critics have often praised the different scribal versions of texts that were produced: Bernard Cerquiglini has argued that scribes, who were used to copying the divinely authorized and ruled language of Latin, rejoiced to copy literature in their mother tongue, which was 'not yet forced into the shackles of established forms'; therefore, they 'manipulated' the manuscripts of the 'open' text in a 'joyful excess' (Cerquiglini 1999: 21, 33–4). We could condemn the modern edition for obscuring this joyful 'variance' by removing it, whether in a 'critical' edition, through the reconstruction of an authorial version, or in a 'best-text' or 'scribal' edition, through the recording of only one manuscript.

Reproduction despite Change

However, rewriting is not always a radical attempt to change things. Tim Machan has warned that while variation might exist on the textual surface, the underlying ideas might remain the same, shared across a deeply traditional and conservative culture by different people; Middle English poets and scribes, he suggests, were more interested in the essential meaning of their poem – the praise of the saints, say – than they were in the mere wording or literary niceties (Machan 1994: 141–2, 155, 165–76). For example, one jolly carol contains the following stanza in the aforementioned manuscript Sloane 2593 and, in variant form, in manuscript Douce 302 in the Bodleian Library in Oxford:

Wolcu*m* be ye, Stefne *and* Jon,	Welcu*m* be ye, Steuen *and* Jone,
Wlcu*m*, Innoce*n*tes eue*r*ychon,	Welcu*m*, child*er*n eue*r*echone,
Wolcu*m*, Thomas, mart*er* on;	Wellcu*m*, Thomas, mart*er* allon;
Wolcu*m*, Yol.	Welcu*m*, Yole, for eu*er* *and* ay.
(ed. Greene 1977: no. 7.B,	(ed. Greene 1977: no. 7.A)
where the spelling in the	
manuscript is modified slightly)	

Besides some tiny differences of spelling and wording, which might reflect varying attempts to reproduce a text transmitted orally in writing, there is only one big difference: between 'Innoce*n*tes' and 'child*er*n'. Yet even this is not a difference in thought, for the children are obviously the innocents slaughtered by Herod, since they appear in a sequence after St Stephen and St John the Evangelist and before St Thomas Becket, which is when their feast-day falls in the calendar (28 December). The accidents of the language change but the substance of the ideas remains. There is some difference in register between 'Innoce*n*tes' and 'child*er*n', the former perhaps evoking the theological connotations of innocence, the latter the pathos of children – a pathos common in the manuscript from which the latter version comes, the anthology ascribed to John Audelay (see entries nos 108, 117.a, 122.A, 412, 428 in ed. Greene 1977; compare Jane Griffiths' essay above). Yet it is difficult to decide whether this 'editorial' change is deliberate or not, substantial or accidental (in all senses of those words).

Moreover, many scribes copied already-edited texts without realizing that the lone exemplar that they were copying differed from others. As Ralph Hanna has noted, each copy of a Middle English work was unique and it was often the only copy, or one of very few copies, known to its readers; it was known only to one or very few readers too (Hanna 1992: 120–2). When scribes copied changed texts, the change was often inherited, and carefully reproduced. When, as sometimes happened, scribes or readers *did* find that their copy differed from another, they often tried to erase the difference – much as modern editors do. Such carefulness often occurs in copies of widely circulated works with considerable prestige, from the fourteenth-century poem *The Pricke of Conscience* to Lydgate's *Fall of Princes* over a century later. For example, in 1476 a Norfolk estate-manager and his son transcribed *The Canterbury Tales* but, because they changed exemplars in the process of copying, they omitted *The Clerk's Tale* and *The Canon's Yeoman's Tale*. When, having finished, they noticed the absence of these tales, they crossed out the colophon concluding the work and added the missing tales 'in the next leef [. . .] for the book of Caunt*er*bury is nat yet ended' (Beadle 1997: 116–17). Similarly, three philosophical sections of *Troilus and Criseyde* were missing in some copies, maybe because they were later stages of Chaucer's work; one scribe who discovered that these sections were missing in his copy later copied them on separate sheets of paper, with red symbols to mark where to insert them into his existing book (San Marino, CA, Huntington Library, MS HM 114, fols 262r, 277v, 318r). The same scribe also copied a text of *Piers Plowman* that conflated Langland's A-text, B-text and C-text to form a new text, perhaps aiming for the most complete one possible (Bowers 2004: 140). These are well-known and extreme cases, but there are countless other, tinier ones. Even carols, transmitted usually with frequent variation that suggests oral circulation, could have extra slips of parchment added, for missing stanzas discovered, somehow, later (London, British Library, MS Sloane 2593, fol. 12; ed. Greene 1977: no. 123.B). In such corrections, the manuscript that results differs still from other copies, because the additions must fit where physically possible rather than where perfectly correct – and the manuscript reveals change between different stages of copying. But these differences and changes, it might be thought, are intended to prevent the received text changing further.

Scribes also sought to prevent further change in the process of textual reproduction by correcting their copies. Such corrections are a little-known element of scribes' work, and some theories of textual instability dismiss their significance (Zumthor 1992: 46), but they are quite common. For example, in the aforementioned copy of *Troilus and Criseyde* (San Marino, CA, Huntington Library, MS HM 114) there are some 213 corrections by the scribe (as far as I can count), most of them written later, to judge by the colour of the ink and the scribe's difficulty of squeezing them in. Over a quarter (60) are so pernickety as to correct the spelling of particular words and a third (71) to correct the tiniest grammatical words, on the presumption that the poem should make sense. About a quarter of them (54) restore the decasyllabic metre, though this restoration usually seems incidental to corrections of other features. In the act of copying the text, scribes sometimes undid the changes to it that made their version differ from others. In nearly two-thirds of his corrections (135), the scribe of the Huntington Library manuscript of *Troilus and Criseyde*, for example, returns the line to the form chosen by the most thorough modern editor (compare Windeatt 1984). A sample of twenty-four manuscripts from the Huntington Library in California suggests that scribes and readers frequently corrected and checked their manuscripts and that nearly 82 per cent of corrections by scribes or early readers turned the text into the form reproduced in the best available modern edition. This rough sample suggests that at least *some* scribes of Middle English corrected Middle English literature in some effort to cancel out variation in their texts, or changes that had been made to them. Their motives for doing so are still not entirely clear, but the process might fairly be compared to the efforts of some modern editors to remove variation from the textual tradition.

However, beyond this superficial continuity between manuscripts and modern editions there are subtle differences in how scribes and editors pursue the 'correct' text. The commonest manuscript corrections, of grammatical slips, of confusing spellings or of small omissions that obviously disrupt stanzaic form, could all easily be made by a sensible read-through of the copied text: this could explain the emending of the spelling 'purgarie' to 'purgatorie' or spotting that in Lydgate's *Fall of Princes* one rhyme royal stanza 'lakketh a verse', that is, lacks one of its seven lines (Durham, University Library, MS Cosin V.iii.24, fol. 12v; London, British Library, MS Additional 21410, fols 71r, 114v). Only certain types of correction would seem to have required the consultation of different copies, which is the essence of modern 'critical' editing: for example, somebody spotted that the same copy of *The Fall of Princes* 'here lakketh vj balades', or six complete rhyme royal stanzas, a precise number that one could not simply guess – although the calculation was one stanza out (London, British Library, MS Additional 21410, fol. 114r). People seem likelier – it is hard to prove – to check the exemplars from which they copied than to collate further exemplars. Such checks would often have been required to add words in a grammatically or metrically inessential position or to add passages of some length. This may explain why the person who oversaw the work of some scribes copying devotional prose for an East Anglian nunnery was able to complete the second half of many doublets in the manuscript they produced – 'pees' into 'pees and reste', say – and to add passages up to a line long in some margins (Durham, University Library, MS Cosin V.iii.24, for example fols 52r, 55r). Some seemingly professional scribes of secular works marked their copies, after checking, with the abbreviation for *corrigitur* (Latin for 'it is corrected') or *examinatur* ('it is examined') at the foot of the page (for example San Marino, CA, Huntington Library, MSS Ellesmere 26.A.13 and HM 268). Yet behind these procedures there might be monastic discipline or the scribe's professional pride and method rather than the philological zeal of some editors.

Finally, for the scribe of Middle English, for whom change is the norm, the decision to keep the text the same is striking; for the modern editor – influenced by traditions of humanist editing and assumptions about the fixity of print – the decision to undo change is normal. So the editorial process of preventing the text from changing has itself changed over time.

Reproduction and Reception

The decision to change the text or to prevent change is, for the scribe, just one of the decisions made in considering how to package what is copied for a new occasion or readership. The operators of a printing press usually have fairly constant material conditions for the whole print-run of any text and (except in rare cases of private or subscription printing) tailor a book not to a very precisely defined reader but to widespread sales. Scribes, by contrast, produced each copy, even of the same text, in changed material conditions, and most often with a specific purchaser, patron, library or community in mind; therefore they packaged the text in changing visual and material forms. For example, the charming lyric 'Ther is no rose' is once written informally on the flyleaf of a book, along with a grace for use at a meal, and once adorned in red and blue with musical notation on a roll for formal performance (ed. Griffiths 1995: 281). Such changes in presentation affect larger works too. So scribes sometimes reproduce Chaucer's *Boece* with lots of scholarly apparatus, or some attempt at a Middle English/ Latin bilingual edition, and sometimes with less apparatus (Wakelin 2007: 12–21). How scribes introduce a text might change too: in one manuscript of *Boece* a later reader noted that it was 'translated by Chaucer, knight of Richard II' (Cambridge, Pembroke College, MS 215, fol. 1r: 'translatum per Chawcers armigerum Ricardi 2di'), thus increasing the work's value and Chaucer's rank for any future reader of the book.

From the late fourteenth century onwards, scribes elaborated the presentation of Middle English literature quite considerably. One big increase was in the number of complex marginal notes or systems of textual division that scribes supplied in some – not all – of the copies of ambitious poems such as Gower's *Confessio Amantis*, Chaucer's *Canterbury Tales* and *Troilus and Criseyde* (and one manuscript of *The House of Fame*), Hoccleve's *Regement of Princes*, Lydgate's *Fall of Princes* and his 'biography' of the Virgin Mary, *The Lyf of Our Lady*, and various anonymous recondite fifteenth-century poems and translations (Wakelin 2007: 39–41, 55, 58, 66; Keiser 1995: 208–12). These marginalia comment on the texts in a variety of ways, most often by providing sources, allegorical interpretations or historical or mythological explanations. That these marginalia proliferate from the period of Gower and Chaucer onwards may reflect, or perhaps nurture, growing respect for English literature from that period, as do other changes in the quality, material form and appearance of English manuscripts at that time (Pearsall 1995; compare Alexandra Gillespie's essay in this volume). Many marginalia win respect for English literature by citing sources or analogues in Latin literature, which was, throughout this period, better respected for its learnedness. For example, in the curious dream vision *The Court of Sapience* the brief suggestion that crystal can cure 'seke men' is justified by a quotation from the Latin encyclopaedia by Bartholomaeus Anglicus ('Bartholomew the Englishman') about curing 'colic and troubles of the bowels as long as there is no constipation' (ed. Harvey 1984: 105, line 976: 'colicam et viscerum passionem, si non assit constipacio'). These marginal notes in some ways continue the interest in Latin literature suggested by the practice of translation in this period (sketched by Helen Cooper in this volume). Yet besides their Latin content, the visual form of the marginalia also suggests that the English text is as worthy of elaborate notes and commentaries as were copies of the Bible or classical poetry in the thirteenth, fourteenth and fifteenth centuries. Some of these marginalia have a more playful intent: the Latin marginalia in the aforementioned Ellesmere manuscript of *The Wife of Bath's Prologue* record the lines from the Bible and from St Jerome that the Wife quotes out of context (translated in ed. Benson 1987: 864–72) and so poke fun at her as much as they glorify Chaucer. But more often such marginalia made English literature look like the important texts that deserved effortful and serious reading in schools and that carried authority.

In some cases this attention to the text's reception began with the authors themselves. The poets John Gower and Thomas Hoccleve clearly prepared Latin marginalia for their poems, as did the authors of various learned fifteenth-century poems and translations. The marginalia on Chaucer's works only occur in a few copies, albeit early ones; they might have been intended by him, or might have been added by the scribes who copied his works. Even when marginalia definitely seem to be the work of later scribes and readers, they often continue the work of the original marginalia. So the marginalia and textual divisions in some copies of Lydgate's works seem to be by him, although more were added by other people, often highlighting similar things (Wakelin 2007: 41–2; Keiser 1995: 215). Similarly, one scholar in the 1440s added to one hundred of Hoccleve's notes to *The Regement of Princes* over fifty more similar notes, including spotting two allusions to Gower's *Confessio Amantis* (Cambridge, Corpus Christi College, MS 496, especially fols 33v–34r). And just as Langland rewrote his *Piers Plowman*, so scribes and readers edited the poem by providing intriguing marginalia (catalogued by Benson and Blanchfield 1997), guiding its reception, sometimes drawing the poem to the attention of 'ȝe lewede ermytes' or 'ȝe ryche men' in the direct tone of some of the poem's monologues (San Marino, CA, Huntington Library, MS HM 143, fols 42r, 68r). Such apparatus was devised, then, both by the original writers of such works and by the scribes who reproduced them, in a continuing process of steering the text's reception as much as its reproduction.

In some of the attention to careful reproduction, and in some of the attention to reception, there might seem to be more of a divide between manuscripts before and after the half century around 1400 than between manuscripts and some 'modern' editions. Editors tend not to reproduce these marginalia found in early manuscripts; but editors do provide footnotes, introductions and so on of their own, which offer sources, summaries and other guides to interpreting the text. Both manuscripts and editions, then, sometimes not only reproduce the text but also change its meaning by framing it within paratexts that guide its interpretation and reception. Against this longer trajectory of continued changes by scribes, readers and even authors, the changes made by more recent editors might be viewed with equanimity. Any 'giving out' or editing changes a text, as the editor gives the text to future readers rather than past writers. But it is vital to be informed of the changes made in editions, in manuscripts, and between manuscripts and printed or digital editions, changes that prevent perfect reproduction.

References

Primary texts

Beadle, Richard and King, Pamela, eds. (1984). *York Mystery Plays: A Selection in Modern Spelling*. Oxford: Clarendon Press.
Benson, Larry D., gen. ed. (1987). *The Riverside Chaucer*. Boston: Houghton Mifflin.

Bestul, Thomas, ed. (2000). *Walter Hilton: The Scale of Perfection.* Kalamazoo: Medieval Institute Publications.

Blake, N.F., ed. (1980). *Geoffrey Chaucer: The Canterbury Tales, Edited from the Hengwrt Manuscript.* London: Edward Arnold.

Blayney, Margaret S., ed. (1974–80). *Fifteenth-Century English Translations of Alain Chartier's Le Traité de l'Espérance and Le Quadrilogue Invectif.* EETS OS 270, 281. London: Oxford University Press.

Brook, G.L., ed. (1948). *The Harley Lyrics: The Middle English Lyrics of MS. Harley 2253.* Manchester: Manchester University Press.

Brook, G.L. and Leslie, R.F., eds. (1963–78). *Laȝamon: Brut.* EETS OS 250, 277. London: Oxford University Press.

Burrow, J.A. and Doyle, A.I., eds. (2002). *Thomas Hoccleve: A Facsimile of the Autograph Verse Manuscripts.* EETS SS 19. Oxford: Oxford University Press.

Cartlidge, Neil, ed. (2001). *The Owl and the Nightingale: Text and Translation.* Exeter: University of Exeter Press.

Casson, L.F., ed. (1949). *The Romance of Sir Degrevant.* EETS OS 221. London: Oxford University Press.

Greene, Richard Leighton, ed. (1977). *The Early English Carols.* 2nd edn, revd. Oxford: Clarendon Press.

Griffiths, Jeremy, ed. (1995). 'Unrecorded Middle English Verse in the Library of Holkham Hall, Norfolk'. *Medium Ævum,* 64, 278–84.

Hirsh, John C., ed. (2005). *Medieval Lyric: Middle English Lyrics, Ballads, and Carols.* Oxford: Blackwell.

Kane, George and Donaldson, E. Talbot, eds. (1988). *Piers Plowman: The B Version.* Revd edn. London: Athlone Press.

Lester, G.A., ed. (1981). *Three Late Medieval Morality Plays.* London: Ernest Benn.

Millett, Bella, ed. (2005). *Ancrene Wisse: A Corrected Edition of the Text in Cambridge, Corpus Christi College, MS 402, with Variants from Other Manuscripts.* EETS OS 325. Oxford: Oxford University Press.

Ruggiers, Paul G., ed. (1979). *The Canterbury Tales. A Facsimile and Transcription of the Hengwrt Manuscript, with Variants from the Ellesmere Manuscript.* With introductions by Donald C. Baker and A.I. Doyle and M.B. Parkes. Norman, OK: University of Oklahoma Press.

Russell, George and Kane, George, eds. (1997). *Piers Plowman: The C Version.* London: Athlone Press.

Tolkien, J.R.R., ed. (1962). *Ancrene Wisse: The English Text of the Ancrene Riwle.* EETS OS 249. London: Oxford University Press.

Wilson, Edward, ed. (1981). *The Winchester Anthology: A Facsimile of British Library Additional Manuscript 60577.* Cambridge: D.S. Brewer.

Windeatt, B.A., ed. (1984). *Geoffrey Chaucer: Troilus and Criseyde.* London: Longman.

Secondary sources and suggestions for further reading

Beadle, Richard (1997). 'Geoffrey Spirleng (*c.* 1426–*c.* 1494): A Scribe of the *Canterbury Tales* in His Time'. In P.R. Robinson and Rivkah Zim, eds.,

Of the Making of Books: Essays Presented to M.B. Parkes (pp. 116–46). Aldershot: Scolar Press.

Beadle, Richard (1998). 'Facsimiles of Middle English Manuscripts'. In Vincent P. McCarren and Douglas Moffat, eds., *A Guide to Editing Middle English* (pp. 319–31). Ann Arbor: University of Michigan Press.

Benson, C. David and Blanchfield, Lynne S. (1997). *The Manuscripts of Piers Plowman: The B-Version*. Cambridge: D.S. Brewer.

Bowers, John, M. (2004). 'Two Professional Readers of Chaucer and Langland: Scribe D and the HM 114 Scribe'. *Studies in the Age of Chaucer*, 26, 113–46.

Brantley, Jessica (2007). *Reading in the Wilderness: Private Devotion and Public Performance in Late Medieval England*. Chicago: University of Chicago Press.

Cerquiglini, Bernard (1999). *In Praise of the Variant: A Critical History of Philology* (Betsy Wing, trans.). Baltimore: Johns Hopkins University Press.

Fellows, Jennifer (1998). 'Author, Author, Author . . . : An Apology for Parallel Texts'. In Vincent P. McCarren and Douglas Moffat, eds., *A Guide to Editing Middle English* (pp. 15–24). Ann Arbor: University of Michigan Press.

Hanna, Ralph, III (1992). 'Producing Manuscripts and Editions'. In A.J. Minnis and Charlotte Brewer, eds., *Crux and Controversy in Middle English Textual Criticism* (pp. 109–30). Cambridge: D.S. Brewer.

Keiser, George (1995). 'Serving the Needs of Readers: Textual Division in Some Late-Medieval English Texts'. In Richard Beadle and A.J. Piper, eds., *New Science out of Old Books: Studies in Manuscripts and Early Printed Books in Honour of A.I. Doyle* (pp. 207–26). Aldershot: Scolar Press.

McGann, Jerome J. (1983). *A Critique of Modern Textual Criticism*. Charlottesville: University Press of Virginia.

McGann, Jerome J. (1991). *The Textual Condition*. Princeton: Princeton University Press.

Machan, Tim William (1994). *Textual Criticism and Middle English Texts*. Charlottesville: University Press of Virginia.

McKenzie, D.F. (1999). *Bibliography and the Sociology of Texts*. Revd edn. Cambridge: Cambridge University Press.

Moffat, Douglas with McCarren, Vincent P. (1998). 'A Bibliographical Essay on Editing Methods and Authorial and Scribal Intention'. In Vincent P. McCarren and Douglas Moffat, eds., *A Guide to Editing Middle English* (pp. 25–57). Ann Arbor: University of Michigan Press.

Mooney, Linne R. (2006). 'Chaucer's Scribe'. *Speculum*, 81, 97–138.

Pearsall, Derek (1985). 'Editing Medieval Texts: Some Developments and Some Problems'. In Jerome J. McGann, ed., *Textual Criticism and Literary Interpretation* (pp. 92–106). Chicago: University of Chicago Press.

Pearsall, Derek (1992). 'Authorial Revision in Some Late-Medieval English Texts'. In A.J. Minnis and Charlotte Brewer, eds., *Crux and Controversy in Middle English Textual Criticism* (pp. 39–48). Cambridge: D.S. Brewer.

Pearsall, Derek (1995). 'The Ellesmere Chaucer and Contemporary English Literary Manuscripts'. In Martin Stevens and Daniel Woodward, eds., *The Ellesmere Chaucer: Essays in Interpretation* (pp. 263–80). San Marino, CA: Huntington Library.

Scott, Kathleen L. (1996). *Later Gothic Manuscripts, 1390–1490*. A Survey of Manuscripts Illuminated in the British Isles Vol. 6. London: Harvey Miller.

Solopova, Elizabeth (2000). 'Layout, Punctuation, and Stanza Patterns in the English Verse'. In Susanna Fein, ed., *Studies in the Harley Manuscript* (pp. 377–89). Kalamazoo: Medieval Institute Publications.

Tschann, Judith (1985). 'The Layout of *Sir Thopas* in the Ellesmere, Hengwrt, Cambridge Dd.4.24 and Cambridge Gg.4.27 Manuscripts'. *Chaucer Review*, 20, 1–13.

Wakelin, Daniel (2006). 'The Carol in Writing: Three Anthologies from Fifteenth-Century Norfolk'. *Journal of the Early Book Society*, 9, 25–49.

Wakelin, Daniel (2007). *Humanism, Reading, and English Literature 1430–1530*. Oxford: Oxford University Press.

Windeatt, B.A. (1979). 'The Scribes as Chaucer's Early Critics'. *Studies in the Age of Chaucer*, 1, 119–42.

Zumthor, Paul (1992). *Toward a Medieval Poetics* (Philip Bennett, trans.). Minneapolis: University of Minnesota Press.

Chapter 11

The Afterlife of Middle English Literature

David Matthews

'Middle English', as Jeremy Smith's essay in this volume has discussed, is a technical term that was coined in the nineteenth century to refer to a specific phase of the English language. It came into widespread use in the 1870s, when it was popularized by a group of influential English philologists – particularly Walter Skeat, Henry Sweet and Richard Morris – who extended its application to the literature that was composed between *c.* 1100 and *c.* 1500. Prior to the nineteenth century, there was no term that designated what we understand as 'Middle English'. In the sixteenth century, scholars developed the study of Old English (see Berkhout and Gatch, eds., 1982; Frantzen 1990); they also promoted the idea of a Renaissance, distinguishing it from the Middle Ages (Ferguson 1948: 73). But neither the sixteenth-century scholars nor any others before the nineteenth century developed an idea of Middle English. And so, before the 1870s, there was no concept of 'Middle English literature' as such. The isolation of Middle English literature as a distinctive body of writing is a relatively recent phenomenon.

That specific literary as well as linguistic features characterize the writing that was produced in the Middle English period has been the theme of this volume; but different ages have perceived different features in the writings that survive from the Middle Ages. As now, readers' conceptions of these writings were partly determined by the editions that they used (compare Daniel Wakelin's essay above). But they have also been determined by broader cultural conditions that have pertained at various times. This essay will discuss these issues by returning, first, to the earliest phase of the understanding and reconceiving of Middle English literature, soon after 1500. It will then consider the seventeenth century, when interest in Middle English literature declined; and then the eighteenth and nineteenth centuries, which saw a revival of interest in the literature. After 1870, Middle English literature became a subject of academic study, and the way it was shaped in the following years has been crucial to how we think about it now. In the past few years, this essay will argue, the most important set of changes since the 1870s has been taking place, creating various prospects and problems for the perception of Middle English in the future.

The Sixteenth Century: Survivals

Through its large-scale destruction of the monastic houses of England, the Reformation of the English Church under the second of the Tudor monarchs, Henry VIII, constituted a highly visible and self-conscious break with the medieval past (see especially Duffy 1992: 478–503). Yet despite the new attitude of suspicion towards the Middle Ages that was engendered by the Reformation, there was not a straightforward break with the *literary* past of England. Instead, there was considerable continuity, with several late-medieval texts remaining available and being reproduced in the new technology of print (discussed in detail in Gillespie 2006).

At the end of the fifteenth century, for example, Geoffrey Chaucer's work had been published by the first English printer, William Caxton, who produced an edition of *The Canterbury Tales* in 1476. This was followed by editions printed by Caxton's successors Wynkyn de Worde and Richard Pynson. In the early days of print both Chaucer's contemporary John Gower and their fifteenth-century successor John Lydgate were routinely placed alongside Chaucer in a triumvirate of English greats: around 1470, in his *Active Policy of a Prince*, the poet George Ashby referred to them as 'Maisters Gower, Chaucer & Lydgate, / Primier poets of this nacion' (ed. Spurgeon 1925: Vol. I, 54).

Interest in all three writers continued in the sixteenth century. William Thynne, a royal servant under Henry VIII, produced a lavish folio edition of Chaucer's works (the first that claimed to include all his writings) in 1532. Thynne's edition was augmented twice more in the 1540s, and it was succeeded by John Stow's edition of 1561, and by

Thomas Speght's two editions of 1598 and 1602. The year 1532 also saw the printing of John Gower's major English work, the *Confessio Amantis*, by Thomas Berthelette, King's Printer to Henry VIII. Lydgate's *Troy Book* was printed by Pynson in 1513 and again by Thomas Marshe in 1555. In addition, Sir Thomas Malory's fifteenth-century Arthurian prose romance, entitled *Le Morte Darthur* by Caxton at its first printing in 1485, was reprinted by Wynkyn de Worde in 1498 and 1529, by William Copland in 1557, and by Thomas East around 1578. And a polemicist and printer named Robert Crowley produced three impressions of an edition of the B-text of *Piers Plowman* in 1550.

In the sixteenth century a printed book usually represented a substantial investment for a printer. At least some of these works seem to have been produced speculatively – in the hope that they would be sold – so the fact that they appeared at all suggests a lively ongoing interest in the medieval literary past. Medieval literature also continued to circulate in manuscripts. While the extent of such circulation is difficult to quantify, it is another indicator of ongoing interest in the medieval literary past in the sixteenth century.

This somewhat rosy picture of the level of interest in Middle English literature in the sixteenth century must, however, be qualified. The 'Middle English literature' that was read in this period consisted principally of texts written after 1350. Almost all of what, in the twentieth century, would be dubbed 'Ricardian poetry' (Burrow 1971) – poetry composed during the reign of Richard II (1377–99) – was known and was available (except for the works of the *Gawain*-poet, which were not read until the nineteenth century). Along with Lydgate and Malory, this formed the core of the sixteenth-century knowledge of Middle English. But there was little interest in, or knowledge of, anything composed before about 1350.

Furthermore, the print runs of each edition of Middle English texts would have been small (as was the tendency in the sixteenth century), and each book comparatively expensive. This means that these works probably reached only a very limited group of readers. In his editions of Chaucer's works, for example, Speght writes of how he first became interested in the poet at Peterhouse, Cambridge – not because he was studying his work (classical, not vernacular literature, formed the curriculum), but because there was a circle of men at Peterhouse who were interested in Chaucer. This highlights what was probably the principal forum for reading Chaucer and most other medieval writing in the late sixteenth century: small coteries of learned men.

What did such readers find interesting and important about Chaucer and other Middle English writing? It is rarely the case that a writer or editor expresses a simple, uncomplicated love of Middle English poetry. All Middle English literature, even Chaucer, was thought a little unrefined for sixteenth-century tastes. Even such clear enthusiasts of Chaucer as Speght, and his collaborator Francis Beaumont, felt the need to excuse Chaucer from the charge of 'inciuilitie' that such works as *The Miller's Tale* inevitably provoked (ed. Spurgeon 1925: Vol. I, 146; Brewer 1978: Vol. I, 137). Simply *enjoying* Chaucer or Gower was not enough; most sixteenth-century commentators thought that literature must have a moral purpose, that it should say something that could instruct the reader. So Wynkyn de Worde, offering *Le Morte Darthur* to the public in 1498, thought the work ought to be read often, as it depicts 'the gracious, knightly, and virtuous war of most noble knights', and because 'by the oft reading thereof ye shall greatly desire to accustom yourself in following of those gracious knightly deeds, that is to say, to dread God, and to love rightwiseness, faithfully and courageously to serve your sovereign prince' (ed. Parins 1988: 52). To read Malory makes one want to become more like an ideal chivalrous knight.

Gower and Chaucer, too, were seen as exemplary and instructive. This is best shown by the fact that they continued to be printed under the increasingly strict censorship and royal control of printing that characterized the reign of Henry VIII. In 1542–3, the parliamentary *Acte for thadvauncement of true Religion and for thabolishment of the contrarie* banned the printing of a great range of works, exempting only certain religious and instructive genres. The writings of Chaucer and Gower seem to have fallen into these categories, suggesting that the two poets were regarded favourably because of their moral instructiveness.

Those who objected to medieval literature also did so on moral grounds. In two works, *The Scholemaster* (1570) and *Toxophilis* (1545), the scholar Roger Ascham, one-time tutor to Elizabeth I, expressed strong views on some medieval texts. He believed that everyone should read Chaucer's *Pardoner's Tale* because of its critique of gambling. But he also deeply disapproved of Malory's *Morte Darthur*, which consisted principally, he famously claimed, of 'open mans slaughter, and bold bawdrye', and he felt that such 'vayne woordes doo woorke no smal thinge in vayne, ignoraunt, and younge mindes' (ed. Parins 1988: 57, 56).

These moral concerns were never far away from literary evaluations in the period. While Chaucer was generally approved of, it was clearly felt that his more bawdy writings needed to be excused. At the end of the sixteenth century, Francis Beaumont went to considerable lengths to apologize for the fabliaux told by the Miller, Reeve and Cook, arguing that these characters could not tell 'such honest and good tales' as those of the Knight, Man of Law or Clerk, as that would be unrealistic (ed. Spurgeon 1925: Vol. I, 146; Brewer 1978: Vol. I, 137). Because Chaucer aimed 'to describe all men liuing in those daies,' he could not leave 'vntouched these filthie delights of the baser sort of people' (ed. Brewer 1978: Vol. I, 138). The implication is that literature was expected to be decorous, but there may be mitigating factors – such as the author's supreme observation of the world around him – if it is not.

A further mitigating factor concerning Chaucer was the idea that he had been a kind of Protestant before Protestantism, someone who prefigured the reform of the English Church. Either ignoring, or perhaps remaining unaware of, the fact that anticlericalism is common in fourteenth-century writing, editors took Chaucer's criticisms of representatives of the Church as evidence of his reformist sensibility. As each new Chaucer edition appeared in the sixteenth century, new material was added to his work, much of it offering support for the notion of Chaucer as reformer (and most of it not, in fact, by Chaucer). Most notable among these additions, a fifteenth-century poem entitled *The Plowman's Tale* and a prose tract, *Jack Upland* – both of them expressing some of the sentiments of the early reformers known as Lollards – helped to give the impression that Chaucer was truly at home in a reformed Church.

As Wynkyn de Worde's comments on Malory, quoted above, suggest, a belief in the instructive capacity of old literature could be closely allied to a belief in its propagandist value: reading Malory could, in de Worde's view, lead to increased awe for the sovereign. As censorship became more severe in the course of Henry VIII's reign, it was a prudent move for any printer to promote the idea that the books he issued upheld established discourses of regal power or patriotism. In his 1532 edition of Gower's *Confessio Amantis*, Thomas Berthelette wrote, with Gower and Chaucer in mind, that 'so longe . . . as letters [literature] shal endure & continue, this noble royalme shall be the better . . .'. The implication is that a great kingdom has a cultural heritage of which it should be proud and on which it depends for its reputation. As the king's official printer, Berthelette had good reason to want to promote this idea.

This was particularly necessary as the climate of opinion about the Middle Ages changed. Henry VIII and his ministers fostered an atmosphere of increasing distrust for the medieval, Catholic past. It was part of Ascham's complaint about *Le Morte Darthur*, for example, that the work came from a time when 'Papistrie' was a 'standyng poole' covering England, and literature was produced by 'idle Monks, or wanton Chanons' (ed. Parins 1988: 56). The fact that Malory himself was not a cleric did not stop Ascham implicating his work in the degeneracy that was then thought to have characterized medieval Catholicism.

Yet despite such attitudes as Ascham's, as the Dissolution brought about a very visible destruction of the medieval English past, there were those who felt the need to preserve literature, artefacts and reputations against the ravages of time. The Tudor chronicler Edward Hall made a general warning against 'Obliuion the cancard [cankered] enemie to Fame and renoune[,] the suckyng serpe[n]t of auncient memory' (quoted in Ellis 2000: v). Tudor editors refer to the oblivion into which literature, in particular, risked falling. William Thynne, in his 1532 Chaucer edition, noted his retrieval of 'trewe copies' of the works of Chaucer that have remained 'almost vnknowen and in oblyuion', while at the end of the century Speght was commended by his collaborator Francis Beaumont for salvaging Chaucer from obscurity – for restoring '*Chaucer* both aliue again and yong again' (ed. Brewer 1978: Vol. I, 89, 137).

Over the course of the sixteenth century, Chaucer came to surpass Gower and Lydgate as the pre-eminent medieval English poet, the two lavish editions by Speght at the very end of the period suggesting stronger interest than ever. And it is clear that Middle English was still read at the end of the century in the wider literary world. Edmund Spenser was a great admirer of Chaucer and drew on Arthurian literature for his major work, *The Faerie Queene*. In the theatre, in the years 1599–1602 there were several plays that drew on Chaucer's work, which may reflect interest sparked by Speght's two editions (Thompson 1978: 30). In 1608, William Shakespeare used the poet Gower as the chorus for his play *Pericles*. Chaucer, Gower and Malory, at least, had been absorbed into the literary culture at large.

Yet interest in Middle English overall was declining markedly by the end of the century. As has already been noted, in the 1550s it was theoretically possible to purchase an edition of the complete works of Chaucer, Gower's *Confessio Amantis*, some of Lydgate, *Le Morte Darthur* and *Piers Plowman*. But after Crowley's edition of 1550, nobody edited Langland until 1813; Gower's *Confessio* disappeared until 1810. Fresh editions of Malory and, above all, of Chaucer continued to appear in the sixteenth century. But by the beginning of the seventeenth century, Middle English literature was becoming unfashionable, and it was also regarded as difficult to read. In his 1602 edition, Speght provided the first glossary of Chaucer's language, clearly suggesting that readers were having difficulties with this. More than Protestant disapproval of all things Catholic, it was the simple fact of linguistic change that contributed to the decline in interest in medieval English literature. As Francis Beaumont said of Chaucer's words, they 'are growne too hard and vnpleasant' (ed. Spurgeon 1925: Vol. I, 145; Brewer 1978: Vol. I, 136).

The Seventeenth Century: Decline

The justifications produced in the sixteenth century for continued interest in late Middle English literature were not enough in the seventeenth century. The medieval period was more than ever regarded as a time of obscurity and superstition, the dead past against which a self-consciously renascent culture needed to define itself (compare Ferguson 1948: 73).

In addition, expectations of verse changed in the course of the sixteenth century and the roughness of a great deal of medieval verse became less acceptable to the more polished standards of the later Tudor writers. Chaucer was excluded from the general opprobrium: given, in the editions of Speght, the kind of elaborate treatment more usually accorded to classical writers, he was now regarded as the model, the father of English verse. His pioneering use of iambic pentameter was probably the crucial difference that separated him from other medieval poets and linked him to the age of Shakespeare. But Gower and Lydgate were now less read, if still regarded as belonging in the pantheon of 'primier poets'. A separation occurred at this point: Chaucer was regarded as standing apart from all other Middle English literature, and it would be three centuries before this situation changed.

Even so, neither iambic pentameter nor his refashioned role as proto-Protestant was enough to secure Chaucer a place in seventeenth-century readers' predilections. After Speght's second edition of 1602 there would be no new Chaucer edition in the seventeenth century. Chaucer's status as the first great English poet, however, remained a commonplace: he is 'of all admir'd', as John Fletcher and William Shakespeare put it in 1613 in the prologue to *The Two Noble Kinsmen*, a play based on *The Knight's Tale* (ed. Spurgeon 1925: Vol. I, 187). Henry

Peacham, in his educational tract *The Compleat Gentleman* (1622), thought that his readers should 'account him among the best of your English bookes in your librarie' (ed. Spurgeon 1925: Vol. I, 197; Brewer 1978: Vol. I, 148).

Concerns about the poet's now-archaic language were, nevertheless, frequent. Some time between 1620 and 1635, Ben Jonson warned against the emulation of this language in his own day – against '*Chaucerismes* . . . which were better expung'd and banish'd' (ed. Spurgeon 1925: Vol. I, 194). In 1635, the scholar Francis Kynaston published part of a translation of Chaucer's *Troilus and Criseyde*, specifically because the original was now difficult to understand. Significantly, he translated it not into English but *Latin*, in order to preserve Chaucer's work in what he thought a more durable, unchanging form. In a prefatory poem to this translation, another Oxford scholar, Edward Foulis, argued that '. . . time can silence *Chaucers* tongue / But not his witte . . .' and confidently announced of Kynaston's work, 'Thus the Translation will become / Th' Originall . . .' (ed. Brewer 1978: Vol. I, 153; cf. Vol. I, 211).

Other Middle English texts were faring even worse. As has been noted, after the 1550s most Middle English verse was not re-edited until the early nineteenth century. In 1634, a printer named William Stansby produced an edition of Malory's *Morte Darthur* but thereafter this work, too, would go unprinted until 1816. Such Middle English writing as did appear in the course of the seventeenth century tended to be published in increasingly low formats. For example, the fourteenth-century fictitious travel narrative *Mandeville's Travels* was enormously popular, appearing in many editions (see Bennett 1954). But these were cheap, chapbook printings, usually in modernized English. Similarly the Middle English romances *Bevis of Hampton* and *Guy of Warwick* were popular in partially modernized versions that had little to do with the original texts in medieval manuscripts. It was the stories these texts told, and not the language in which they were told, that attracted interest in the seventeenth century.

While the booksellers who compiled and sold this material tried to perpetuate claims about the moral, exemplary and patriotic value of such old literature – offering Bevis, for example, as an ideal English hero – it was difficult to disguise the real selling-point of *Bevis*, *Guy* and Mandeville's fanciful travels. This was, simply, that they offered an escapist world of marvels and fantasy. The conventional idea that the Middle Ages represented a time of primitive credulity and superstition had become entrenched, and to most seventeenth-century readers, late-medieval writings were proverbial for their unrealistic character and mendacity. Tales of Bevis and Guy and even of King Arthur had become synonymous with outrageous fiction. The satirist Henry Parrot wrote a poem on the kinds of people who patronized bookstalls and spoke of the 'Countrey-Farmer' who says to the bookseller, 'Shewe mee King *Arthur, Bevis,* or *Syr Guye*'; the bookseller responds, 'Those are the Bookes he onely loves to buye' (Parrot 1615: 11r). Such works, it is implied, appeal to uncultivated, rustic tastes, and it is clear that King Arthur has sunk to the level of Bevis and Guy.

By then even Chaucer was implicated in the view that medieval literature was synonymous with lies. Despite his veneration by poets and dramatists, already in the sixteenth century 'Canterbury Tale' could be used to mean an obvious fiction: in his 1575 *Book of Falconrie*, for example, George Turberville refers to 'a verie old womans fable or Cantorburie tale . . .' (ed. Spurgeon 1925: Vol. I, 111). Later, the phrase was often used to mean a tall story or yarn. In Thomas Fuller's widely read *History of the Worthies of England* (1662), 'Canterbury Tales' are said to be writings 'meerly made to marre precious time, and please fanciful people', while in 1709 the editor of the *Tatler*, Richard Steele, bemoaned the way young men adorn their stories so that a fifteen-minute anecdote 'grows into a long *Canterbury* Tale of Two Hours . . .' (ed. Spurgeon 1925: Vol. I, 239, 311).

So in the seventeenth century Middle English literature was positioned as a sub-literature: it filled popular, cheaply produced books which, to judge by their numbers, and the frequency of their appearance, were widely enjoyed by ordinary people. Peacham's ideal seventeenth-century gentleman was expected to have Chaucer's books in his library, but Peacham says nothing about actually reading them. Oblivion, once mobilized as a trope justifying early Tudor editors' publication of medieval texts, now overwhelmed Middle English writing.

1700–1870: Revival

In the course of the eighteenth century Great Britain (then a relatively new political entity) became a world power as a result of military domination and the Industrial Revolution. Throughout the century, literary education and general thinking about literature continued to be dominated by classical models. Yet there was also a turning away from such models and a search for an alternative in something indigenous to Britain. For some scholars, the medieval period was of increasing interest: these scholars wanted to trace *native* origins for the nation of Great Britain. The Middle Ages and medieval literature were still regarded as primitive, but this suited the narrative of eighteenth-century Whig history, which saw a barbarous past as the necessary platform for present progress and perfection (see Spadafora 1990: 213–52). From the 1760s in particular, there was a rediscovery of medieval artefacts and literature, which led to a full-scale revival in the Romantic period.

Later, in the Victorian period, surplus wealth and rising imperial domination led to a growth in national confidence. New universities were established in the nineteenth century along with – late in the century – a national system of elementary education. In this context, study of the medieval past and, within it, Middle English literature and language grew quickly. Though scepticism about the Middle Ages persisted – it was still regarded as an era of superstition – inescapably the period was a past that could not be ignored. The growth of parliamentary democracy in the nineteenth century, for example, led to increased interest in Parliament's thirteenth-century origins. By mid-century the revival of interest in the Middle Ages encompassed a broad range of cultural phenomena: in architecture and art as well as literature and theatre, scholarship and popular entertainment.

However, at the beginning of the eighteenth century there were only occasional indicators of the interest in Middle English writing that was to come. A few antiquarians searched out previously obscure vernacular chronicles. Most notable among them, Thomas Hearne, at Oxford University, edited the early Middle English chronicle attributed to Robert of Gloucester in 1724. In the same period, scholarly interest in *Mandeville's Travels* was renewed by the first edition of the version of the text in MS Cotton Titus C.xvi (now in the British Library in London), which was published in 1725. This is the basis for all modern editions of the work.

It is significant, however, that Hearne and his work were considered dull by many of his contemporaries. Hearne is usually thought to be 'Wormius' in Pope's *Dunciad*, of whom it is said: 'To future ages may thy dulness last, / As thou preserv'st the dulness of the past!' (ed. Rogers 1993: 504). The most celebrated offering of a Middle English work in this period, predictably enough, was in the field of Chaucer studies. John Dryden's translation of parts of *The Canterbury Tales* appeared with a prefatory essay on Chaucer in his *Fables, Ancient and Modern* in 1700. At the time Dryden was Poet Laureate; his weighty authority gave new impetus to the idea that Chaucer was the Father of English Poetry. Fresh interest in Chaucer was sparked, and in 1721 a new edition of Chaucer's complete works appeared, the first since 1602.

These major editions of Chaucer, Robert of Gloucester and Mandeville, issued in the space of four years, suggest a miniature revival in the reading of Middle English. Once again, however, what looks to be the case retrospectively was not necessarily so at the time. Dryden, for example, had no interest in discussing Chaucer's place as a medieval author. 'From *Chaucer*,' he wrote, 'the Purity of the *English* Tongue began': the poet represents a *beginning* for Dryden – the beginning of modern poetry, not the culmination of medieval literature (ed. Spurgeon 1925: Vol. I, 273; Brewer 1978: Vol. I, 162). Dryden's concern was to lift Chaucer *out* of dusty antiquarianism and out of the Middle Ages altogether (see Patterson 1991: 13–22, especially 15).

Dryden was particularly interested in *The Canterbury Tales* and felt that part of that text's value lay in its realistic depiction of English people of the past. All 'the various Manners and Humours (as we now call them) of the whole *English* Nation, in his Age' were to be found in *The Canterbury Tales*. 'Not a single Character has escap'd him', Dryden wrote: 'We have our Fore-fathers and Great Grand-dames all before us, as they were in *Chaucer*'s Days' (ed. Brewer 1978: Vol. I, 166, 167). In 1775, the classicist Thomas Tyrwhitt published an edition of *The Canterbury Tales*, in which he showed that Chaucerian metre was more regular than had been thought. Tyrwhitt, like Dryden, helped to promote the idea that *The Canterbury Tales* constituted Chaucer's masterwork, his great portrait of fourteenth-century life.

At the same time, the genre of medieval romance was being explored for opposite reasons. In romance and its incredibilities, an antidote to neo-classical realism was found. As suggested above, the general lack of realism in medieval literature had been used to condemn it, but now its fantastic character was celebrated as a virtue by its adherents. The chief apologist was the Oxford professor Thomas Warton. In his landmark *History of English Poetry* (1774–81), Warton outlined the conventional view that the consolidation of Protestantism and the rejection of Catholic superstition had allowed the establishment of enlightened reason in England by the seventeenth century. The Middle Ages 'propagated a general propensity to the Marvellous, and strengthened the belief of spectres, demons, witches, and incantations' (Warton 1778: Vol. II, 462). But for Warton this was positive, as it was conducive to poetry. There are fictions, he argued, 'that are more valuable than reality' (463). He advocated the reading of chivalric romances as

imaginative texts, counterposing them to 'obscure fragments of unin-
structive morality or uninteresting history' (209) that, he said (probably with Hearne in mind), was the preoccupation of an earlier
generation of antiquarians. In his lengthy discussions of medieval
literature, Warton brought to light masses of Middle English material
that had not been read for centuries.

Warton's work remained popular in the nineteenth century, influ-
encing, among other things, the early novels and poems of Walter Scott,
which have a medieval setting. Medievalism took a variety of forms,
too manifold to examine here (see Chandler 1971; Girouard 1981;
Poulson 1999). At one level, it influenced popular forms of art and
entertainment – in the wake of Walter Scott's romantic novel *Ivanhoe*,
for example, the spectacle of knights jousting became a common one
at the circus (Girouard 1981: 90–2). At another, more official level,
medievalism led by the 1840s to the Gothic Revival in architecture,
which saw many public buildings constructed in the neo-Gothic
style – most notably the Houses of Parliament, which were rebuilt
after a fire destroyed the medieval Westminster Hall in 1834. The
Ecclesiological Society, founded in 1845, argued that the architectural
style of the period from the late thirteenth to the fourteenth centuries
(known as 'Decorated') was the true Gothic style in England. In the
second edition of *The Seven Lamps of Architecture*, John Ruskin wrote,
'I have no doubt that the only style proper for modern northern work
is the Northern Gothic of the thirteenth century' (Ruskin 1907:
xxviii). In an era of rapidly advancing technology and the spread of
industry's dark Satanic mills, many writers and artists looked back to
a supposed time of pre-industrial harmony in the Middle Ages.
Concerned with the growing numbers of the working classes, Ruskin
idealized medieval labour. There was as much 'mechanical ingenuity',
he argued, 'required to build a cathedral as to cut a tunnel or con-
trive a locomotive' (Ruskin 1907: 217). The same idealization of the
Middle Ages is reflected in the lushly Edenic scenes of the Pre-
Raphaelites' pseudo-medievalist paintings.

In these favourable circumstances, the rediscovery of Middle
English literature accelerated. New texts, some of which later became
canonical in Middle English, were unearthed in the first half of
the nineteenth century. One man alone – Frederic Madden, a self-
educated scholar and Keeper of Manuscripts in the British Museum –
discovered the romances of *Havelok the Dane* and *William of Palerne*; found
the manuscript containing *Pearl*, *Patience*, *Cleanness* and *Sir Gawain and
the Green Knight*; found and edited the two texts of Laȝamon's early

Middle English Arthurian verse chronicle, the *Brut*, and edited the Wycliffite Bible, the translation of the Bible into Middle English by the followers of John Wyclif (see the essays by Marilyn Corrie and Helen Cooper in this volume).

Madden's work opened the way for the increasing formalization of the study of Middle English later in the century. Frederick Furnivall, a lawyer and medieval enthusiast, established the Early English Text Society ('EETS') in 1864, to further the printing of medieval texts. Four years later he established a Chaucer Society, in order to give formal support to the study of the poet. It was only at this time that a general perception grew that Geoffrey Chaucer was intimately related to the larger context of Middle English. Furnivall's associate, the Anglo-Saxonist W.W. Skeat, along with Richard Morris, a philologist-clergyman, produced the first English textbook of Middle English, *Specimens of Early English*, in several editions from 1871 onwards. Despite their use of the more general term 'Early English', it was not long before 'Middle English' came into currency. Now, for the first time, a strong sense of continuity was perceived in the period between the Norman Conquest and the end of the Middle Ages. EETS and the Skeat-Morris textbooks promoted the view that Laȝamon's *Brut*, the 'Katherine Group' of saints' lives (see Catherine Sanok's essay above), the romances of Bevis and Guy, Gower, Chaucer, Langland, Malory and a host of others all belonged in a single (if long and diverse) period: that of Middle English literature.

While he encouraged the study of Middle English in schools and universities, Furnivall was not principally concerned to establish the subject as an academic discipline. He had originally been inspired by Alfred Tennyson's Arthurian poems and believed that popular medievalism, in Tennyson's *Idylls of the King*, Scott's *Ivanhoe* and countless other works largely forgotten today, might be used to encourage people to read the real literature of England's medieval past. He was targeting an enlightened reading public – the kind of public he might reasonably conclude was being created by such things as the Forster Education Act of 1870, which brought in a nationwide system of elementary schooling.

But Furnivall overestimated the impact of popular medievalism. Alongside the enthusiasm for the Middle Ages in the nineteenth century there were many statements of scepticism. The old idea, deriving from the sixteenth century, that the Middle Ages were a time of Catholic superstition and barbarism did not die easily – if it has died at all. The popularity of nineteenth-century medievalism did *not* translate into a broad interest in actual medieval texts in England in the years after the establishment of Furnivall's societies. Partly, of course, this was to do with the obvious difficulty that many of the texts presented. Who would swap Tennyson's *Idylls* or William Morris's *Defence of Guenevere* for Laȝamon's *Brut*? Why take the trouble to read thousands of alliterative lines of early Middle English when what seemed like a medieval atmosphere was delivered in Tennyson's or Morris's elegant verse?

The philologists and enthusiasts of the nineteenth century were not good at – or even particularly interested in – articulating in belle-lettristic terms what readers might *enjoy* about Middle English writings. Many of them were motivated by their interest in the history of the English language rather than any feeling for literature. Skeat's students, for example, would be asked in examinations to explain vocabulary in *The Canterbury Tales* and to parse Chaucerian sentences; they would be expected to know the origins of words (ed. Matthews 2000: 239–41). Frederick Furnivall tried to communicate some of his passion for medieval literature, but in place of literary appreciation he offered, as the justification for printing and reading Middle English, 'duty to England.' It was a national obligation, in his view, that old texts should be brought out of obscurity, the oblivion that had been warned of in the sixteenth century. Furnivall said little about *liking* the texts; on another occasion, he depicted editing them as a kind of grim manual labour, calling for 'men who know they have a work to do, and mean to do it; men who can look 270 manuscripts and books in the face, and say quietly, "Well, at 9 a-year, we shall clear you off in 30 years" . . .' (quoted in Matthews 1999: 148).

Furnivall was simply perpetuating a longstanding tradition: earlier editors of Middle English were often quite frank about what they saw as the *lack* of literary value of their material. They were excavating it for its valuable contribution to a sense of the English past, and rarely for its poetic beauty or narrative appeal. When Frederic Madden stumbled on the hitherto unknown poem *Sir Gawain and the Green Knight* one day in 1828, for example, he knew he had come across something significant. But Madden's long introduction to the poem does not mention the enigmatic and intricate narrative details of Gawain's quest for the Green Chapel that have kept modern readers fascinated. And if Madden, the poem's first modern reader, was surprised to discover that Gawain's host in the castle in which he lodges was the Green Knight all along, he does not mention it. Instead, he focused on what he considered to be the poem's valuable illustrations of fourteenth-century detail. He saw the head-dress of Bertilak's lady as an accurate description of 'the female coiffure in the reigns of Richard the Second and Henry the Fourth'. And he dwelt on the stanzas in the second fitt of the poem in which Gawain is armed, seeing them as 'valuable for the minute description they contain of the mode of completely arming a knight at the close of the fourteenth century' (Madden, ed., 1839: 324, 314).

There is no doubt that by the last third of the nineteenth century Middle English literature was printed and read as never before. However, its readers were encouraged to value it for reasons very different from those for which it is read now.

1870 to the Present: Expansion and Consolidation

Between 1870 and the First World War there was unprecedented scholarship devoted to producing and reading texts in Middle English. When its great proselytizer, Frederick Furnivall, died in 1910, Middle English looked more secure than it ever had done. The better-known authors, such as Langland, Chaucer and Gower, had appeared in authoritative, highly scholarly editions (Skeat edited Langland and Chaucer, G.C. Macaulay Gower). Malory's *Morte Darthur* had been re-edited several times in the late nineteenth century. Fresh editions of *Pearl* and *Sir Gawain and the Green Knight* (the relative newcomers on the Middle English scene) also appeared. At the same time, literature that had been untouched for centuries was rediscovered: the wealth of Middle English religious prose was explored, chiefly by the prolific German scholar Carl Horstmann in his many editions of saints' lives and the work of the fourteenth-century English mystic and hermit Richard Rolle. In addition, much that is now taken for granted – such as the way Middle English is pronounced – was first established at this time. There was a great spirit of co-operation between British and German scholars, and broad acceptance of the Germans' rigorous philological method, which placed linguistic considerations ahead of literary ones. The late nineteenth century also saw the American academy becoming heavily involved in Middle English, initially because of connections between Frederick Furnivall and scholars at Harvard University, who promoted the publications of EETS and the Chaucer Society.

In short, Middle English studies in its current shape was established in the period 1870–1918. By the end of that period there was more

Middle English to read and more people interested in, and capable of, reading it than ever before. Then in the years after the First World War, the university study of English rapidly expanded and Middle English became a central part of the curriculum.

There were, as ever, dissenting voices. Perhaps the most famous of late nineteenth-century judgements on Chaucer was that of the poet and influential critic Matthew Arnold, in 'The Study of Poetry' (1880). Like many before him, Arnold saw Chaucer as forming a break with the medieval past, producing superior verse to that of his predecessors. By revalidating the old idea of Chaucer as Father of English Poetry, Arnold appeared to reaffirm Chaucer's place in English poetic tradition. Yet Arnold went on to say that 'Chaucer is not one of the great classics' because he lacked 'the high and excellent seriousness which Aristotle assigns as one of the grand virtues of poetry' (ed. Spurgeon 1925: Vol. II, 128–9; Brewer 1978: Vol. II, 219). Throughout the seventeenth and eighteenth centuries criticism derived from Greek and Roman writers (and especially Aristotle) had helped to suppress medieval literature. At the height of the revival of Middle English, Matthew Arnold once again invoked Aristotle to draw a line between Chaucer and the truly weighty writers of modernity who succeeded him.

Arnold's judgement stands as a reminder of the way that, since the Tudor period, Middle English literature has always stood on, or sometimes beyond, the boundaries of literary respectability. Yet his judgement did not, of course, prevent the study of Middle English from prospering in universities throughout much of the twentieth century. Early in the century, the literature began to be read, as now, from a critical perspective, with Chaucer's works leading the way. After the First World War, Germanic philology became much less fashionable in the Anglo-American world. Theme, character and authorial genius, rather than sound-changes, dialect and source study, became the focus of interest. R.K. Root's *The Poetry of Chaucer* (1906) and G.L. Kittredge's *Chaucer and His Poetry* (1915) were the first of a long series of influential monographs on Chaucer to emerge from the American academy, in which Middle English became subject to a more thoroughly literary-critical form of analysis (see further Patterson 1987: chapter 1, especially 14–18).

Of course philology and language study remained crucial to reading Middle English (and they are still). The popular image of philology as dry and scientific led to a view of Middle English scholarship as conservative and slow to change. And it is true that when departments of English around the world began to absorb French-inspired theory in the 1970s, Anglo-American medieval studies were resistant. But by the 1990s the frameworks of gender studies, queer theory, historical materialism, psychoanalytic criticism and deconstruction were being applied to Middle English texts. Theoretical approaches to medieval literature had come to exist alongside more traditional, empirical lines of enquiry. Moreover, there has been a broadening of the subject in recent years, with the opening up of previously neglected areas of Middle English: fifteenth-century verse, for example, and religious prose.

All of this, of course, is *academic* study. Frederick Furnivall's dream of wider *public* acceptance of Middle English has never been realized. It is possible to argue that Chaucer became better known in the first half of the twentieth century among an enlightened, educated reading public: dozens of children's versions of Chaucer, for example, were produced in the late nineteenth century and the first half of the twentieth, partly in order to establish Chaucer's classic status among young readers (Matthews 2000a). And there were also the notable attempts of Virginia Woolf and G.K. Chesterton to offer criticism of the poet aimed explicitly at a non-academic general public: Woolf in an essay ('The Pastons and Chaucer') published in 1925 and Chesterton in his book *Chaucer*, first published in 1932. But as Stephanie Trigg has argued, these critical experiments did not create the kind of publicly oriented appreciation that their authors desired for Chaucer (Trigg 2002: 186–94). And beyond Chaucer, and perhaps Malory, most of the rest of Middle English has been read exclusively within the scholarly world.

As in the nineteenth century, part of the explanation for this is, obviously enough, the linguistic challenges raised by the material. Today, general readers buy Dickens, Trollope and the Brontës in great numbers and there is fierce competition among the rival series that publish them. A series of successful films can cause a boom in the reading of Jane Austen. Seamus Heaney's translation of the long and difficult Old English poem *Beowulf* has also been a major success among the general reading public. Yet no edition or translation of Chaucer has achieved anything like the same status. *Beowulf* has somehow achieved a reputation that eludes most of Middle English literature.

One striking facet of recent work in Middle English has been a fresh emphasis on continuity rather than rupture between the late-medieval and early-modern periods. The major literary histories that have appeared from the university presses of Cambridge and Oxford, for example, see Middle English in a context that includes the reign of Henry VIII and the beginnings of the English Reformation (see Wallace, ed., 1999; Simpson 2002). James Simpson's volume in the Oxford English Literary History begins with 1350, the importance of which is justified by the emergence of a 'newly articulate vernacularity' in the mid-fourteenth century (Simpson 2002: 2). Several other recent works place a renewed emphasis on the mid-fourteenth century: Derek Pearsall's *Chaucer to Spenser: An Anthology of Writing in English 1375–1575* (1999), and Pearsall and Duncan Wu's *Poetry from Chaucer to Spenser* (2002), for example.

Pragmatically, what such works represent is an attempt to retrieve later Middle English for modernity by linking it to the Renaissance. As Linda Georgianna, author of the first volume in the Oxford English Literary History, has put it, the chronological division between her volume (which covers the medieval period up to 1350) and James Simpson's was 'simply the necessary result of a prior decision to figure the years 1350–1550 as a period that could borrow some cultural capital from the term *early modern*' (Georgianna 2003: 153).

It is striking that such reconfigurations actually stage a return to the Tudor view of Middle English. It was suggested at the beginning of this essay that the earliest retrieval of Middle English, in the Tudor period, was confined to literature after 1350, with a corresponding focus on how Chaucer and his contemporaries could be linked to Tudor writers. In the twenty-first century, this configuration is being revived in a way that implies it is not 1066 or 1100 that marks a beginning for Middle English, but the active lifetime of Chaucer. While this might be viewed as a beneficial reconnection of early English literary history with the tradition established in the early modern period, in practice it also lends itself to a fresh split within Middle English. In a way reminiscent of Dryden in 1700, recent scholars could be seen as wanting to lift Chaucer and his contemporaries out of a medieval context in order to piggy-back them on to the more successful Shakespeare.

How Middle English literature will be perceived in the future is difficult to predict. On the one hand it is surely the case that there are more people than ever before reading it. But on the other, unless the future involves a broadening of the Middle English texts that are read, the field will divide so that Chaucer can be studied alongside his fellow geniuses Spenser and Shakespeare, while everything else becomes the specialist subject of the very few left to research it.

What does Middle English have to recommend it that no other period of literature has? The field is vast, uneven, often infuriating,

a

a

David Matthews

sometimes tedious – to the great perplexity of generations of readers since 1500. More positively, for the native English speaker, for a relatively small linguistic effort, a huge literature is unlocked. And, at a time when, as I have suggested, the links between late fourteenth-century writing (in particular) and early modern literature are being affirmed, it is worth remembering the attraction of the fundamental *difference* of medieval writing and its contexts of production, which this book has explored. Between about 1550 and 1800, readers of Middle English grappled, often uncomprehendingly, with the deep-seated otherness of the literature – which is precisely why so much effort was expended on comparing it with the more familiar classics, or with post-medieval literature. It was only in the nineteenth century that many scholars, writers and artists began to see the appeal of the otherness of Middle English. Our approach can perhaps be somewhere between the two. We can still find in Middle English literature connections with our current preoccupations, as much recent work on it shows. At the same time, it is a literature that always attracts by its pastness, its difference and its capacity to surprise.

References

Primary texts

Brewer, Derek, ed. (1978). *Chaucer: The Critical Heritage*. London: Routledge & Kegan Paul.

Madden, Frederic, ed. (1839). *Syr Gawayne: A Collection of Ancient Romance-Poems*. Edinburgh: Bannatyne Club.

Matthews, David, ed. (2000). *The Invention of Middle English: An Anthology of Sources*. Turnhout: Brepols.

Parins, Marylyn Jackson, ed. (1988). *Malory: The Critical Heritage*. London: Routledge.

Parrot, Henry (1615). *The Mastive, or Young-Whelpe of the Olde Dogge: Epigrams and Satyrs*. London: Thomas Creede.

Pearsall, Derek, ed. (1999). *Chaucer to Spenser: An Anthology of Writing in English 1375–1575*. Oxford: Blackwell.

Rogers, Pat, ed. (1993). *Alexander Pope*. Oxford: Oxford University Press.

Ruskin, John (1907). *The Seven Lamps of Architecture*. 2nd edn, reprd. London: J.M. Dent.

Spurgeon, Caroline, ed. (1925). *Five Hundred Years of Chaucer Criticism and Allusion (1357–1900)*. 3 vols. London: Kegan Paul.

Warton, Thomas (1774–81). *The History of English Poetry*. 4 vols. Reprd 1998, with an introduction by David Fairer. London: Routledge/Thoemmes.

Secondary sources and suggestions for further reading

Bennett, Josephine Waters (1954). *The Rediscovery of Sir John Mandeville*. New York: Kraus.

Berkhout, Carl T. and Gatch, Milton McC., eds. (1982). *Anglo-Saxon Scholarship: The First Three Centuries*. Boston, MA: G.K. Hall.

Burrow, John (1971). *Ricardian Poetry: Chaucer, Langland, Gower and the Gawain Poet*. London: Routledge & Kegan Paul.

Cannon, Christopher (1998). *The Making of Chaucer's English: A Study of Words*. Cambridge Studies in Medieval Literature 39. Cambridge: Cambridge University Press.

Chandler, Alice (1971). *A Dream of Order: The Medieval Ideal in Nineteenth-Century English Literature*. London: Routledge & Kegan Paul.

Chesterton, G.K. (1932). *Chaucer*. London: Faber & Faber.

Colley, Linda (1992). *Britons: Forging the Nation 1707–1837*. New Haven: Yale University Press.

Cooper, Helen (2004). *The English Romance in Time: Transforming Motifs from Geoffrey of Monmouth to the Death of Shakespeare*. Oxford: Oxford University Press.

Duffy, Eamon (1992). *The Stripping of the Altars: Traditional Religion in England c. 1400–c. 1580*. New Haven: Yale University Press.

Ellis, Steve (2000). *Chaucer at Large: The Poet in the Modern Imagination*. Minneapolis: University of Minnesota Press.

Ferguson, Wallace K. (1948). *The Renaissance in Historical Thought: Five Centuries of Interpretation*. Boston: Houghton Mifflin.

Frantzen, Allen J. (1990). *Desire for Origins: New Language, Old English, and Teaching the Tradition*. New Brunswick: Rutgers University Press.

Georgianna, Linda (2003). 'Periodization and Politics: The Case of the Missing Twelfth Century in English Literary History'. *Modern Language Quarterly*, 64, 153–68.

Georgianna, Linda (forthcoming). *To 1350: The Literary Cultures of Early England*. The Oxford English Literary History Vol. 1. Oxford: Oxford University Press.

Gillespie, Alexandra (2006). *Print Culture and the Medieval Author: Chaucer, Lydgate, and Their Books, 1473–1557*. Oxford: Oxford University Press.

Girouard, Mark (1981). *The Return to Camelot: Chivalry and the English Gentleman*. New Haven: Yale University Press.

Kittredge, G.L. (1915). *Chaucer and His Poetry*. Cambridge, MA: Harvard University Press.

Lerer, Seth (1993). *Chaucer and His Readers: Imagining the Author in Late-Medieval England*. Princeton: Princeton University Press.

McMullan, Gordon and Matthews, David, eds. (2007). *Reading the Medieval in Early Modern England*. Cambridge: Cambridge University Press.

Matthews, David (1999). *The Making of Middle English, 1765–1910*. Minneapolis: University of Minnesota Press.

Matthews, David (2000a). 'Infantilizing the Father: Chaucer Translations and Moral Regulation'. *Studies in the Age of Chaucer*, 22, 93–114.

Palmer, D.J. (1965). *The Rise of English Studies*. London: Oxford University Press.

Patterson, Lee (1987). *Negotiating the Past: The Historical Understanding of Medieval Literature*. Madison: University of Wisconsin Press.

Patterson, Lee (1991). *Chaucer and the Subject of History*. Madison: University of Wisconsin Press.

Pearsall, Derek and Wu, Duncan, eds. (2002). *Poetry from Chaucer to Spenser*. Oxford: Blackwell.

Poulson, Christine (1999). *The Quest for the Grail: Arthurian Legend in British Art 1840–1920*. Manchester: Manchester University Press.

Simpson, James (2002). *1350–1547: Reform and Cultural Revolution*. The Oxford English Literary History Vol. 2. Oxford: Oxford University Press.

Spadafora, David (1990). *The Idea of Progress in Eighteenth-Century Britain*. New Haven: Yale University Press.

Thompson, Ann (1978). *Shakespeare's Chaucer: A Study in Literary Origins*. Liverpool: Liverpool University Press.

Trigg, Stephanie (2002). *Congenial Souls: Reading Chaucer from Medieval to Postmodern*. Minneapolis: University of Minnesota Press.

Utz, Richard J. (2002). *Chaucer and the Discourse of German Philology*. Turnhout: Brepols.

Wallace, David, ed. (1999). *The Cambridge History of Medieval English Literature*. Cambridge: Cambridge University Press.

Woolf, Virginia (1925). 'The Pastons and Chaucer'. In *The Common Reader* (pp. 13–38). London: Harcourt, Brace & Co.

Index

Page numbers in **bold** refer to illustrations.

'A God, and yet a man?' 25

Aegidius Romanus: *De regimine principum*, Hoccleve's use of 136

Ælfric 147

ages of man: symbolism of 10

Agnes, St 62

Alan of Lille: quoted 9

Albertanus of Brescia: and original of Chaucer's *Tale of Melibee* 180

Alliterative Morte Arthure, The 175

Ancrene Wisse 39, 64, 71, 107–8; adapted for lay use 221; chivalric allegory in 65, 71; revision of 220; and romance 71–2; Tolkien's edition of 212; translation of Bible in 35

Anglo-Norman dialect of French 100, 148, 166; words from, in English 152

Anglo-Norman literature 148, 166; chronicles 77–8, 79, 83, 85; poetry 112, 166; romances 80; ~ , in translation 174; translations into 170; for women 107, 170; women in 89

Anglo-Saxon Chronicle, The 83

Anglo-Saxon England: books in 100; Normans and 77, 83, 93, 147, 166; in romances 83

Anne, Queen (wife of Richard II): and *Legend of Good Women* 73, 220

Annunciation: images of 15–16

antifeminism: and defences of women 68; literature of 54–5, 60

Apollonius of Tyre: English adaptations of 177

architecture: symbolism of 11

Aristotle: theories of, on causation 123; ~ , on poetry 247; ~ , on women 55

Arnold, Matthew: on Chaucer 247

Art of Good Lywyng and Deyng, The: woodcut from **14**

artes memorativae 102

Arthur of Brittany 82

Arthurian legend 78, 79; *see also* Malory, Sir Thomas, *Le Morte Darthur*; romances; *Sir Gawain and the Green Knight*

Arundel, Archbishop Thomas:
approves Love's *Mirror* . . . 173;
Constitutions of, against
heterodoxy 47–8, 49, 110, 200;
interrogation of suspected heretic
by *see* Thorpe, William, *Testimony
of*
Ascham, Roger: views of, on Chaucer
and Malory 235, 237
Ashby, George: on Chaucer, Gower
and Lydgate 233
Assembly of Ladies, The 73
astrology: and symbolism 11
Athelstan, King 83
Audelay, John: anthology ascribed
to 223; requests readers' prayers
127
Augustine, St: *De doctrina Christiana*,
quoted 10; Hoccleve's use of 136
authors: and concept of 'authority'
(*auctoritas*) 123–4; cult of, in Italy
129; medieval views on 120–38;
self-naming by, in request for
prayers 126–7; unidentified in
medieval manuscripts 125
Awntyrs off Arthure, The 19–20

Bartholomaeus Anglicus: encyclopaedia
of, referred to 227
Battle of Maldon, The 147
Beaufort, Margaret: as patron of
printed texts 113
Beaumont, Francis: and Chaucer 235,
236, 237, 238
Bede 78, 79; *Ecclesiastical History* 78;
Life of St Cuthbert 78
Benedeit: *Voyage of Saint Brendan,
The* 170
Beowulf 147, 150, 166: Heaney's
translation of 248
Berthelette, Thomas: edition of
Gower's *Confessio Amantis* 234,
236
bestiaries: symbolism in 10–11
Bevis of Hampton: popularity of,
in seventeenth century 239

Bible: accessibility of 34, 109–10;
and apocrypha 36; Authorized
Version of 37; 'consumption'
of 33–4; English translations of
171, *see also* Wyclif, John, Bible
translation; French translation of
171; and history 77–8; Hoccleve's
use of 136; interpretation of 32;
printed 35; in Protestant tradition
37; as source for stories 167–8;
Latin text of, revered 171;
translated from Latin 34–5, 173;
translations of 170–2; teaching of
35, 36
Biblia pauperum 35
Boccaccio: and Chaucer 133–4, 181;
and cult of the author 129; *De
casibus virorum illustrium*, and
Lydgate's *Fall of Princes* 135;
Decameron 181; *Il Filostrato*, and
Chaucer's *Troilus and Criseyde*
133–4, 181; *Teseida* 181; ~ ,
commentary on 137
Boethius: *De consolatione philosophiae*
48, 133, 134, 182; ~ , and
Chaucer's *Troilus and Criseyde*
179–80; ~ , translations of 169,
177
Bokenham, Osbern: female readership
of 73; *Legends of Holy Women*,
as laywomen's reading 67
Bonaventure, St: *Meditationes vitae
Christi* wrongly attributed to 173
*Book of the Knight of La Tour-Landry,
The* 67
Book of Ghostly Grace, The 41
book production 99–101, 103–5,
110, 116; bureaucracy and 114;
centralization of 115; and
Christian education 108–9;
commercialization of 114;
commissioning of 104; costs
of 103–4, 105; courts as focus
for 110–11; guilds relating to
114; lay involvement in 108;
monasteries and 106–7, 108;

patronage and 105; secular institutions and 110–13; technical innovations in 103, *see also* printing; town-centred 113–16

Brendan, St: voyage of 170

Brook, G.L.: *The Harley Lyrics* 213

Brunanburh, Battle of: OE poem on 83

Brut (prose): historical material in 85

Bury, Richard: *Philobiblon* 104

Cannon, Christopher: on anchoritic literature 71

Canterbury Cathedral: windows of, typologically explained 11–12

Capgrave, John 112: life of St Katherine 62, 173

carols 25–6, 28; omissions/insertions in 224; religious poetry made into 221–2; variant wording of 222–3

Caxton, William 101, 211; edition of *Canterbury Tales* 233; edition of *Le Morte Darthur* 176, 234; *Eneydos* 177; *Recuyell of the Historyes of Troye* 177; as translator 176

Cazelles, Brigitte: on virgin martyr legends 71

Cecilia, St 62

Celtic languages: in medieval Britain 148

Cerquiglini, Bernard: on scribal input to texts 222

'Chandos Herald' 112

Chandos, Sir John 112

Charles d'Orléans: lyrics by 112

Chartier, Alain: *Le Traité de l'Espérance*, textual variants in 217

Chaucer, Geoffrey 2; and authorship 122, 123–4, 129–34; and Boccaccio 129, 181–2; career of 111, 115; considered as Church reformer 236; and Dante 182–4; as 'early modern' writer 249; editions of, early printed 233–4, 237; ~ , later 242; ~ , modern scholarly 246; influenced by French, Italian and Latin poets 129; as 'makere' 99–100; manuscripts of 113; ~ , omissions/ insertions in 223–4; ~ , parallel text editions of 217; monographs on 247; and Ovid 177; and patronage 99–100, 111, 115, 196; and Peasants' Revolt 191; plays based on 237; Renaissance views on 93, 235–6, 237; reputation of 233–6; ~ , modern 248; ~ , pre-eminent 237, 238; spurious additions to *œuvre* of 236; as translator 4, 178–86; transmission of, and printing 1, 233–4; and Virgil 177, 184–5; and women 3, 54, 60–2, 89–90

—: *An ABC* 185

—: *Boece see* translations of Boethius' *De consolatione philosophiae*

—: *Book of the Duchess, The*: and patronage 196

—: *Canterbury Tales, The*: Chaucer's self-effacement in 128; constancy as theme in 59; manuscripts of 116, 217, 218, 221, 222; ~ , marginalia/apparatus added to 226, 228; patience as theme in 60–1; printed copy of 109; revisions of, authorial 221; synonymous with lies 240; translated by Dryden 241; Wife of Bath, character of 60, 61–2, 69–70, 89

—: —: *Canon's Yeoman's Tale*: omitted from Hengwrt manuscript 218

—: —: *Clerk's Tale*: character of Griselda in 60–1, 68

—: —: *Friar's Tale*: and Dante 182

—: —: *Knight's Tale*: and Boccaccio's *Teseida* 181; as source for Fletcher and Shakespeare's *Two Noble Kinsmen* 238

—: —: *Melibee, Tale of*: original of 180–1

Chaucer, Geoffrey (*cont'd*)
—: —: *Merchant's Tale*: paraphrase of Song of Songs in 172, 180
—: —: *Miller's Tale*: 'inciuilitie' of 235
—: —: *Monk's Tale*: and Dante 182, 183
—: —: *Nun's Priest's Tale* 206; and Gower's *Vox Clamantis* 192–3; and Peasants' Revolt 191–2
—: —: *Pardoner's Tale*: as anti-gambling tract 235
—: —: *Parson's Tale*: source material for 185
—: —: *Physician's Tale* 59
—: —: *Reeve's Tale*: different dialects used in 161
—: —: *Second Nun's Tale* 62, 182, 183; and legend of St Cecilia 185
—: —: *Sir Thopas, Tale of* 180, 181
—: —: *Wife of Bath's Tale* 68–9; and Dante 182
—: *Complaint of Venus, The* 179
—: *Complaint to His Purse* 113
—: *Former Age, The*: and Boethius' poetry 179
—: *Gentilesse*: and Boethius' poetry 179
—: *House of Fame, The* 115, 129–31, 190; and Dante's *Divine Comedy* 184; ending of 131, 134; and historical events 189–90; and Latin authors 129; marginalia/apparatus added to manuscript of 226; narrator/author figure in 129–30, 131
—: *Legend of Good Women, The* 54, 111; Alceste as model of constancy in 58–9; audience of 73–4; and concept of authority 123–4; Medea as character in 91–2; Ovid's *Heroides* as source for 185; textual variation in Prologue to 220–1
—: *Parliament of Fowls, The* 113, 214; and concept of authority 123–4

—: *Romaunt of the Rose, The*: Fragment A, as translation of *Le Roman de la Rose* 178–9
—: translation of Boethius' *De consolatione philosophiae* (*Boece*) 169, 177, 179; presentation of manuscripts of 226
—: *Troilus and Criseyde* 54; and Boccaccio's *Il Filostrato* 133–4, 181, 182; and Boethius' *De consolatione philosophiae* 179–80; character of Criseyde in 54, 89, 90; and Dante 182–3; history and the individual in 85–6; 'Lollius' as authority for 132, 181–2; marginalia/apparatus added to manuscripts of 226; narrator/author figure in 132–3; scribal input into Huntington Library (MS HM 114) manuscript of 224; poet's farewell to 99–100; problem of ending of 90–1; sexual morality in 58; sources for 133, 181–2; translated into Latin 239; Usk's use of 115
Chaucer Society 244; and America 246
Chesterton, G.K.: and Chaucer 248
Chrétien de Troyes 70–1; Grail story, source claimed for 175; *Yvain*, and *Ywain and Gawain* 168
Christ: as feeding the faithful 23–4, 41, 43, 48; as knightly hero 20, 21, 65; as lover 64–5; Passion of *see* Passion of Christ; patience of, as exemplar 60; wounds of 12, 26
chronicles 77–8, 83; and documentary authority 78–9; Latin 78–9, 83
Church (Roman Catholic): and confession 43, 200–1; Eucharistic doctrine of 43; in Middle Ages 32, 33; and Reformation 77; teachings of 42, 43–51, 200–1
Church Fathers: Hoccleve's use of 136; *see also* Augustine, St

Clanchy, Michael: on development of written French in England 148
Claudian: eulogy translated 177–8
Cleanness: biblical material in 37–8, 42; quoted 37, 38; rediscovered 243
Cloud of Unknowing, The: and religious images 13
colour symbolism 11
Copland, William: edition of *Le Morte Darthur* 234
Cornburgh, Avery 67
Corpus Christi: drama performed at feast of 93, 114, 167; *see also* mystery play cycles
Corpus Christi Carol, The 20
Court of Sapience, The: marginalia in 227
Crowley, Robert: edition of *Piers Plowman* (B-text) 234
Crucifixion: images of 15, 17, 20–1, 26; as joust 21; meditations on 38
Cursor Mundi 35, 108–9; differing dialects in manuscripts of 159–61; subject of 35, 36, 170–1

Dance of Death ('danse macabre') 19; at St Paul's (London) 19
Dante: and cult of the author 129; *Divine Comedy* 182; *La Vita Nuova*, commentary on 137
De arte lacrimandi 17
De custodia interioris hominis 39
De heretico comburendo 47, 200
De institutione inclusarum 26
Deschamps, Eustache: calls Chaucer a great translator 178
devotional literature 172; in translation 173
devotional practices 13–17, 21
Diodorus Siculus: *Bibliotheca historica*, Skelton's translation of 138
Dissolution of monastries: and destruction of medieval heritage 237; *see also* Reformation
Dives and Pauper 44, 107

Domesday Book: written in Latin 148
Donatus: *Ars grammatica* 157
Douglas, Gavin: translation of Virgil's *Æneid* (*Eneados*) 89, 177
Dream of the Rood 166
Dryden, John: and Chaucer 241, 242; *Fables Ancient and Modern* 241
Dunbar, William: 'Done is a battell . . .' 20

Early English Text Society (EETS) 244; and America 246
East, Thomas: edition of *Le Morte Darthur* 234
Easter Sepulchres 18
Ecclesiological Society: promotes medieval architecture 243
education 102, 106; of clergy 106; of laity 108
Edward I: and land rights 78
Edward III: glorified by Minot 194–5
Edward IV: oral culture in court of 101–2, 105; and Wars of the Roses 202–3
Eleanor of Aquitaine 81
Elizabeth I: translation of Boethius 177
Elizabeth of Spalbeck, St: contemplates devotional image 15
Ellesmere manuscript of *Canterbury Tales* (San Marino, CA, Huntington Library, MS Ellesmere 26.C.9) 116, 217, 218, 221; marginalia in 227
English literature: periodization of 1, 249
Eve 60; as opposite of Virgin Mary 55
Everyman 48; priesthood and sacraments supported in 48–9

Fèvre, Jean le: *Le Livre de Leesce* 54; translation of *Lamentations of Matheolus* 54
Fèvre, Raoul le: prose history of Troy 177

Findern manuscript (Cambridge,
Cambridge University Library,
MS Ff.1.6) 113, 214; lyrics in 73,
214
Fletcher, John: *Two Noble Kinsmen*,
and Chaucer's *Knight's Tale* 238
Fortune/Fortuna (goddess) 57–8;
images of 19; wheel of 19
Foulis, Edward: on Chaucer's
language 239
Four Daughters of God 39
Fourth Lateran Council 43, 44, 45,
106
Francis, St 107
Franciscans: as *joculatores Dei* 107; and
meditation on Crucifixion 38
French: Anglo-Norman *see* Anglo-
Norman dialect of French;
grammar of, as influence on
English 153–4; as language of
cultured élite 149, 151, 166;
as language of record 149; and
Middle English vocabulary 145,
149, 151–3, 169; Norman *see*
Norman French; romances,
translated 174; teaching of 149;
writings in, in ME period 80,
101
friars 107
Froissart, Jean 112
Fuller, Thomas: disparages *Canterbury
Tales* 240
Furnivall, Frederick: promotes
medieval literature 244–5, 246,
248

Gaimar: verse history of England 84
Galen: views of, on women 55–6
Gaunt, Simon: on virginity and
sexuality 63
Gawain-poet: and biblical narrative
37–8; and French 152; and
religious teaching 3; and social
criticism 112; *see also Cleanness*;
Patience; *Pearl*; *Sir Gawain and the
Green Knight*

Geoffrey of Monmouth 78, 79; and
giants in Britain 85; *Historia regum
Britanniae*, French version of 82;
~ , influence of 79; ~ , source
book for, a fiction 174; use of
sources by 79
Geoffrey de Vinsauf: Chaucer and
192; *Poetria nova* 148
Georgianna, Linda: volume in Oxford
English Literary History 249
Gertrude the Great: account of St
Mechtild 40–1
Gildas 79
glosses: of vocabulary in translations
169; *see also* manuscripts, Middle
English literary,
marginalia/apparatus in
Goldsmiths' Company (London):
as patron 105
Gospel of Nicodemus 36
Gospel of 'Pseudo-Matthew' 36
Gothic Revival 243
Gower, John: decline of interest in
238; Latin marginalia prepared
by 227; and patronage 115; and
Peasants' Revolt 191; reputation
of 233, 234; as sergeant-at-law
115
—: *Confessio Amantis* 2, 57; and
Apollonius of Tyre 177; constancy
as theme in 59; early printed
editions of 234, 237; historical
narratives in 86; marginalia/
apparatus added to 136–7, 226
—: *Cronica Tripertita*: figure of Richard
II in 197
—: *Vox Clamantis*: Chaucer and 192–3;
and Peasants' Revolt 191; rhetoric
of 191–3
Grail romances 21, 175; *see also
under* Malory, 'Tale of the
Sankgreal'
grapheme: defined 157
Great Vowel Shift 146
Gregory the Great: Hoccleve's use of
136

Grosseteste, Robert 39: *Le Château d'amour* 39
Gui de Warewic 83
Guido de Columnis 90; *De destructione Troiae* 87
Guillaume de Machaut: and cult of the author 129
Guy of Warwick: popularity of, in seventeenth century 239

Hall, Edward: on risk of oblivion 237
Hanna, Ralph: on uniqueness of manuscripts 223
Havelok the Dane 84; rediscovered 243
Hearne, Thomas 241; edition of Robert of Gloucester 241, 242
Hengwrt manuscript of *Canterbury Tales* (Aberystwyth, National Library of Wales, MS Peniarth 392D) 116, 217, 218; order of tales in 221
Henry II 81; French verse and the court of 80, 81
Henry III: *Proclamation* (1258) in English 162–3
Henry IV (Henry Bolingbroke) 196–7, 202; figure of, in *Richard the Redeless* 199
Henry V 202; and Hoccleve's *Regement of Princes* 136, 195
Henry VI: piety of 12; and Wars of the Roses 202
Henry VIII: censorship in reign of 235, 236; fosters distrust of Catholic Middle Ages 236–7
Henry of Huntingdon 77–8; and Anglo-Saxon 83
Henryson, Robert 2; and symbolism 9
—: *Bludy Serk, The* 21
—: *Fables* 10: 'The Cock and the Jasp' 10; 'The Paddock and the Mouse' 10
—: *Garmont of Gud Ladeis, The* 9
—: *Orpheus and Eurydice* 9–10; Christian symbolism in 11

—: *Testament of Cresseid, The* 9
—: *Thre Deid Pollis, The* 19
heraldry: symbolism of 11
Herebert, William 38
heresy 3; Lollards condemned for 47, 110, 200
Hilton, Walter: on religious images 13
—: *On the Mixed Life*: audience of 44
—: *Scale of Perfection*: audience of 44; pilgrimage symbolism in 27
history: courtly poetic representations of 93; and documentation 78–9; and imperial ambition 80; and the individual 85–9; 'matters' of 80; in medieval literary culture 77–80, 85, 86–8; and the present 78, 79, 80; and rights 78; and women 88
Hoccleve, Thomas: and authorship 122; as Clerk of the Privy Seal 115, 136; Latin marginalia prepared by 227; and patronage 115, 196, 220
—: *Dialogue with a Friend* 54, 220
—: *Letter of Cupid* 54; quoted 56
—: *Poem to Sir John Oldcastle* 195; Henry V in 195–6
—: *Regement of Princes*: glosses on 136; and Hundred Years War 195; marginalia/apparatus added to manuscripts of 136, 226, 228; sources of 136
Holkham picture bible 35
Horstmann, Carl: edits Middle English religious texts 246
household: concept of, in Middle Ages 111; dissemination of books by 113
Hue de Rotelande: *Ipomedon*, source claimed for 175
Hull, Dame Eleanor: translation of Psalms 171
Humphrey, Duke of Gloucester: Palladius translated for 177; as patron 105, 112, 220

Hundred Years War 194
hunting: as courtly pastime 19

'I haue a gentil cook' 214
'I synge of a mayden': different
   editorial treatments of 215–16
images, religious *see* religious images
'Imago Pietatis' 18
'In a þestri stude I stod . . .' 213
'In noontyde of a somers day' 19
Incarnation: lyrics on 25–6
*Instructions for a Devout and Literate
   Layman* 10
Isidore of Seville: on 'interpretation'
   167

Jack Upland: added to Chaucer's *œuvre*
   236
Jacobus de Cessolis: *De ludo scaccorum*,
   Hoccleve's use of 136
Jean de Meun: translation of Boethius
   179; *see also Roman de la Rose, Le*
John, King 82; loses Normandy 149
John of Grimestone 38
John of Salisbury: *Policraticus* 148
Jonson, Ben: warns against
   'Chaucerisms' 239
journeys *see* quests; pilgrimage
Julian of Norwich 2; 'shewings' of
   26–8, 41–3; as writer 74, 108
Juliana, St 63

Katherine of Alexandria, St: life of 62,
   63, 173
Kempe, Margery 2; as author 74,
   137–8; devotional practices of 15,
   16–17, 17–18; rediscovery of 74
—: *The Book of Margery Kempe* 15;
   dictated to priest 104, 138;
   rediscovery of 74; subject matter
   of 137
King Horn 213
Kittredge, G.L.: *Chaucer and His Poetry*
   247
knighthood: and love 70–1; and male
   identity 70

Kynaston, Francis: Latin translation of
   Troilus and Criseyde by 239

lais, Breton: sources acknowledged in 175
Langland, William: a clerk? 115;
   critiques Church and clergy 44–6;
   in holy orders 115; and religious
   teaching 3, 32–3
—: *Piers Plowman* 2, 86; Christ as
   knight in 21; Christ as reformer
   in 60; early printed edition of
   234, 237; Holy Church in 32;
   Langland's authorial presence
   in 126; marginalia/apparatus in
   manuscripts of 228; and oral
   culture 102; pilgrimage symbolism
   in 27, 45; rewritings of 220;
   salvation of the just in 45–6;
   satirizes corruption 115; scribal
   input to text(s) of 222, 223, 224,
   228; texts of, conflated 224; textual
   problems/variants in 218–19, 220;
   Victorian edition of 237
lapidaries: symbolism in 11
Latin: in Anglo-Saxon England 148,
   151; and English vocabulary in
   Renaissance 146; marginalia/
   apparatus in, to vernacular
   works 136–7, 227; knowledge
   of, equated with literacy 73;
   as language of learned 34; as
   language of record in medieval
   England 148, 166; as literary
   language 148; texts in 100, 101,
   106–7; words in Middle English
   151; ~ , mediated by French 152
Laurent de Premierfait: translates
   Boccaccio's *De casibus virorum
   illustrium* 135
Laȝamon: Brut 81–3, 87, 174–5, 213,
   245; ~ , authorial presence in
   125–6; ~ , edited by Madden
   243–4; ~ , history and the
   individual in 85; ~ , parallel texts
   of 217; and Wace 82, 83; writes
   down his own text 104

Les Echecs amoureux: and Lydgate's
    Reson and Sensuallyte 135
'Lily Crucifixion' 15
Linguistic Atlas of Late Mediaeval English
    158
literacy: and education 102, 106; of
    the laity 33, 103, 105–6; of the
    religious 102–3, 106
Lollards: attacked by Love 48;
    legislation (*De heretico comburendo*)
    against 47, 200; rejection of
    Church doctrines by 47; and
    vernacular texts 109–10; and
    voices of the disempowered
    199–201
London: as New Troy 191
Love, Nicholas: *Mirror of the Blessed Life
    of Jesus Christ* 16, 33, 34, 39; as
    translation of *Meditationes vitae
    Christi* 173
Lydgate, John: on Chaucer's
    translations from Dante 183; and
    concept of authorship 122, 134–5;
    decline of interest in 238; diction
    of 135, 151; female readership of
    73; marginalia/apparatus added
    to manuscripts of 135, 228; and
    patronage 73, 105, 107, 112;
    and *pietà* 17; reputation of, post-
    medieval 233; transmission of,
    and printing 1, 237; and women
    90, 91, 92
—: *Fall of Princes, The* 90, 122; copies
    of 108; early printed edition of
    120–2, 138; and Boccaccio's *De
    casibus virorum illustrium* 135;
    marginalia/apparatus added by
    scribes to 226; woodcut title page
    of (1527) 120–2, **121**, 123
—: *Life of St Alban, The* 105
—: *Life of St Edmund, The*: copies of
    108
—: *Life of St Margaret, The* 73
—: *Lyf of Our Lady, The*: marginalia/
    apparatus added by scribes to
    226

—: *Reson and Sensuallyte*: Latin
    marginalia to 135–6
—: *Testament, The* 17
—: *Troy Book, The* 90; character of
    Medea in 91, 92–3; early printed
    editions of 234; illustrated
    manuscript of 214
—: 'Vppon the cross nailid I was for
    the': as carol 221
Lynne, Margaret and Beatrice 67
lyrics: antifeminist 54–5; authorship of
    125; in Findern family manuscript
    73; in MS Harley 2253 213;
    religious 25–6; written in long
    lines 216

Macaulay, G.C.: edition of Gower 246
Machan, Tim: on scribal priorities 222
Madden, Frederic: and rediscovery of
    Middle English literature 243–4,
    245
Magna Carta: written in Latin 148;
    translated into Anglo-Norman 148
'maker' (poet): concept of 40
Malory, Sir Thomas 2, 49;
    imprisonment of 203, 204;
    requests readers' prayers 127;
    and sources of *Le Morte Darthur*
    50, 175–6
—: *Le Morte Darthur*: diction of
    rupture in 204, 205–6; doctrinal
    orthodoxy of 51; editions of, early
    printed 234, 237; ~ , nineteenth-
    century 246; as model for
    conduct 235, 236; 'The Healing
    of Sir Urry' 204–5; 'The Most
    Piteous Tale of the Morte Arthur
    Saunz Guerdon' 50; sexual
    morality in 58; social context
    and 202, 204, 205; 'Tale of the
    Sankgreal' 28, 205; ~ , Real
    Presence in 50–1; ~ , sacrament
    of penance in 50; ~ , symbolism
    in 21–5; and Wars of the Roses
    202, 203
Man of Sorrows *see* 'Imago Pietatis'

Mandeville's Travels: popularity of, in seventeenth century 239; text in MS Cotton Titus C.xvi, edition of 241, 242

Mannyng, Robert: *Handlyng Synne* 107; ~ , title of, as translation of *Manuel des péchés* 169; verse chronicle 84; ~ , authorial presence in 125, 126

manuscript miscellanies 112, 113, 213

manuscripts: Middle English literary 211–12, 216–22, *see also at* MSS *for individual manuscripts*; of the Bible 35; copying of 5, 116; editing of 213–19; illustrated 214; marginalia/apparatus in 135–7, 226–8; miscellaneous contents of 214; modern editions of 4, 211–13, 217, 219, 228; ownership of, by laywomen 66–7, 214; reproduction of 226–8; scribal input to 221–2; textual variation between 216–17, 219–26

Margaret of Antioch, St 62, 63

Marie de France: *Guigemar* 70, 71; *lais* 70

marriage: as political symbol 56; re-evaluation of 65; and social order 58; and virginity 62, 67

Marshe, Thomas: edition of Lydgate's *Troy Book* 234

Mary, the Virgin: apocryphal stories of 36; at Crucifixion 38; devotion to 15–16; in mystery plays 93, 94–5; as opposite of Eve 55

Mary of Oignies 15

Matthew of Paris 107

Mechtild of Hackeborn, St 40

medievalism: nineteenth-century 243, 244–5

Meditationes vitae Christi 33, 39, 173

men: as category 68; identity of 70–1

mendicant orders 107

Mercers' guild (London): *Petition . . .* 163

Michael of Northgate: *Ayenbite of Inwyt* 107

Middle English language: adaptations in 4, *see also* translation and adaptation; challenging to early modern readers 238, 239, 245, 248; characteristics of 3–4, 145–6; defined 145, 232; dialects in 159–61, 162; and French 146, 151–3; French grammatical influences on 153–4; functions of 149, 162–3; historical context of 147–9; inflections reduced in 145–6, 155, 156; and Latin 146, 149, 151, 152; as literary language 163; and Norse 149–51; phonology of 146; pronouns in 150–1; in public documents 162–3; spelling of 158–9; spoken by majority 149; standardization of 163; status of 146, 166, 176; translations into 4, *see also* translation and adaptation; variability of 149; verb forms in 155–6; vocabulary of 145, 149–53

Middle English literature: antiquarianism and 241, 243; authors' role in 5, 100, 122–38; ~ , and oral culture 102, 105, 189; availability of, to contemporaries 105, 108–9; 'best-text' editions of 218; contexts for 2–3, 4; decline of interest in 237–9, 240; development of 5; dialect in 159–62; diplomatic editions of 212–13; facsimile editions of 212; and historical events 189–206; illustrations in manuscripts of 214; and literary histories 248–9; manuscript miscellanies and 213; manuscripts of *see* manuscripts, Middle English literary; parallel texts of 217; perceptions of, modern 4, 249–50; periodization of 1–2, 248–9; philology in study of 245, 246, 247; popularization of, stalled 248; printed editions of 4, 211–12, 213; production of 3, 5, *see also* book production; readership of 100–1; reception of, in post-medieval period 232–8; revisions of 219–20; revival of interest in 240–6; status of, under Normans 79; ~ , debased in seventeenth century 239–40; study of 2, 233, 244, 245, 246–50; texts of, dignified by marginalia/apparatus 227; ~ , owned by religious 109; textual criticism and editing of 218–19; use of sources in 50–1, 132–5, 166–86; voices of the disempowered in 199–201

Minnis, Alastair 125

Minot, Laurence: poems on Hundred Years War 194–5

minstrels 101–2

Mirk, John: *Instructions for Parish Priests* 44

Mirror of Simple Souls, The 173; Latin version of 173

misogyny: in medieval literature 55, 90, 93

Monk of Farne: on Christ's body 13

monks: textual production by 106–7, 108; criticized 78

Moone, Hawisia: queries sacraments of Church 47

Morris, Richard: and definition of Middle English 232, 244; *Specimens of Early English* 244

Morris, William: *Defence of Guenevere* 245

Mort le roi Artu, La 50

Mortimer, Anne, Countess of March: as Lydgate's patron 73

MSS: Aberystwyth, National Library of Wales, Peniarth 392D *see* Hengwrt manuscript

Cambridge, Cambridge University Library, Ff.1.6 *see* Findern manuscript

Cambridge, Magdalene College, Pepys 2006 113

Cambridge, Trinity College, R.3.8: Midland English text of *Cursor Mundi* 159, 160–1

London, British Library, Additional 37049: illustration in 214

London, British Library, Additional 60577 (the 'Winchester Anthology') 212

London, British Library, Cotton Caligula A.ix: varied contents of 213

London, British Library, Cotton Nero A.x 162

London, British Library, Cotton Titus C.xvi: editions of *Mandeville's Travels* based on 241

London, British Library, Cotton Vespasian A.iii: Northern English text of *Cursor Mundi* 159–60, 161

London, British Library, Harley 2253: contents of 112–13, 213; scribal convention relating to lyrics in 216; and trilingualism 214

London, British Library, Sloane 2593 213–14; carol in 222

Oxford, Bodleian Library, Douce 302 127; carol in 222

Oxford, Bodleian Library, Eng. poet. a.1 *see* Vernon manuscript

San Marino, CA, Huntington Library, Ellesmere 26.C.9 *see* Ellesmere manuscript

San Marino, CA, Huntington Library, HM 114 222, 223–4

Mum and the Sothsegger: author of, a scrivener? 115

'My deþ ich loue my lyf ich hate' 213

Mystère d'Adam, Le 35–6, 37

mystery play cycles 3; as aid to biblical instruction 35; and Latin liturgical drama 93–4; as salvation history 80, 93; women in 93; *see also* *N-Town Play*; Wakefield mystery cycle; York mystery cycle

mythology, classical: and Christian symbolism 11

N-Town Play, The: stage direction in 16

Nativity: apocryphal details of 36; carol on 25–6, 28–9

Navigatio Sancti Brendani: translated into Anglo-Norman 170

Neckham, Alexander: *De naturis rerum* 148

Nicholas of Guildford 127–8

Norman French 145; in England 148, *see also* Anglo-Norman dialect of French

Norse: in medieval Britain 147, 148, 149–51; phrasal verbs in 156; grammar of, as influence on English 154, 156

numerology 11

'O man unkynde' 214

Old English language: adjectival paradigms in 155; Anglian dialect of 149, 150; defined 145; dialects of 147, 149; inflections in 145; ~ , and word order 154–5, 156; Latin words in 151; Norse words in 149–50; standardization of, to West Saxon 147, 149–50; studied in sixteenth century 232; verb forms in 155–6

Old English literature 147; in Middle English period 1, 83, 147

Oldcastle, Sir John 85

oral culture, medieval 101, 105

Orm: *Ormulum* 35, 170; ~ , spelling-system in 158; on problems of 'rime' and verbatim translation 179

Ovid: and Chaucer 177; and Gower 177; *Heroides*, and Chaucer 129, 185

Owl and the Nightingale, The 213; author's self-naming in 127–8

Oxford English Literary History 249

Palladius: translation of 177

Parker-Library-on-the-Web project 212

Passion of Christ: as battle 20; Instruments of 12; meditations on 38, 64

pastimes: symbolism of 11

Patience 37; rediscovered 243

patronage 83, 99–100, 105, 107, 111–12, 115; as influence on representation of historical events 193–4

Peacham, Henry: recommends Chaucer 238–9, 240

Pearl 37; dialect in 162; editions of 246; rediscovered 243; spiritual love in 72

Pearsall, Derek: *Chaucer to Spenser* 249; *Poetry from Chaucer to Spenser* 249

Peasants' Revolt 115, 190, 193; contemporary accounts of 190–1, 193

Pecham, Archbishop John: Constitutions of 44; and lay education 106, 108, 109

pelican: symbolism of 23–4

penance 43; sacrament of, rejected by Lollards 47

Peter Lombard: commentary on Psalms 171

Petrarch: Chaucer's use of, in *Troilus and Criseyde* 133, 134, 182; and cult of the author 129

Petrus Comestor (Manducator) 34: *Historia scholastica* 34

Philip (VI) of Valois, King of France: vilified by Minot 194

phoneme: defined 157

pietà images: and devotional practice 17
pilgrimage: as penance 43, 44;
     symbolism of 11, 27
Pinkhurst, Adam (scribe) 116, 163
Plowman's Tale, The: added to
     Chaucer's *œuvre* 236
'poesye' 80, 86; concept of 5
Porete, Marguerite: burned for heresy
     173
prayers for the dead 78
Pre-Raphaelites: medievalism of 243
Pricke of Conscience, The 108–9;
     manuscripts of 223
printing 1, 101; and religious
     institutions 108; and reproduction
     of texts 226
Priscian: *Institutiones grammaticae* 157
prose fiction 176
Psalms 34; translated 171
Pynson, Richard: edition of *Canterbury
     Tales* 109, 233; edition of
     Lydgate's *Fall of Princes* 120,
     122, 138; edition of Lydgate's
     Troy Book 234

quests: symbolism of 11
Quintilian: Hoccleve's use of 136

Real Presence: in Grail Quest in
     Le Morte Darthur 50; *see also*
     transubstantiation
Reformation 32; as break with Middle
     Ages 233, 237; mystery plays
     ended at 93; and prayers for the
     dead 78
religious images 12–13; contemplation
     of 13–17, 26; printed **14**; *see also*
     Annunciation; Crucifixion
religious truth: Church as source of
     32–3
Renaud de Louens: *Le Livre de
     Melibée* . . . 180
Richard II 196–9; deposition of 196–7;
     and London 191; and Peasants'
     Revolt 190; Westminster Abbey
     portrait of **198**, 199

Richard Cœur de Lyon: representation of
     Richard I in 84
Richard the Redeless: author of, a
     scrivener? 115; figure of Richard
     II in 197, 199
Robert of Basevorn: *Forma praedicandi*
     123
Robert of Gloucester: Hearne's edition
     of 241, 242
Rolle, Richard 108; on Christ's body
     13; edited by Horstmann 246;
     Incendium amoris 137; translation
     of Psalter 171
Roman d'Enéas, Le 80, 87; female role
     in 80–1, 89
Roman de la Rose, Le 178
Roman de Thèbes, Le 80
romances: historical matter in 83–4;
     interest in 1, 242; and patronage
     83; popular appeal of English
     174; in prose 176; in translation
     173–4; *see also* Grail romances;
     Sir Gawain and the Green Knight
Root, R.K.: *The Poetry of Chaucer*
     247
Ruskin, John: promotes medieval
     architecture 243

Sainte-Maure, Benoît de: *Le Roman de
     Troie* 80, 87
saints' lives 62, 67, 172–3, *see also*
     virgin martyrs
Salih, Sarah 63
Sawles Ward: audience of 39
Scott, Walter: *Ivanhoe* 243, 244
scribes: adaptations of texts by, for
     target readership 226; carefulness
     of 223–4, 225, 228; changes to
     texts by 159, 221–2, 225–6;
     and collation of texts 225;
     exemplars used by, unique to
     them 223; corrections by 224–5;
     and *difficiliores lectiones* 222;
     marginalia/apparatus added by
     226–7; range of work produced
     by 163

scriptoria 108

Scripture, Holy *see* Bible

Secreta secretorum (Pseudo-Aristotle): Hoccleve's use of 136

senses: symbolism of 10

sexual morality: and social order 57–9

Shakespeare: *Pericles* 177; ~ , character of Gower in 237; *Two Noble Kinsmen,* and Chaucer's *Knight's Tale* 238

Shirley, John: and *Storie of Asneth* manuscript 67

sickness: symbolism of 9, 10

Simpson, James: volume in Oxford English Literary History 249

sin: symbolism of 10

Sir Degrevaunt: parallel texts of 217

Sir Gawain and the Green Knight 2, 28; absence of direct French source for 174; editions of 245, 246; girdle as symbol in 28, 87–8, 92; language of 174; manuscript of 37, 243, 245; matter of Troy in 86–7; women vilified in 92; *see also* Gawain-poet

Sir Percyvell of Galles 175

Sir Tristrem 174

Skeat, Walter William: and definition of Middle English 232, 244; editions of Chaucer and Langland 246; *Specimens of Early English* 244

Skelton, John: authorial persona of 123, 138; *Dolorus Dethe . . .* 138; translation of Diodorus Siculus' *Bibliotheca historica* 138

Somer Soneday 19

speech–writing relationship 157–9; and orthography 158–9

Speght, Thomas: and Chaucer 234, 235, 237; editions of Chaucer 234, 237, 238; glosses Chaucerian language 238

Spenser, Edmund: *Faerie Queene,* and medieval literature 237

Stanzaic Morte Arthur, The 50

Storie of Asneth, The: manuscript of 67; and spiritual value of marriage 65–7

Stansby, William: edition of *Le Morte Darthur* 239

Steele, Richard: disparages *Canterbury Tales* 240

Stow, John: edition of Chaucer 233

Strang, Barbara: on Middle English dialects 159

Straw, Jack 129

Strohm, Paul 56

Sudbury, Archbishop Simon: murder of 190, 191

Summit, Jennifer: on 'lost woman writer' 74

Sweet, Henry: and definition of Middle English 232

symbolism: in ME literature 9–28; and authority 11; as memory prompt 12–13; of nature 11; *see also* colour symbolism

Tale of Beryn, The 12

Tennyson, Alfred: *Idylls of the King* 244, 245

'Ther is no rose' 226

Thomas of Chobham: *Summa de arte praedicandi,* quoted 10–11

Thomas of Hales: *Luve Ron* 107

Thorpe, William 202, 206; *Testimony of* 200–1

Three Dead Kings, The 19

Three Living and the Three Dead, the (topos) 19

Thynne, William: edition of Chaucer 233, 237

Tolkien, J.R.R.: diplomatic edition of *Ancrene Wisse* 212

tombs: as memento mori 18

translation and adaptation 166–86; of Bible *see* Bible, translations of; of classical (Latin) sources 176–7; and interpretation 167, 168, 170; and originality 167; patronage of

170; problems of 168–9; range of relationships between original and translation 168; of religious texts 172–3; *sensus* versus *sententia* in 180; source texts for 167; and textual difficulties 169; word-for-word 167–8; *see also* Chaucer, Geoffrey, as translator
transubstantiation 18; Love's treatise on 48; rejected by Lollards 47
Trevet, Nicholas: Latin glosses on Boethius 179
Trigg, Stephanie: on appreciation of Chaucer 248
Tudor dynasty 77, 233
Turberville, George: disparages *Canterbury Tales* 240
typology 11–12, 36
Tyrwhitt, Thomas: edition of *Canterbury Tales* 242

universities: foundation of 107
Ursula, St: legend of 79
Usk, Thomas 115–16; *Appeal* 163; *Testament of Love* 115; and *Troilus and Criseyde* 115, 116

Vegetius: translations of 177
Vernicle, cult of the 26
Vernon manuscript (Oxford, Bodleian Library, MS Eng. poet. a.1): and oral performance 105
'vierge ouvrante' images 16
Virgil: *Æneid*, and *Le Roman d'Enéas* 81; ~ , Chaucer and 129, 184–5, 193
virgin martyrs: legends of 62, 67, 71; and eroticism 63; as models for wives, 67, 68
virginity: and eroticism 63–5; medieval views on 56, 63; as protest against social norms 62–3; as spiritual marriage 63, 65
visions 40–3; *see also* Julian of Norwich; Kempe, Margery; Mechtild of Hackeborn

Vulgate 34, 35; apocrypha found in 36; exegesis of, and imaginative writing 39; manuscripts of 36; *see also* Bible

Wace: French version of *Historia regum Britanniae* 82, 174–5; and patronage 105, 111; *Le Roman de Brut* 148; *Le Roman de Rou* 105, 148
Wakefield mystery cycle: Crucifixion in 21; *Play of the Resurrection* 18; *Salutation of Elizabeth*, language of 94
Walter of Bibbesworth: *Le Tretiz de langage* 149
Walter of Oxford: fictitious source for Geoffrey of Monmouth's *Historia regum Britanniae* 174
Walton, John: translation of Boethius 177
Warenne, Isabel de, Countess of Arundel 107
Warton, Thomas: promotes medieval romances 242–3
Warwick, Richard Neville, Earl of (the Kingmaker) 202–3
William of Palerne: rediscovered 243
William Thorpe, Testimony of see Thorpe, William
Winstead, Karen: on female readers of saints' lives 73
Wohunge of Ure Lauerd, Þe 64, 65, 71
women: Aristotelian views on 55–6; and authorship 137; as book owners 73; constancy of 58–9; and drama 73; and literary culture 72–3; and marriage *see* marriage; in Middle Ages 3; in Middle English literature 54–5, 67–72; and misogyny 55, 93; patience of 60–1, 62; as patrons 105; as readers 66–7, 72–3; role of, in medieval historical narratives 85, 89; stereotyping of 55, 68–9, 70; as visionaries 40–1,

women (*cont'd*)
    see also Julian of Norwich; Kempe,
    Margery; Mechtild of Hackeborn;
    as writers 74
Woolf, Virginia: and Chaucer 248
Worcester: as centre of Anglo-Saxon
    culture 147; 'tremulous hand'
    scribe of 147
Worcester, William: *Boke of Noblesse*,
    revisions of 220
Worde, Wynkyn de: edition of
    Canterbury Tales 233; edition of
    Le Morte Darthur 234, 235
writing, and speech *see* speech–writing
    relationship
Wu, Duncan: *Poetry from Chaucer to
    Spenser* 249

Wulfstan (Anglo-Saxon writer)
    147
Wyclif, John: Bible translation 34–5,
    171–2, 173, 200; ~ , edited by
    Madden 244; condemned as
    heretical 110; dissemination of
    views of 199–200; Latin works
    by 109; rejects Church's teachings
    46–7; vernacular works by 109;
    see also Lollards
Wynter, Simon: life of St Jerome
    111–12

York mystery cycle: opening of
    39–40
Ywain and Gawain: and Chrétien de
    Troyes' *Yvain* 168, 174